Mystics Dictionary
of
Spirit Language

By
Ken Ludden

An Ankahr Muse Publication

Mystics Dictionary of Spirit Language
English

This book is intended as a reference book companion to the full Mystical Apprenticeship training program of Ankahr Muse, and should not be used for any other purpose.

First published by Lulu, February 10, 2012

ISBN 978-1-105-51281-0

Printed in the United States of America

Introduction

Throughout the apprentices course of study they must translate over 5000 images, and from those images develop suitable messages. The mastering of Spirit Language is the very foundation of all Ankahr Muse skills for the Ankahr Muse Practitioner (AMP). Having mastered Spirit Language allows the apprentice to decipher messages coming directly from spirit—such as dream interpretation, vision divination, and many visionary images. Once the apprentice has also accomplished the ability to develop messages that are independent from their own point of view, prejudices and personally acquired doctrines, then Spirit will speak directly to the apprentice on a regular basis.

The Mystic Dictionary of Spirit Language is designed specifically as an aid to correct translation of elements found in vision images, dreams and even serendipitously observed items in the manifest. The definitions here are derived from the essential function or form of each item in the manifest realm, and is intended as a universal language for all humans who are alive. This First Edition is the premier publication of a Spirit Language Dictionary, and is part of the effort of Ankahr Muse to usher in the new Yin era.

By making this information available to the general public, it will guide them in their own quests to comprehend the messages from spirit they experience. Not only does it allow them to translate dreams they an d others find perplexing, but it will also allow them to find spirit meaning in many other areas: art works, spontaneous visions, visions others have shared with them, tea leaves, crystals and many more avenues to sight.

There will be expanded releases of this dictionary periodically through the coming years, as it is a dynamic document. As apprentices continuously uncover more elements not defined in this current volume, the dictionary will be expanded.

One of the most significant elements this dictionary offers is the fact that as any person becomes familiar, and at all levels on the road to fluency, it opens the door for Spirit to make more direct contact in the form of vision. But for those in the general public who use this reference guide, it is vitally important to recognize that knowing definitions alone does not make one fluent in a language, and there are many times that these definitions are not applicable. Read the Mystic Apprentice textbook series [1] to get a better idea of the larger context that real time uses of this language applies.

[1] The complete Mystic Apprentice 6-volume textbook series is available to be purchased online worldwide at: http://www.lulu.com/spotlight/kenatcirclecenterdotorg on the web, and are also available through Barnes and Nobel, Google Books, Amazon, and Alibris, as well as other book vendors world wide.

Mystics Dictionary of Spirit Language
English

A

ABOVE – 1) indicates that which comes from or of the divine; 2) heaven; 3) pineal gland; 4) god.

ABSINTHE – 1) self-induced and controlled change of mind; 2) elective madness; 3) artificial muse or to call upon an artificial muse particularly to impress or align with social elements.

ABYSS – 1) pitfall; 2) subconscious; 3) womb of the earth.

ACE – 1) singular, distinctive; 2) essence of, or characteristic, that renders the item unique; 3) that essential element from which one's uniqueness comes; 4) one's primary gift; 4) the first impetus that sets something in motion; 5) spark from which a new consciousness grows.

ACORN – 1) represents fertility, or that from which an entire life comes; 2) fecundity; 3) draws attention to an element in life that causes ultimate spiritual growth.

ACROBAT – 1) one who performs in inspired state before others, but is not on path when so doing; 2) one who is most agile when inspired, but lacks grounding; 3) state of inspired action in another that gets attention, leads or encourages others to be inspired; 4) risk involved from allowing free response to inspiration without regard to one's path; 5) uselessness of inspiration that, while impressive, does not advance one on one's given path.

ADAM –1) origin of humanity; 2) mythic beginning of earthly life; 3) vulnerability to temptation; 4) incompleteness of one person alone and isolated.

ADAM KADMON – 1) in the religious writings of kabbalah, a phrase meaning "primal man", the oldest rabbinical source for the term "Adam ha-Ḳadmoni" is num. r. x., where Adam is styled, not as usually, "ha-rishon" (*the first*), "ha-kadmoni" (*the original*); 2) the perfect or complete man, comparable to the Anthropos of gnosticism and manichaeism (*there is also a similar concept in Alevi and sufic philosophy called al-insān al-kāmil* (الإنسان الكامل)); 2) first man and/or woman; 3) the world soul, or universal soul of humanity.

ADAPT – 1) to alter, change, adjust or transform for the purpose of sharing; 2) change or alter to fit needed specifications.

ADAPTOR – 1) object that serves to facilitate sharing in which form must be altered to suit recipient; 2) that which accomplishes change or alteration to needed specifications.

ADDICT – 1) one who is unable to experience life without a filter of protection; 2) one who is lost and unable to embrace, love or accept self; 3) one who can only exist when out of connection to real world.

ADMINISTRATION – 1) force that makes sure that everything is working properly without actively participating in it; 2) the act of giving something needed; 3) control by means of organization, monitoring, or advising.

ADZ – 1) represents that one has an opportunity to take action that will refine one's life; 2) need to take action to transform, limit, define or refine one's life.

AFRICA – 1) represents the portion of the universal commitment to all of manifest existence that represents the origins of the strongest and most capable beings.

AGATE – 1) barrier reduced to mere obstacle that has special, beneficial properties; 2) symbol of protection against the results of being tempted or beguiled; 2) a protective obstacle against outside forces based on its color.

AGING – 1) transforming completely who one is; 2) unfolding of one's destiny; 3) becoming of what one is meant to be; 4) maturation process.

AIR – 1) inspiration; 2) breath of life.

AIR [COLD] – 1) need for inspiration is met with that which is unconceivable, uncomfortable, or difficult to fit into this world.

AIR [HOT] – 1) need for inspiration is met with that which is intrusive, brutal and uncomfortable; 2) outgoing communication is intrusive, brutal and uncomfortable for those who receive it.

AIR [WALKING ON, TAKING STEPS ON] – 1) very elevated, so much so that one is no longer on path; 2) one takes an inspired path without grounding; 3) so inspired that one is out of touch with reality.

AIR CONDITIONER – 1) a man-made construction in manifest that alters inspiration so that what is taken in is unconceivable, uncomfortable, or difficult to fit into this world; 2) changing inspiration into that which is not easily fit into the manifest realm; 3) deliberately out of touch with nature.

AIRPLANE – 1) vehicle that can take one to a new place through inspiration, but without remaining on one's path; 2) inspired means to a goal that avoids actual path; 3) using inspiration to avoid work on path.

AKASHA RECORD – 1) supplies the official spiritual record of experiences; 2) suggests to consult one who has ability to see the spiritual blueprint for one's specific life.

AKASHIC RECORD – 1) supplies the official spiritual record of experiences; 2) suggests that one might consult one who has ability to see the spiritual blueprint for one's specific life.

ALARM CLOCK – 1) use of marker in time to alert or prepare; 2) pre-planned time to enter full consciousness on the manifest plain; 3) self-determination in time.

ALBATROSS – 1) opinion that weighs one down; 2) element of fate set forth in one's life by outside opinion learned at early age that defines one's life afterward; 3) connection with opinion that no longer is inspiring, only confining or debilitating.

ALBUS ⁞∴ - 1) meditative symbol related to the astrological signs of mercury, cancer; 2) geomantic sign meaning pure spiritual intellect; 3) spiritual wisdom; 4) sagacity or clear thought; 5) bringing or inviting change.

ALCHEMY – 1) elemental charge of chi within things of the manifest that can unleash or make manifest results coming from the power of this charge; 2) informed magical use of elements in the manifest realm.

ALCOHOL – 1) delusion causing, self-inflicted change: 2) change that causes delusion.

ALEXANDRITE – 1) that which brings spiritual knowledge which, depending on source of light, is either of the heart (*spiritual light*) or of abundance (*manufactured light*); 2) change from heart to abundance depending on spiritual presence.

ALIEN – 1) sentient being of known origin; 2) manifest being with origin from the void; 3) of unfamiliar origin, foreign being.

ALLEYWAY – 1) open but little used path of transition, often hidden by society; 2) where dwelling places of souls are very close.

ALLIGATOR – 1) being equally comfortable in spirit or manifest, and able to transition with agility from one state to the other; 2) relationship between spirit and manifest in which only actions in manifest will nourish the soul.

ALLOY – 1) represents the natural state of an essential metal; 2) suggests relationship with or connection to an essential form of specific material in manifest.

ALMOND – 1) represents the natural provision of nurture that holds wisdom; 2) encourages one to find nourishment from life that is result of patience, persistence and determined path of risks taken.

ALTAR – 1) represents a sacred place in manifest; 2) elevated structure in manifest to house divinity; 3) suggests one take an action of service that is also personal sacrifice but done with pure heart and in alignment with spiritual purpose.

ALUMINUM – 1) precious neutrality that is either reflective of self, or impartial depending on orientation; [FOIL] 2) precious neutrality that is either reflective of self or impartial depending on orientation used to cover, wrap, preserve or hide things.

ALUMINUM FOIL – 1) represents precious neutrality that is either reflective of self or impartial depending on orientation used to cover, wrap, preserve or hide things.

AMBER – 1) remnant of flow of life that was interrupted and kept in stasis for a long time; 2) passion about the past in life; 3) what can be learned if one looks back to a single moment in time, as if time had stopped there.

AMBULANCE – 1) quick means to arrive at life-saving resource; 2) placing overall survival over demands of path in the immediate.

AMETHYST – 1) resource of divine illumination through spiritual flow and heart's truth; 2) delivering illumination in manifest through spiritual flow and heart's truth.

AMMUNITION DEPOT – 1) this represents a storage place of commitments designed to ultimately cause destruction and death; 2) suggests an answer is to be found in one's mechanism that stores resentments' poisons.

AMPHIBIAN – 1) represents a being that is equally at home in spiritual and manifest states.

AMPHIBIOUS – 1) indicates one is able to bridge difference between spiritual state and manifest state; 2) suggests that one develop the ability to find balance between spiritual state and manifest state in one's life at the moment.

ANCESTOR – 1) elders of blood line; 2) guides with direct connection to the one being guided; 3) wisdom that is passed down through generations; 4) species knowledge.

ANCHOR – **1)** obstinate resistance to change held in place by series of perpetual and precious cycles taken together as logical reasoning to remain unchanged; 2) conservative nature that does not allow change; 3) sacred structure that stabilizes in extreme change.

ANGEL – 1) represents the visual, sensory, auditory or otherwise tangible manifestation of spirit; 2) suggests an answer may bne found through one who is the deliverer of messages from spirit in dream state, meditation or vision.

ANIMAL – 1) the essential manifestation of a living creature; 2) the biological essence of an individual without consideration of human traits; 3) the basic manifestation of being.

ANIMAL PRINT – 1) represents natural confusion; 2) indicates that associated elements of the vision are in a state of natural confusion.

ANKH – 1) meditative symbol that represents the Egyptian word ankh meaning "life" or "to live"; 2) the universe; 3) all life, both the human and the divine; 4) the key of knowledge of mysteries and hidden wisdom; 5) power, authority; 6) combination of male and female symbols, therefore represents the union of the two generative principles of heaven and earth; it also signifies immortality.

ANKLE – 1) highlights the connection between one's movement on one's path and direction on one's path; 2) suggests one focus on the connection between one's movement and direction on their path..

ANT – 1) represents the force of change that introduces industriousness, order, structure, organization; 2) suggests the elements of industriousness, order, structure and organization be sought.

ANTARCTICA – 1) that pure spiritual state which grounds the universal commitment to manifest existence.

ANTIPERSPIRANT – 1) represents that externally applied element, usually spiritual in nature, which prevents internal change from becoming external change that is either offensive or will have unwanted effect on belief system.

ANTIQUES – 1) represents that things from the past that, depending on the item, represent essential function item represented in the past; 2) suggests an answer may be found by considering, seeking out or being mindful of things from the past.

APARTMENT – 1) represents one's dwelling place of the soul in urban life; 2) suggests one find a place where each individual has their own singular space within an **APARTMENT BUILDING**.

APARTMENT BUILDING – 1) spiritual dwelling place for the many in society; 2) society, or societal structure that many people build; 3) additive creation of society, not a destructive creation; 4) societal vehicle so that many may to pass through change; 5) arriving at a new place so long as societal views and requirements are accepted and adhered to; 6) structure where many different people who have the same spiritual make-up reside; 7) organized spiritual community.

APPLAUSE – 1) people's actions as a group that show appreciation; 2) acts of recognition from others as a group.

APPLE – 1) represents one develop or utilize a commitment to nourishment through the outer heart to get to spiritual nurture and growth.

APPLE CORE – 1) represents the central element of a commitment that does not participate in function of commitment, but allows for it to be reproduced elsewhere; 2) axis between polar opposites around which commitment is centered.

APPLE TREE – 1) life of knowledge; 2) life filled with the results from having lived life; 3) life that results in offering of commitment to nourishment through the outer heart to get to spiritual nurture and growth.

APPOINTMENT BOOK – 1) one's view of the future; 2) record of agreed upon commitments; 3) one's intended projection of organization.

AQUARIUS – 1) represents a visionary; 2) eleventh sign of the zodiac; 3) of the eleventh house, Aquarians are considered the house of friends, working on behalf of others; 4) fixed air sign for an individual; 5) represented in our solar system by the planet Uranus and Saturn; 6) a thinker; 7) symbol for purpose for an individual to learn and plan for the future and to adapt to changes that are coming; 8) making "something special" from what others thought was nothing or just pieces of junk; 9) symbol of the water bearer, "carrying water" is a uniquely human act, done to insure personal survival and growth through change; 10) an act of the intellect that shows thoughtful preparation for the future, one who prepares self and others for change to come; 11) one who can create drastic change now if thought necessary; 12) one who brings new ideas into the world; 13) represents consciousness.

ARCHWAY – 1) structure in life that allows for pursuit of the new; 2) fixed patterns of living that lead to new path's; 3) new directions.

ARCTIC – 1) signifies that purely spiritual state that connects the universal commitment to manifest existence and divinity.

ARK – 1) vessel that carries divine power; 2) structure on earth that contains divine commitment; 3) results from combination of life and effort that will transport man and animal through ultimate change; 4) survival by divine right.

ARM – 1) represents how one embraces the world; 2) means by which to encompass; 3) suggests focus on those things which one holds close and dear.

ARMOUR – 1) represents presence of precious protection for those who expect confrontation; 2) suggests one find the absolute, precious determination to survive; 3) points to the need for preparation to survive any and all tests.

ARMPIT – 1) center of vision, another eye; 2) vision that supports task and embrace of the world; 3) union between task and one's embrace of the world that brings vision to the heart.

ARMY – 1) social recognition and preparedness for potential need for defense; 2) recognition that there is the possibility of danger and structure for being prepared for it; 3) being realistic about this world through readiness rather than exacerbating discord.

ARROW – 1) emotional statement; 2) action that shows desire to affect others; 3) idea or thought that goes outward from you and takes on a life of its own; 4) action with an intended purpose, yet once done cannot be controlled, nor can one know the ultimate outcome.

ARROW FEATHERS – 1) represents when one's opinions are used to guide an idea or concept put into action in the world.

ARROW SHAFT – 1) represents the obstacles and hassles in life that must be dealt with by means of an emotional or intentional action directed at others; 2) element of necessity in emotional outburst or deliberate action with intent to affect others.

ARROWHEAD – 1) represents a pyramid containing wisdom that guides actions that have intent to affect others; 2) result from meeting one's obstacles that give both impetus and potential for taking actions that will affect others; 3) exact reason or intention that leads one's deliberate and inwardly compelled actions to impact others or the world.

ART – 1) manifestation of creative effort to communicate to others; 2) refined manner of communication being so refined as to exactly and creatively have specific desired impact; 3) means by which spirit guides the world forward; 4) vision so perfectly expressed that its essential function is to revolutionize feeling, thinking and formation of future potentials; 5) effective commentary that compels new direction, creative thinking, original actions or forging path ahead.

ASH – 1) that which is left behind as the essential result of light- and heat-generating encounter of pure balance between yin and yang; 2) aftermath of conflict that served purpose of balance and is now complete.

ASH [GREY] – 1) represents neutral material left behind after an impassioned encounter.

ASH [WHITE] – 1) represents the spiritual essence in manifest world that is left behind after impassioned encounter.

ASHTRAY – 1) represents the successful accomplishment of a peace treaty in the recent past; 2) container for that which is left behind as the essential result of a light- and heat-generating encounter of pure balance between yin and yang; 3) that which contains the aftermath of conflict that served purpose of balance and is now complete.

ASIA – 1) represents the part of the universal commitment to manifest existence that is centered on respect of ancient wisdom, tradition, family lineage and simplicity.

ASP – 1) one who has ability to beguile, but with deadly impact; 2) indicative of the fact that when one manipulates others, it ends the relationship, the effective spiritual journey of the other, and the spiritual death of self.

ASSIMILATION CHAKRA – REFERRED FROM **DIGESTION CHAKRA**] - 1) how one takes in the world and puts to use *(as nurture and nourishment)* that which is gained from such encounters; 2) way in which one makes constructive use of what is encountered in life.

ASSIMILATION CHAKRA – ALSO CALLED THE **MINERAL CHAKRA**] 1) represents that which holds one's foundations of life, health, security, ability to procreate and the sexual aspects of life; 2) stands for one's religious beliefs, shame, and ethnics, which have become the foundation of one's world view.

ASTEROID – **1)** represents celestial event that is both commitment and obstacle; 2) suggests importance of a fated event of celestial origins; 3) shows an intersection of paths with the potential to lead to a conflict of commitments on large scale; 3) commitment to fate, and facing what obstacles and conflicts may arise.

ASTROLOGER'S FINGER THAT POINTS UP – 1) direction of attention to planetary dance that will have effect on the earth; 2) ironic or playful recognition of fate, destiny and futility of resistance to spiritual intention for life.

ATOM – 1) energetic confluence of elements causing illusion of manifest; 2) building block of manifest; 3) essential facts that make all things equal and illusionary.

ATTIC – 1) place where old ideas, traditions, and thoughts that affect your view, but not the current foundation, are stored; 2) residual place where all that is obsolete is found; 3) potential for treasure in that which is considered obsolete; 4) value of lost, but not forgotten, ancient wisdom.

ATTRIBUTE – 1) relative meaning through association [*e.g., the color of a long sleeve shirt indicates way in which one embraces the world*]; 2) assigned meaning; 3) outstanding feature.

AUNT – 1) peripheral association that is extremely close and in union with one; 2) signifies peripheral familial lineage as relevant to one's specific moment in time.

AUSTRALIA – 1) represents that portion of the universal commitment to manifest existence that embraces the full spectrum of the balance of nature.

AUTHOR – 1) one who shares wisdom gained in life; 2) one who takes initiative to bring a new, or specific, body of thought or knowledge into being in the manifest realm.

AUTUMN – 1) represents maturity; 2) indicative of cycle of regeneration that includes destruction and decay as integral part of rebirth.

AVALANCHE – 1) represents the natural state in human life where pure spirituality suddenly encompasses and overwhelms one; 2) the sudden and unexpected death of a person, place or thing; 3) a **SHAKTI-PAD** that changes one's entire spiritual essence in an instant.

AVERAGE PERSON FINGER DOWN – 1) indication of the process of maintaining elements of life; 2) message to pay attention to the practical considerations of the path or the manifest realm.

AVERAGE PERSON FINGER UP – 1) indication of the process of celestial order coming into one's life, becoming aware of it; 2) represents there is a message one must pay attention to as it comes from the divine and applies to one's life; 3) reminder that life ends and one must ultimately take place in spiritual realm.

AVIATOR - 1) one who knows how to guide others in inspiration toward goal; 2) visionary and inspirational catalyst; 3) one who makes false promise that goals can be achieved without need of toil along path.

AWL – 1) precious emotion that, when used in active assault against natural protection against change, will puncture that protection; 2) emotional assault that will penetrate natural protection against change.

AXE – 1) image blending wand and sword, indicating the handling the things that one must with tremendous feeling; 2) dealing with something necessary that must be discarded, thrown out or cut off.

B

BABAJI – 1) reference to Avatar: Babaji[2].

BABOON – 1) of a nature to want to take in everything that life has to offer, but is prone to hierarchy and systems of dominance; 2) open to any and all experiences; 3) considers every possibility.

BABY – 1) innocence; 2) new direction; 3) new path.

BABY CARRIAGE – 1) easy beginning in life, not connected to demands of path; 2) naïveté to the demands of life from the very start; 3) born with a silver spoon in mouth, prone to entitlement life trap.

BACK – [ON BACK] 1) takes responsibility for; [AS OPPOSITE TO FRONT] 2) where one has come from, that which brings you to the present; 3) where history and future meet in the moment that one is in.

back itching – 1) one must actively take responsibility.

BACK OF HEAD – 1) what one used to think; 2) old belief.

back tingling – 1) feeling the need to take responsibility.

BACKPACK – 1) the structure which allows one to take full responsibility for any number of things; 2) sense of responsibility that will carry a diversity of causes; 3) that which takes on a burden for

---

[2] The immortal master lives today near Badrinath, in the upper Himalayan Mountains. His body has not aged since the age of sixteen, when centuries ago he attained the supreme state of enlightenment and divine transformation. this followed his initiation into the scientific art of kriya yoga by two deathless masters, the siddhas Agastyar and Boganathar, who belonged to the "18 siddha tradition", famous among the Tamil speaking people of southern India.

which responsibility is taken; 4) that which allows one to carry a heavy load from the past being brought forward into the present reality.

BACTERIA – 1) represents the unseen helpers or hinderers of health, digestion or assimilation; 2) the unseen dangers.

BAD LUCK – 1) represents spirit presence manifesting in lives of those who refuse to, or do not, take faithful actions.

BADGE – 1) outward showing of rank, or position; 2) show of gregarious nature; 3) need to promote one's self, one's position, one's personality.

BAIT – 1) device by which others are drawn in; 2) lure used to snare with.

BAKERY – 1) where nourishment for life is prepared; 2) readying the soul; 3) use of passion, inspiration and cleverness together to promote life, nurture and nourishment.

BALCONY – 1) within the structure of the dwelling place of the soul, an elevated place from which one can view the world; 2) place in swelling of the soul from which the world can view one; 3) spiritual place from which one displays one's spiritual nature and openness to others.

BALD – 1) mind is organic and available; 2) without thought of any sort; 3) unable to use intellect; 4) incapable of intelligence; 5) inability to understand, remember or figure things out.

BALL – 1) commitment; 2) sphere or realm; 3) cause for unity; 4) that which connects people.

BALLERINA – 1) represents one who is responsible for universal communication; 2) most capable of pure honesty; 3) embodiment of spirit on earth for all to see.

BALLOON – 1) represents that one has developed a commitment from inspiration; 2) hollow commitment.

BALSA – 1) life that is so perfectly inspired that it lacks substance; 2) life that is vapid, as if hollow; 3) pointless existence.

BAMBOO – 1) life that develops very quickly, but lacks center or substance; 2) state in life where development is artificially accelerated that renders one without substance; 3) popular culture in life that is superficial, has mass following, and while somewhat flexible, is rigid and is hollow or vapid at core.

BANANA – 1) nourishing thought that is necessary; 2) existential ponderings that lead to spirit nourishment.

BAND – 1) represents group that is purely spiritual in unity and coordination; 2) like minded and of spiritual nature.

BAND-AID – 1) represents a belief system that is applied briefly in order to get through an ordeal; 2) temporary beliefs to fortify boundaries.

BANDANA – 1) vivid belief system that contains thoughts and prevents inspiration; 2) vivid belief system that establishes the nature of one's connection with the divine; 3) vivid belief system that allows one to usurp that system and claim it as a personal identity; 4) putting one's belief system and the nature of one's connection to the divine in clear view.

BANGS – 1) represents present thoughts not well developed, and intentionally or purposefully blocking spiritual vision.

BANK – [RIVER] 1) natural border to fluid change; [FINANCIAL] 2) control or stagnation in flow of human energy to get things accomplished; 3) means of hording for self-serving ends.

BANK ACCOUNT – 1) represents a personal cache to hoard; 2) way to avoid participation in flow that is arranged in advance; 3) suggests one is placing one's fear-based projections in front of active fluidity and growth in life.

BANK CHECK – 1) represents a record of one's idea about a sum of money to be transferred or distributed via this tool.

BANNER – 1) belief system about how one projects things into the world; 2) celebration of self while showing off that celebration to the world.

BAR – 1) location in barrier for exchange; 2) point of passage between two divided zones; 3) resource for self delusion; 4) location for hiding from reality; 5) means of altering one's self to avoid reality; 6) place where illusion of fun supplants active participation in life.

BARB – 1) emotional public outburst that may harm if encountered, but serves as deterrent to those who might otherwise approach; 2) pointed emotional public event that is designed to keep others away; 3) public display of defensiveness that ensures isolation and loneliness.

BARBED WIRE– 1) that which publicly strictly enforces difference, where it is universally dangerous not to be separate; 2) public means of strictly enforcing difference yet easily dismantled and taken down; 3) precious public line of reasoning riddled with specific emotional ideas; 4) represents that which maintains intersection between important ideas on both sides feeling mutual and emotionally charged need for self-protection; 5) string of public, and sudden emotions and ideas that are different and yet equal.

BARBED WIRE FENCE – 1) very strictly enforced difference, where it is dangerous not to be separate; 2) strictly enforced difference yet easily dismantled and taken down; 3) precious line of reasoning riddled with specific emotional ideas; 4) intersection between important ideas on both sides feeling mutual and emotionally charged need for self-protection; 5) emotions and ideas that are different and yet equal.

BARKING DOG – 1) represents an active warning coming from a close companion.

BARN – 1) dwelling place of nourishment for the soul; 2) area in life where base nature is honored and well kept so it is ready for use; 3) place where animal strengths are well tended in preparation for hard labor; 4) barracks for military readiness.

BARNACLE – 1) encrusted hardness from too much continuous change without periods of stability; 2) where defensiveness from constant instability becomes living thing; 3) underbelly of caustic results from too much constant change, not shown to others.

BARRETTE – 1) indicates a required, and sometimes precious, tool for organizing thoughts.

BASEBALL – 1) commitment to succeeding in tasks which must be done; 2) commitment to playful enactment of one's duties in life.

BASEMENT – 1) when base nature becomes empty foundation of spiritual dwelling place; 2) where one hides or stores things related to, or relegated to, one's base nature.

BASKET – 1) interwoven network of life skills and results that carry forward that which is necessary; 2) using life itself with which to carry forward that which will be needed; 3) life structure that will sustain nourishment when action is taken to do so.

BASS CLEF – 1) societal organization of spiritual foundations; 2) means upon which expression of spiritual foundations is based; 3) way of homogenizing spiritual expression so all may participate.

BAT – 1) inspired acts of darkness; 2) that which comes to life only in the dark; 3) ability to navigate and remain inspired through times of darkness.

BATH – 1) self-inflicted and highly controlled change that nurtures; 2) provision for changing only that which is most necessary in life; 3) in control of when, how, where and how much one changes; 4) changing to suit one's self only.

BATHROOM – 1) aspect of the soul that has to do with change, restoration, cleansing and eliminating.

BATHTUB – 1) represents a location for self-contained and controlled changes.

BATHTUB RING – 1) represents all that remains after one has controlled any and all changes in one's life.

BATON – 1) necessary hassle; 2) problem or situation that must be dealt with; 3) element of life one uses to take care of things that demand action; [ORCHESTRAL CONDUCTOR'S BATON] 4) necessary tool of Mediumship; 5) necessary tool of channeling; 6) required ritual, tool, device or process that allows one to facilitate the delivery of spirit into the manifest.

BATTERY – 1) represents necessary and needed reserve of energy; 2) location of shakti generator.

BEACH – 1) represents wisdom resulting from having endured huge change; 2) new shore on which one arrives after enduring change; 3) location of wisdom from which one faces and encounters huge change.

BEACH BUGGY – 1) means for skirting change while also avoiding wisdom and one's path; 2) futile avoidance of change.

BEACH TOWEL – 1) means of keeping separate from wisdom while exposed to it; 2) way to remove and protect against change when on boarder where wisdom has resulted from having endured hug change.

BEAD – 1) commitment that can be related to a thought or belief; 2) minor commitment put on display for sake of others.

BEADED PURSE – 1) that which one uses to transport tools anticipated as needed, but also adorned with minor commitments to show and impress others; 2) collection of minor commitments that collectively represent the tools one has to face anticipated needs.

BEAR – 1) state of hibernation; 2) cycle oriented individual; [MOTHER BEAR] 3) fierce protector.

BEARD – 1) manner of expressing one's self is thoughtful; 2) *(long beard)* one expresses one's self in a manner that shows great, developed thoughtfulness.

BEATING DRUM – 1) conveyance of information that informs anyone who hears it; 2) non-specific delivery of information.

BEAVER – 1) enterprising by means of using life itself to prepare for and manage change; 2) suggests one has the ability to thrive in long periods of change.

BED – 1) area in dwelling place of the soul for retreat and restoration of powers; 2) meditation chamber in spiritual dwelling; 3) location of restoring and recuperating rest.

BEDROOM – 1) represents the aspect of the soul's dwelling place that is about the connection to the unconscious/spirit or about rest; 2) structured place in manifest that is restorative.

BEE – 1) represents that the industriousness of accomplishing what one needs by getting the most out of each experience in life; 2) industriousness of nature; 3) miraculous ability to be inspired even where it seems impossible.

BEE STING – 1) emotional action that immobilizes the opponent so one can go on working in an inspired way; [BEE DYING AFTER STINGING] 2) fulfillment of nature; 3) to be fulfilled in ultimate way.

BEELZEBUB – 1) – 1) one term for perversion of the mind and thought;

2) particular concept of state where intellect's thought or belief regarding the spiritual self that makes one become one's own enemy; 3) embodiment of self-destruction; 4) name for state when one is in danger to self from within one's mind.

BEER – 1) self-induced intellectual change that is in constant state of commitment to inspiration; 2) change that nourishes the intellect.

BEETLE – 1) spirit of divine nature; 2) ancestral spirit still at work long after passing over.

BEIGE – 1) spirituality is practical when one has vast experience; 2) represents significance of earth experience to spiritual being.

BEING SOILED – 1) one possessed something and wouldn't let it go, but suddenly has; 2) long held possessions that are no longer necessary and it can cause harm if one doesn't let go

BELL – 1) represents significant of the sound of the universe; 2) vibration of the planets and the earth; 3) celestial body.

BELLY BUTTON – 1) represents one's participation in the flow of generations through time; 2) evidence of one's temporal, and initiating, connection between origin and essence.

BELT – 1) that which connects or protects the intersection between foundation and assimilation; 2) practical, precious and/or dark perpetually applied stricture that holds foundation and movement on path in synch.

BELT BUCKLE – 1) means, sometimes precious, that secures that which connects or protects the intersection between foundation and assimilation; 2) stricture that holds foundation and movement on path in synch.

BENCH – 1) that which elevates you yet allows you to rest; [WOODEN BENCH] 2) taking life and creating something that elevates one and that one can rest on; 3) a thing that is for the good of many.

BERET – 1) represents one's belief system, which is also one's gift, that is means of connecting with the divine *[specific color dictates more of nature of that connecting thing, or state of the connection]*.

BERRY – 1) lessons from life; 2) after the experiences mature, the lessons from them nurture us.

BIBLE – 1) combined wisdom of mankind encompassing lineage, mythology and spiritual practice; 2) collected wisdom of mankind that spiritually guides.

BICUSPID SHELLS – 1) representation of duality in one's base nature; 2) the essential duality in all base natures.

BICUSPID SHELLS - 1) representation of duality of the base nature; 2) the essential duality in mankind's base nature.

BICYCLE – 1) vehicle that moves one forward in life, not quite connected to the path; 2) an opportunity for movement on the path that, because there is duality one can go forward; 3) division becomes unity even though it is separate.

BIDET – 1) societal provision for growth that results from having one's foundation inundated by essence from others; 2) controlled, self-administered change when one feels that one's foundation has been inundated with that which one does not want or need.

BIG RIG – 1) combination of man's works in the world that contain large items with a desire to reach the destination without actually traveling the path; 2) means of service to the many so that things to heavy to carry along the journey on life's path might be available when the goal is met.

BILL – 1) refers to any statement of an idea about value and the manifest world *"now that I have had this experience, it therefore establishes this value to the manifest world"*; 2) statement of one's estimation of value that beyond stating the value is also actively demanding acknowledgment and agreement.

BINOCULARS – 1) ability to see clearly in the manifest; 2) using the manifest structures to bring vision into clear and present view.

BIRD – 1) gossip; 2) personal opinion.

BIRD THAT CANNOT FLY – 1) an opinion that cannot reach far.

BIRTHING – 1) starting a new life, starting a new path; 2) something new that comes from one but that is its own thing and has its own biography; 3) one's ability to nurture and give, and to share one's insights and direction in the beginning with the ultimate goal that the recipient will solidly establish its own independent life.

BLACK – 1) dark; 2) unique; 3) stagnant; 4) separate; 5) unwillingness to change and learn; 6) against self; 7) separate; 8) unique; 9) different.

BLACK HEADPHONES – 1) that which represents controlled connection to exclusive source of dark information.

BLACK HOLE – 1) represents the nature of darkness to attract and absorb that which ventures close; 2) mysterious boundary between astral and spiritual; 3) question of possibility of parallel or alternate universes.

BLACK HOUSE – 1) dwelling place of the soul that is remote or distant; 2) dwelling place of the soul that is stagnant, confining or absent of light; 3) dwelling place of the soul that is unique or different.

BLACK JET – PLANE] 1) dark means of inspiration that removes one from one's path in pursuit of that path's goal; [SEMI-PRECIOUS GEM STONE] 2) darkness that can bring spiritual light.

BLACK LIPS – 1) expresses in

unique, different, separate, or stagnant manner.

BLACK PANTS – 1) one's reasons move on one's path are dark; 2) when one has stopped moving on path; 3) represents having a very unique path that necessitates a solitary or lonely path in life.

BLACK PERSON – [PERSON IN BLACK] 1) a person who is unique, different, stuck or that carries darkness with them; [BLACK SKINNED PERSON IN NATURAL WORLD] 2) a person of the negro race absorbing all light, thus appearing dark; [HUMAN RACE STARTED IN AFRICA ACCORDING TO MANY BELIEFS] 3) kingly; 3) invitation to drop prejudice

BLACK RIMMED GLASSES – 1) refers to a world view framed in darkness.

BLACK SHEEP – 1) represents when one appears as faithless among; 2) one who is shunned or rejected by their community

BLACK TINTED GLASSES – 1) world view in which all is seen as dark, different, exotic, unique, stagnant or separating.

BLACK WATCH – 1) one's devotion to time keeps intercedes between one's embrace of the world and one's actions by imposition of stagnation, uniqueness, judgment or divisiveness; [ON RIGHT WRIST] 2) devotion to time keeps one stagnant in creative endeavors, separating embrace of the world from creative actions in the world; [ON LEFT WRIST] 3) devotion to time interrupts logical flow or effectiveness of linear actions, whereby enslavement to time can sever embrace of the world on the linear side from logical actions in the world; [EITHER SIDE] 4) able to be interrupted from anything if time constraints intervene.

BLACK OR DARK RIMMED GLASSES – 1) sees world framed in darkness.

BLADE OF GRASS – 1) one aspect of abundance and nourishment.

BLEEDING FROM EARS – 1) one care what others think; 2) one spends, or wastes, life force on the opinions of others.

BLIMP – 1) inspired commitment that is vapid and hollow yet able to transport and travel great distances without being found out, mainly due to the outward appearance of neutrality.

BLIND LEAD DOG – 1) signifies one's spiritual familiar who serves as one's companion with vision or other spiritual gift so that they may maximize their gift of vision.

BLOCKAGE – 1) represents that which inhibits or completely blocks flow.

BLOOD – 1) life force, connects one to one's heart and thus represents emotions; 2) experience of being connected to manifest form (*hungry, cold, timid, frustrated, horny*) that leads to emotions.

BLOOD DRAINING – 1) represents

one is draining one's own life force.

BLOOD OFFERING – [WEDDING DAY TRADITION, OFFERING A CUP OF BLOOD TO EACH OTHER] 1) represents an offering or sharing of an experience of complete love for each other.

BLOOD STONE – 1) symbol of the obstacle represented by the Christian story of Jesus Christ dying for the sins of mankind; 2) obstacle represented by abundance that also contains deep feelings and strong connection to earthly things.

BLOWING OUT A CANDLE – 1) a life that ends early; 2) a life that ends early is an inspiration to others regarding the value of their own life.

BLUE HOUSE – 1) dwelling place of the soul is changing; 2) dwelling place of the soul allows growth and change.

BLUE LIPS – 1) manner of expressing is changing; 2) manner of expressing is fluid; 3) expresses through flow; 4) expresses in ever-changing manner.

BLUE PANTS - 1) when one's path has completely changed; 2) being suddenly beset by disease, catastrophes or major changes.

BLUE RIMMED GLASSES – 1) represents that one's world view is framed with flow, growth or perpetual change.

BLUE SUEDE SHOES – [AS FOOT IN VISION] 1) direction on path is changing or fluid; [AS BETWEEN FOOT AND PATH] 2) connection with path is through flow and change, or separated from path due to change or flow.

BLUE TINTED GLASSES – 1) world viewed as place of constant change; 2) world viewed as unstable, unpredictable.

BLUEPRINT – 1) structure is temporary or protean; 2) ideas, upon which to build, are fluid or changing; 3) change and growth result in new structures.

BOAT – 1) process of change, i.e., means of survival, way of dealing with change, or vehicle of getting through change; 2) a half commitment to a particular vehicle to survive change; [HUGE SOLID BOAT] 3) vehicle used to navigate, survive and manage change is solid and strong, can contain many; [ROW BOAT] 4) one manages, navigates and survives by working through change; [SAILBOAT] 5) one's soul in life remaining inspired allows for survival and navigation of change; [SMALL WOODEN BOAT] 6) destructive creation of life becomes vehicle for getting through change, all of life is being stripped down to survive change.

BODY – 1) physical manifestation of spirit.

BOILING WATER – 1) represents being in a state of agitated flow, growth or change; 2) actively changing, growing or flowing; 3) state of evolving growth, change or flow in which many inspired commitments are made, though none last; 4) chaotic growth, change or flow that will continue until nothing more can occur; 5) indicates that one is forcing growth, flow or change to become inspiration due to repressed feelings that must become expressed.

BOMB – 1) commitment used as invasive means to destroy; 2) repression leads to destruction; 3) when inspiration fails a commitment, it is destroyed along with everything in close proximity.

BONE – 1) spiritual structure that supports life; 2) strong internal spiritual nature translates to strong physical manifest nature.

BOOK – 1) accumulated and shared wisdom; [PAGES IN A BOOK] 2) bits of wisdom; [ONE PAGE OF A BOOK] 3) a single, individual idea of wisdom.

BOOK-LOCK-KEY – 1) represents that one is required to have the key, or way to comprehend information, and that key is at hand; 2) one must use willingness as a way to get information, the willingness is there.

BOOKSTORE – 1) market place for wisdom; 2) place where one goes to find resources of wisdom.

BOTTLE – 1) that which holds an experience one then takes in, which alters one's consciousness and experience; 2) contained or isolated experience that alters or has some effect on one; 3) an intentional alteration of removing one from the natural flow; [BROKEN BOTTLE] 4) weapon made from that which is designed hold and preserve experiences.

BOTTOM ITCHING – 1) represents that one must rest while remaining connected to one's path.

BOTTOM TINGLING – 1) represents one is feeling the need to rest while remaining connected to one's path.

BOUQUET – 1) represents a collection of experiences that celebrates or gives deference to; 2) selected and arranged experiences from the past that all support one common idea.

BOW – [FOR HUNTING] 1) a hassle or necessary chore secured to a particular concept come together as the impetus for specifically targeted actions with a particular outcome or response in mind; [TIED IN A BOW] 2) a narrow belief system used to hold a group of things in place that is by its nature temporary, and can be undone at any moment.

bow tie - 1) that belief system that can be used to temporarily force a united state of expression among people, places or things that can be undone at any moment by the one who imposed it; 2) that belief system that is temporarily used to complete imposed unification of expression.

BOWL – 1) empty half commitment; 2) container of experiences or possessions specifically for the purpose of nourishment.

BOX - 1) solid practical structure, the result of one's works in the world, that contains things in the manifest world.

BRACELET – 1) how one presents work one does as related to, or separate from, one's embrace of the world; 2) an ongoing or continuous thing that informs the relationship between one's embrace of the world and one's actions in the world.

BRAIDS – 1) not shouldering responsibility for thoughts or ideas, nor allowing them to influence tasks; 2) bringing ideas to the front so they can be seen; 3) unifying spiritual thoughts and ideas.

BRAIN – 1) central, and neutral, core of commitment to manifest being; 2) dense and solid neutrality from which all thought emerges.

BRANCH – 1) a particular aspect of life; [TAROT] 2) suit of wands, as expressed in the following illustrative narrative: *one is walking in the garden after an evening meal, enjoying the stroll in the moonlight when suddenly the branch of a tree falls to block the path. it is impossible to do nothing, for one must either walk around it, step over it, turn back, or remove it from the path before continuing. thus a tree branch represents the things in life which must be dealt with, but have in and of themselves no particular emotional charge.*

BRANCH – 1) reference to **TAROT** suit of **WANDS**; 2) one aspect of life;

BRASS RING – 1) precious passion that is ongoing, inspired, and propels one to take action; 2) action, both precious and passionate, that gives feeling of major fulfillment when taken.

BREAD – 1) life, nourishment of life, staff of life; [FEEDING BIRDS BREAD CRUMBS] 2) taking little bits of life to support one's opinions; 3) all of life wouldn't support the opinion; 4) a justification for insubstantial opinions; 5) what nourishes opinions is little bits of life.

BREAD CRUMBS – 1) represents little bits of life.

BREAST FEEDING - 1) transmitting the spiritual essence of one's heart's path into a new life; 2) transmitting the genetic code of immuno-defense and antibodies to local agents one has been exposed to in life.

BREASTS – 1) natural resource for nourishment and nurture; [HUGE BREASTS] 2) very nurturing, yet if too big they block the heart in which case too much provision of nurture causes lost touch with one's own heart.

BREATH – 1) inspiration that comes from a specific person

BRIDGE – 1) structures or events that sustain change; 2) a path that sustains change; 3) a path that leads through change without having to deeply go into it; 4) the past is still relevant, it is integrated and is a sign of maturity and integrity because one sees the overall path to change; [UNDER A BRIDGE] 5) one has had an opportunity to go through change in a way that all makes sense and the past might be integrated, yet one has chosen to ignore the past as one goes through change.

BRIEFCASE – 1) tools anticipated that will be needed are manmade structures in the manifest; 2) actions are all centered on being equipped with manmade tools.

BROCCOLI – 1) that which is necessary and abundant to sustain nourishment.

BROKEN BOTTLE - 1)weapon made from that which is designed hold and preserve experiences.

BROKEN DOLL – 1) non-living representation of life for playing that no longer can function as intended; 2) false persona intended for amusement and fantasy has been seen through and is no longer effective.

BROKEN LEG – 1) movement on the path is interrupted, no longer possible; 2) means of moving on path is damaged, destroyed or fractured.

BRONZE – 1) represents precious passion that may allow self-reflection if highly polished.

BROOM – 1) ultimate image of service, clearing the path for others; 2) actions of service to clear path for others is mandatory.

BROTHER – 1) fellow or member of close community brought together by circumstances of birth, non-elective; 2) fellow mystic, fellow member of one's spiritual community

BROWN – 1) practicality; 2) being-ness of life; 3) industry of life.

BROWN HORSE – 1) practical quest in life; 2) the practicality of following one's quest in life.

BRUSH – 1) means of organizing thoughts; 2) necessary and non-elective activity of organizing one's thoughts.

BRUSH FIRE – 1) spontaneous passionate outbreak that becomes destructive to young and slight in stature lives due to inspiration; 2) the way inspiration will increase passion to a point of destructiveness to life; 3) out of control destruction to minor forms of life due to passion with too much inspiration.

BUBBLE – 1) represents temporary commitment that is hollow; 2) commitment that is result of sudden inspiration forced in time of change; 3) an isolated life in which the isolation is both temporary and due to sudden inspiration.

BUBBLE GUM – 1) represents useless substance of feelings and spirit that exercises anger and occasionally forms into fleeting inspired, but hollow, commitments that immediately deflate.

BUG – 1) structured society at height of either yin or yang era where individual is relevant only in terms of function to serve overall societal structures; 2) function eclipses identity; 3) place in society.

BULL – 1) represents one has avid determination and persistence.

BULLET HOLE – 1) the crevasse left when one has had the commitment of another forced intrusively into one's life and thus has had one's life destroyed by another being.

BULLETIN BOARD – 1) represents a central exchange of personal wisdom; 2) manmade structure in life that allows indirect communication without privacy; 3) means of communicating without specific target for communication.

BUMBLEBEE – 1) industriousness of accomplishing what one needs by getting the most out of each experience in life by means of alternate states of intellect and darkness; 2) industriousness of nature resulting from the interrelationship between intellect and darkness; 3) miraculous ability to be inspired even where it is logically impossible due to alternating states of darkness and intellect..

BUMPER CARS – 1) represents creating confrontation for amusement; 2) the realm of provocateurs who seek to amuse themselves by causing conflict; 3) playing devil's advocate to avoid actual progress on path.

BUNNY – 1) represents actively participating in material life; 2) erratic progression through life of earthliness; 3) human desires and instincts to procreate and to have fear; 4) nervousness; 5) ability to be inspired one moment and then go deep into darkness; 6) connected to development/origin of the Fibonacci number system.

BUNNY TAIL – 1) represents that which results from having actively participating in material life; 2) results of erratic progression through life of earthliness; 3) reputation for having human desires and instincts to procreate and to have fear; 4) what follows nervousness; 5) aftermath of ability to be inspired one moment and then go deep into darkness.

BURGLAR – 1) event that intrudes on spiritual dwelling place for the purpose of taking away parts of spiritual self; 2) one who intrudes on spiritual dwellings to steal spiritual information or essence; 3) psychic vampire.

BURNING BUILDING – 1) represents the destruction of spiritual dwelling place due to passionate combustion resulting from sudden inspiration; 2) destructive force of passion and inspiration that can destroy spiritual dwelling places and personal identity.

BURNT UMBER – 1) represents dark practicality; 2) dark practicality remaining after passion and inspiration have forced destruction.

BUS – 1) means by which groups can join together to avoid actually interacting with their paths by following a predetermined journey to stated goals; 2) societal provision of illusion of mass progress to spiritual goals that actually detracts individuals from their own development on their paths.

BUSH – 1) an aspect of one's life that isn't your whole life; 2) dwarfed or diminished life.

BUSINESS – 1) structure in man's world that turns activity into flow; 2) one's enterprises in life.

BUTCHER'S SHOP – 1) place to prepare elements for nourishment and making one strong.

BUTTER – 1) solid intellectual result from overworking high spiritual principles of flow; 2) such things as greed, entitlement, superiority, and royal lineage that are the results from over working the highest concepts of spirituality to the point they produce these intellectual structures.

BUTTERFLY – 1) a whim that comes to one; 2) an inspiration; 3) a small, fleeting opinion.

BUTTON – 1) single holiness; 2) any action one takes that removes one from the community [*e.g., meditating rather than going to a party*].

buttox itching – 1) suggests that one must stop and rest while remaining connected to one's path.

BUTTOX TINGLING – 1) represents feeling the need to rest while remaining connected to one's path.

C

CABLE – 1) represents a precious line of thought, idea or reasoning that is very resilient, and made up of many smaller thoughts.

CACTUS – 1) natural abundance represented by presence of life in lifeless areas; 2) sustaining life in harsh environments; 3) survivability.

CAKE – 1) nourishment in celebration; 2) special nourishment that is more celebratory than substantial.

CALAMINE LOTION – 1) flow of spirit and feeling that eases irritation when boundary has been agitated; 2) use in action of spirit and heart to soothe.

CALCULATOR – 1) that which reduces all things to numeric values and their relationships; 2) mechanism of man's world that imitates one function of the brain.

CALENDAR – 1) system of measuring time; 2) organization of manifest in terms of the flow of time.

CAMEL – 1) ability to survive by storing large amounts of water, and able to walk for many miles; 2) infinite ability of nature to adapt to environment.

CAMP – 1) represents a temporary settlement; 2) significant of societal organization around shared resources and combined efforts.

CAN – 1) commitment to a precious extrusion of one's gift(s) that contains nourishment; 2) ability to store resources in advance of need.

CAN OPENER – 1) that which cuts open precious containers of nourishment; 2) ability to have access through tough barriers.

CANDLE – 1) life, mortality; 2) one's life (*at birth the candle is lit, at death it burns out*); [LIGHTING A CANDLE] 3) putting into life a new life; [BLOWING OUT A CANDLE] 4) a life that ends early; 5) a life that ends early is an inspiration to others regarding the value of their own life; [WHITE CANDLE] 6) the spiritual life of an individual.

CANDY - 1) that which does not nourish but pleases; 2) necessary diversion to balance life experience.

CANNON – 1) represents a tunnel that allows for destructive commitments to focus their damage.

CANNON BALL – 1) represents destructive commitment.

CANOE – 1) natural means of navigating change; 2) use of life to progress along life's path; 3) way of living on the river of life.

CANTILEVER – 1) illusion of over-balance; 2) unusual way that balance creates; 3) distribution in unseen and unexpected ways.

CANTOR – 1) indicates one who brings pure spirit through song; 2) representative of spirit for ceremony.

CANYON – 1) the extreme result of change; 2) change through time creates the new.

CAPRICORN – [10TH SIGN OF THE ZODIAC] 1) symbol of life through hard work; 2) the sea goat - 1)tough, stubborn, eats most anything and likes the established order and money; 3) conservative, success through determination; 4) rigid and unforgiving when others stand in their way; 5) moralistic and social, will always ascend; 6) takes up a profession of "law and order", [*i.e. doctor, lawyer, police, teacher*]; 7) likes to show off wealth.

CAR – 1) that which transports one on one's path and gets one where one goes in stable times; 2) to move forward on one's path, yet without connection to the path; 3) progressing yet not participating on the path; 4) not dealing with life; [RACE CAR] 5) equipped to get to a place in a particular way, can go very fast, focused on challenge and overcoming challenge.

CARABOSSE – 1) represents the mythological sorceress who dooms infants at birth; 2) represents conditions at birth that limit one throughout life.

CARAMEL – 1) practical and spiritual nourishment that is more about pleasure than nourishment; 2) practical and spiritual necessary diversion to balance life experience.

CARD – 1) brief offering of personal wisdom and thoughts; 2) expression of sentiment through written word.

CARDBOARD – 1) represents a solid practical idea that is durable but not long lasting.

CARDINAL POINTS – 1) represents elemental aspects.

CAROUSEL – 1) circular pattern in life that is entertaining but accomplishes nothing; 2) Rota – 1) Wheel of Life reference to Tarot; 3) pattern in life that is perpetual and meaningless.

CARPET – 1) things one elects to believe in so life's foundation is comfortable; 2) makes life more comfortable and work better; 3) beliefs that cover things up, soften things and make it warmer; 4) how one chooses one's beliefs so that the foundation is habitable; [FLYING CARPET] 5) the foundation one rests on is taken into the realm of inspiration and used as a vehicle to give illusion of forward movement; 6) beliefs that make the connection to the path very comfortable.

CARRIER PIGEON – 1) opinion that returns to originator; 2) opinion that is designed to sustain its own life and influence many.

CART – 1) manifest structure for carrying a heavy load; 2) life structure to ease burdens.

CARTON – 1) solid practical ideas used to contain; 2) structure of practical ideas that create boundaries and environment.

CARTOON – 1) an extreme, fanciful representation of state of being; 2) discourse through image representation playing base nature against high minded principles, and childish humanity against civilized structures of human endeavor.

CARVED IVORY – 1) represents an ancient grudge that has been kept alive and animated by time; 2) those attitudes for which any attempt to break them down or erode them only makes them more attractive and of greater value.

CARVED JADE – 1) represents obstacle of abundance that has been used as an enhancement or element of decorative pleasure; 2) plentiful and abundant obstacles in all lives that give great benefit..

CARWASH – 1) structure for changing vehicle used for progressing yet not participating on the path back to its original form; 2) way of erasing the results of not having dealt with life.

CASKET – 1) represents structure for returning one's body to the earth at the completion of a cycle; 2) in the act of burying someone one acknowledges life itself by the act of physically admitting that life ends.

CAST – 1) temporary spiritual change that soon becomes barrier that removes ability to embrace the world, take actions, travel on one's path or have any direction on one's path; 2) agency of spirit that has the ability to prevent or inhibit one's ability to embrace the world, take actions, travel on one's path or have any direction on one's path so that they can find spirit.

CASTLE – 1) the spirit and soul of this person is housed in a much protected place; 2) reference to one's position in life; [CASTLE WALL] 3) one's life; [CASTLE ON A HIGH AND STEEP HILL] 4) to get to one's soul's home an incredible barrier must be overcome, this barrier could be physical as well as spiritual, thus one is remote from place of being at home with one's soul, or being physically a long distance away from home.

CASTLE ON A HIGH AND STEEP HILL - 1) to get to one's soul's home an incredible barrier must be overcome, this barrier could be physical as well as spiritual, thus one is remote from place of being at home with one's soul, or being physically a long distance away from home.

CASTLE WALL – 1) represents the sanctity of one's own life; 2) indicative of the extent to which one values and celebrates one's life; 3) represents the need for privacy and the ways in which one insures it will be maintained.

CAT – 1) spirit presence; 2) psychic gift ; 3) familiar.

CATALABUTTE – 1) master of ceremonies; 2) ring master.

CATALOG – 1) book that is collection of available things rather than collection of shared wisdom; 2) to make record of where things are, to record an inventory.

CATALOGUE – 1) see **CATALOG**

CATALYST – 1) that which sets things in motion; 2) impetus; 3) first element to respond to chi flow, or any other flow, that then effects another, then in turn another, etc.

CATERPILLAR – 1) represents the intermediary state between development and inspiration; 2) in phase of being extremely connected to path.

CATHEDRAL – 1) grand palace that is a creation of man made for the purpose of reflecting and embodying the presence of spirit; 2) spirituality and manifest meet in ultimate celebration of achieved symbolic potential, and if manifest and spirit join together then the achievement is fulfillment of that potential.

CATSUP – 1) essence of heart that makes nourishment better; 2) applying essence of heart to make things easier to assimilate.

CAUGHT IN STORM – 1) indicates something very suddenly came and changed one's life completely; 2) represents that even though one may think the situation has passed, it has not.

CAVE – 1) represents the foundation chakra; 2) means by which what is outside of the earth can connect with what is inside.

CD – 1) symbol of sun and source of music; [LIGHT AND MUSIC] 2) double symbol of spirit presence in manifest; [SOMETHING UNEXPECTED COMES UP AND INSERTS ITSELF IN LIFE] 3) wheel of fortune; 4) pentacle or gift from spirit built into one's design for the purpose of assigning one responsibility to care for, develop and fulfill the gift in service of others.

CELEBRITY – 1) being known for what one does; 2) high and visible reputation, yet dehumanized and turned into a brand to market.

CELL – [BIOLOGICAL] 1) single organic unit of larger organism that has simultaneously individual identity of purpose and solid base of identity as part of group; 2) that which collectively with others make up a whole, while maintaining unique purpose and identity; [PRISON CELL] 3) enforced societal dwelling place of the soul assigned to those who have broken the required code of conduct; 4) place of confinement, restriction and imprisonment in society designed to punish those who disobey societal rules, and with hope of breaking occupants' resistance to conformity through rehabilitation to societal code.

CELL MATE – 1) one who is assigned to share the enforced societal dwelling place of the soul assigned to those who have broken the required code of conduct; 2) sharer of place of confinement, restriction and imprisonment in society designed to punish those who disobey societal rules, and with hope of breaking occupants' resistance to conformity through rehabilitation to societal code; 3) life-mate of those who have no spiritual concept of life.

CELLOPHANE – 1) transparent and artificial filter that augments an aspect of everything it covers; 2) represents the power of self-delusion that allows one to augment and accentuate an aspect of reality in one's world view.

CELL-PHONE – 1) represents a tool of communication; 2) remote, impersonal, and dark; 3) distraction of right brain and creative side.

CEMENT – 1) prior obstacle or barrier that has been reduced to dust, apparently freeing one, until change occurs that turns that broken down barrier into an absolute, all-consuming entrapment of barrier; 2) elements of life that, when change is introduced, become imprisonment and trap one in stagnation.

CEMENT MIXER – 1) societal circumstances that agitate the combination of change with prior barriers that have been reduced to apparently freeing one, turning it into an absolute, all-consuming entrapment of barrier; 2) that which takes elements of life at the moment of change to produce imprisonment and trap one in stagnation.

CEMETERY – 1) place on earth where structures for returning bodies to the earth at the completion of a cycle; 2) location where the act of burying someone

one acknowledges life itself by the act of physically admitting that life ends, thus the place itself represents the value of life as accentuated by the illusion of time.

CENTAUR – 1) ego mission from which one cannot free one's self; 2) represents that one's path in life has become an all-consuming mission; 3) when ego has become obsession.

CENTIPEDE – 1) a state in life where there is ultimate connection to one's path on earth without possibility of inspiration.

CERTIFICATE – 1) single idea of mankind acknowledging status of an individual in the manifest and within the structures of time and space, society and human enterprise.

CHAIN – 1) representation of a series of perpetual and precious cycles taken together as logical reasoning to remain unchanged.

CHAIR – 1) single moment in time; 2) a place to rest and repose; 3) one is still on one's path as one's feet are on the ground; [WOODEN] 4) it is made from life; [EMPTY CHAIR] 5) moment in time that is open and unfilled; 6) a promise; 7) another perspective, another moment in time; [CLIMBING OVER CHAIRS] 8) rushing through single moments in time, not taking the time to stop or be in any of the moments.

CHAKRA – 1) portal through which chi flows in and out; [CROWN CHAKRA] 2) connection to the divine; [VISION CHAKRA] 3) being able to have vision through what is often called "the third eye"; [EXPRESSION CHAKRA] 4) being able to express the truth of your spirit essence; [HEART CHAKRA] 5) path of the heart, representing both the non-compromising tempest of soul and greatest tranquility; [ASSIMILATION CHAKRA] 6) which determines how you take in the world and what use you make of it once you've assimilated it; [FOUNDATION CHAKRA] 7) also called the mineral chakra, this holds one's foundations of life, health, security, ability to procreate and the sexual aspects of life, religious beliefs, shame, ethnics, and is the foundation of one's world view; [ROOT CHAKRA] 8) connection to the earth. [DIVINE AXIS] 9) the crown and root chakras work together to complete the cycle of relationship between heaven and earth, which the human being represents..

CHALK – 1) a tool for writing made of the spirit essence of life; 2) the dust remnant of spent spiritual enterprise in life through which one may communicate.

CHALK BOARD – 1) dark place where one's actions can communicate when the dust remnant of spent spiritual enterprise in life is used; 2) the transient opportunity offered by solid darkness to communicate with pure spirit.

CHALK WRITING – 1) message from spirit written by spirit's hand in the spiritual essence of life.

CHAMELEON – 1) ability to blend into background; 2) masking one's presence by assuming the look of the immediate surroundings.

CHAMPAGNE – 1) self-induced change to delusional state by means of mildly poisonous alterations; 2) being perpetually infused with commitment to the point one maintains an extreme and volatile inspirational state.

CHAOS – 1) represents a confluence of unstructured and manic paths, each without reason or discernable direction; 2) diverse elements coming together in a great tangle of highly energized yet unfocused movement.

CHAPEL – 1) place of worship, unique, independent; 2) creative place adapted from an organization to meet specific needs; 3) more friendly environment for those who gather in worship; 4) small, private space that is a creation of man made for the purpose of reflecting and embodying the presence of spirit at an altar of ritual; 5) spirituality and manifest meet in humble, private potential, and if manifest and spirit join together then the achievement is fulfillment of that potential.

CHARCOAL GRILL – 1) contained, focused anger and passion marshaled for use in preparing that which will nourish.

CHARLATAN 1) one who professes knowledge or an ability one does not have; 2) one who gives false representation of skills and abilities.

CHART – 1) organizational patterns of individual invention meant to display system information for others to follow; 2) written record of progress, kept for the purpose of having a body of evidence of patterned occurrences to study, analyze, and use for projections and conclusions about the charted data.

CHECK – TIC MARK] 1) a mark that indicates the item nearest has been accounted for, recorded, inventoried or whatever else it might specifically be designated to mean in a case specific use; [FINANCIAL TOOL] 2) record of one's idea about a sum of money to be transferred or distributed via this tool.

CHEEK – INDICATION OF FACIAL FEATURE] 1) how one is prepared for, and expects, a potentially negative response; [ATTITUDE] 2) displayed lack of concern as to what a reaction may be, with the assumption of a predictable negative response; 3) [*taking it on the cheek*] being prepared to accept physical results of negative reaction to a behavior, statement, fashion, provocative action or other intended display.

CHEESE – 1) made from inheritance and essence of life; 2) the prepared and spiritual evolution from the essence of life; 3) food made from life essence.

CHEESE GRATER – 1) means of breaking down solid food made from life essence for purpose of evenly spreading it throughout that which is consumed.

CHEF'S HAT – 1) connection with divine through highly inspired spirit state.

CHEMICAL ADDITIVE – 1) element added for a designed purpose to an already bonded mixture of elements.

CHEMICAL REACTION – 1) represents an energetic interaction of dissimilar elements joining or repelling each other.

CHEMISTRY – 1) energetic interaction of dissimilar elements joining or repelling each other; 2) inner knowing of true physical compatibility between two beings; 3) the manifest science of spiritual connection and bonding at elemental level.

CHERRY – 1) commitment of emotion or feeling to be taken that leads to itself, and does not sustain one; 2) item with the sole purpose to attract another to help it regenerate itself.

CHERUB – FROM THE HEBREW – 1) KERUBH] 1) represents one gifted with both knowledge and inherent innocence who through these twin gifts is easily inspired; 2) suggestion that through purity and innocence that one can inspire others with one's own presence.

CHEST – 1) represents the heart; 2) the chasm of feeling into which one pulls all that is embraced.

chest itching – 1) one must take direct action from the heart.

chest tingling – 1) represents that one is feeling an urge from the heart.

CHEWING GUM – 1) expression of anger that does not achieve its goal *[example: complaining yet never getting anywhere].*

CHICKEN – 1) an opinion that cannot reach far.

CHILD – 1) not gender specific, one who is still growing and learning; 2) an innocent or innocence itself; 3) accepting of one's fate, doing whatever is next; 4) someone in the beginning of an unfamiliar process.

CHILD'S FINGER DOWN – 1) indication that one is home where they currently are; 2) showing the need for grounding; 3) person being communicated with needs stability in their life.

CHILDHOOD HOME – 1) dwelling place of a child's soul; 2) pure connection with spirit; 3) not compromised by conditionings and the world.

CHIMNEY – 1) escape route for darkness expelled when one is in residence in their soul's dwelling place; 2) manifest structure that channels the excess and expelled product from destructive outbursts of anger, passion that is inflamed with inspiration.

CHIMPANZEE – 1) one who is adept at life; 2) a member of a group that is highly socialized; 3) uninhibited and naturally at home in the world.

CHIN – 1) how one leads when presenting one's self to the world; 2) the first thing that one presents to others when first meeting; 3) one's self-perceived strong suit.

CHINCHILLA – 1) state of spiritual timidity; 2) will release spiritual thoughts if any pressure is applied whatsoever to contradict them.

CHOCOLATE – 1) highly practical consumption of emotionally satisfying things; 2) food with little nourishment value but high relaxation and pleasure value that is very important and practical to include in dietary balance.

CHOP STICKS – 1) in alignment with Law of Unity, where opposition strengthens; 2) practical and necessary act of seeking nourishment.

CHOPPED NUTS - 1) commitment to starting new life that has been broken, shattered and killed; 2) inability to create new life; 3) taking destructive action that kills the possibility of a future.

CHORD – 1) manifestation of spiritual union and harmony through societal structure.

CHRIST – 1) divine consciousness leading humanity by example of love, compassion, forgiveness and patience; 2) consciousness of highest order of example for living; 3) avatar.

CHRISTIAN – 1) one who is called to pattern one's life after the example of the Christ consciousness.

CHRYSALIS – 1) transforming completely who one is; 2) unfolding of one's destiny; 3) becoming of what one is meant to be; 4) maturation process.

CHURCH – 1) place that is a creation of man made for the purpose of reflecting and embodying the presence of spirit; 2) spirituality and manifest meet in potential, and if manifest and spirit join together then the achievement is fulfillment of that potential.

CHURCH KEY – 1) represents the foundation of belief system that by its use opens new avenues of experience and growth in spirit; 2) spiritual willingness as the foundation upon which one must act.

CHURCH-FIGURE FINGER DOWN – 1) indicates presence of a spiritual message saying that the importance or intention of the meaning is found in the underworld and all the temptations.

CHURCH-FIGURE FINGER UP – 1) represents the presence of, or the eventuality of, a spiritual message saying that the importance or intention of the meaning is found in God.

CINDERELLA – 1) transformation through service to elevated state; 2) indicates an individual who is of lowly station in life yet deserves to be seen for their beauty, skills, pure heart and spirit presence.

CINEMA – 1) represents illusion that imitates life visible as a result of light traversing the film to create a projected image.

CINNAMON – 1) practical spice to enhance changes; 2) practicality found in the exotic nature of a thing to enhance all it comes near.

CIRCUIT – 1) represents the potential of fulfillment of flow; 2) completion of chi or energetic system in state of good balance and unobstructed flow.

CIRCUS – 1) fantasy world in temporary dwelling place of the soul meant to inspire, entertain and inform through irony and humor the foibles of the human situation; 2) atmosphere that is highly charged, perpetually thrilling or exciting, and memorable in life.

CITY – 1) organized social behavior; 2) functions and events; 3) structured social life; [OUTSKIRTS OF CITY] 4) something that is not part of normal social structures and social behavior.

CITY BUS – 1) means by which groups in a local area can join together to avoid actually interacting with their paths by following a predetermined journey to stated goals; 2) societal provision of illusion of mass progress to spiritual goals that actually detracts individuals from their own development on their paths.

CLASS – 1) group of students in bond of simultaneous growth; 2) group to which a thing belongs; 3) of elevated status in social structures of manifest realm.

CLASSMATE – 1) represents an equal; 2) someone who is learning the same lesson, at the same time.

CLASSROOM – 1) indicates the location in dwelling place of the soul where designed growth through learning occurs.

CLAUSTROPHOBIA – 1) fear of being confined; 2) strong desire to expand and grow; 3) it is the time and place to go somewhere and take action, move along the path.

CLAW – 1) represents the perfect means of a psychic nature to grasp.

CLAY – 1) represents possibility of practical use of the provision of earth itself to create whatever one wishes, limited only by one's own imagination and facility; 2) represents to make whatever one wants out of living on earth.

CLEAR HOUSE – 1) dwelling place of the soul that offers no privacy and is transparent.

CLEAVE – 1) having shown in action to be one who lives in faith-filled action of service for the highest good of others; 2) to adhere closely; 3) stick; 4) cling; 4) to remain faithful in spite of challenge.

CLEF - **1)** societal organization of spiritual expression; 2) means upon which expression of spiritual expression is based; 3) agreed upon way of homogenizing spiritual expression so all may participate.

CLEFT - 1) that which has been divided; 2) a whole that has been divided into parts, creating a void where there should be unification; 3) reflection that even within a whole there is a balance of opposites.

CLEFT PALLET – 1) when one shows in their manner of expression that they have been divided; 2) manner of expression that has been divided into parts, creating a void where there should be unification; 3) reflection through expression that even within a whole there is a balance of opposites.

CLIMBING OVER CHAIRS – 1) represents rushing through single moments in time; 2) suggests one is not taking the time to stop or be in any of the moments along one's path, and thereby missing one's path.

CLOAK – 1) separateness from, something intentionally hidden; [INSIDE OUT] 2) protects one as one goes into the world, feeling protected in the world; [RIGHT SIDE OUT] 3) a barrier that protects.

CLOGS – BLOCKAGE] 1) that which inhibits or completely blocks flow; [FOOTWEAR] 2) practical potential to sabotage when and if necessary in the manifest realm.

CLOTH - 1) belief system; 2) belief system made up of intricate intersection and interrelationships between a great many different ideas and points of view coming together in time to form a solid network of thought. (*color and various elements and adornments give specifics)*.

CLOTH – 1) belief system; 2) sum total of one's individual beliefs, ideas, concepts, opinions and attitudes that, when taken together, perfectly show how they approach the things of the manifest realsm; [BABY'S CLOTHNG] 3) the inherited belief system upon which one builds their foundation of belief; 4) conceptual, ideological, or intellectually belief that establishes one's manifest destiny *(i.e., born into rich family, or cultural background, well educated parents; etc.)*.

CLOTH GLOVES – 1) activity coming from or pertaining to belief system; 2) what one does in life as result of one's belief system; 3) how one is directed to interact by one's belief system.

CLOTH NAPKIN - 1) belief system, often of pure spirit, that assures that life's nourishment does not overreach its intended function; 2) use of a spiritual belief system to separate nourishment from manner of expression.

CLOTHES – 1) presentation of belief systems; 2) how one chooses to present one's self; 3) outward indication of the state of a person, how they appear, what is apparent to others.

CLOTHES LINE – 1) represents an idea that allows belief systems to be examined, changed and developed.

CLOTHES PINS – 1) represents the practicality of tending to one's belief systems; 2) suggests one maintains one's belief systems and makes sure they change and grow as one's life supports.

CLOTHING – 1) represents taking a belief system in life and with it creating protection; 2) identity and/or personal expression.

CLOUDS – 1) nuance; 2) dream.

CLOVEN HOOF – 1) one's direction on path is divided but not evident; 2) one has hidden motive in direction forward; 3) deep insincerity in forward movement; 4) example not to be trusted.

CLOVERLEAF – 1) represents one who has good fortune in abundance due to being of faith; 2) one who practices the **LAW OF FLOW**; 3) to be protected and provided for by divinity.

CLOWN – 1) one with unusual, flamboyant, startling and entertaining belief systems on display; 2) represents state of selflessness in one who serves the pleasure of another without thought of self, and usually at expense of self in society's view.

CLOWN COLLAR – 1) exaggerated expression of extreme vulnerability to inspiration and excitement.

CLOWN SHOES – 1) exaggerated emphasis of direction on path.

COAL – 1) elemental internal energy source once all life forms are broken down to elements.

COAST – 1) represents one's vulnerability to change; 2) wisdom from constantly dealing with perpetual and inevitable change.

COAT OF ARMS – 1) that to which one belongs as if by right of birth; 2) one who embodies precepts, goals, ideals and beliefs of larger body; 3) one who is faithful to lineage.

COBRA – 1) one's ability to beguile has hidden element of defensiveness that causes one's head to become inflated, and the urge to destroy others emerges; 2) representative of fact that introduction of spiritual elements can cause destructive defensiveness.

COCOA – 1) commitment to practicality in all things.

COCONUT – 1) commitment to the practical, upon examination, leads to spiritual nourishment and opportunity for spiritual growth.

COCONUT MILK – 1) inheritance of a commitment that is practical; 2) practical essence of life as commitment; 3) practical commitment providing the essence of life from spirit; 4) spiritual growth mechanism coming from practical commitment; 5) the essence of spiritual lessons in life that are derived from practical commitments.

COFFEE – 1) practical change administered to self.

COFFIN – 1) represents the returning to the earth, the completion of a cycle; 2) signifies that in the act of burying another, one acknowledges life as one physically admits that life ends

COINS – 1) reference to the suit of pentacles and indicating one's gift; 2) to exchange and take from your abilities and turn it into literal wealth and recognition; 3) success, achievement, money.

COLD AIR – 1) represents that the answer to the request for inspiration is something is unconceivable, uncomfortable, difficult to fit into this world.

COLLAGE – 1) exposition of a person's thought process; 2) how things fit together for one; 3) how one chooses to display internal process.

COLLAPSE – 1) to suddenly be without energy to sustain; 2) inevitable outcome for all manifest elements.

COLLAR – 1) perpetual and ongoing force on a person that controls their actions, thoughts and expressions.

COLLEGE – 1) represents a place for higher learning.

COLOR OF ROOF – 1) this is representative of the quality of one's connection to spirit.

COLORED BOX – 1) structure in manifest for concealing, collecting, storing or hiding; 2) means of achievement is dependent on specific color.

COLORED FINGERNAILS [LONG] – 1) furthest reach of actions bears the influence of specific color; [COLOR SPECIFIC] 2) impact of actions goes beyond the actions themselves.

COLORED FINGERNAILS– SHORT] 1) furthest reach of actions bears the influence of specific color, but impact does not go beyond the actions themselves.

COLORED GLOVES – 1) *(specific color gives precise information regarding the nature of each of the following:)* 1) activity; 2) what one does in life; 3) how one interacts.

COLORED HOUSE – 1) represents the dwelling place of the soul with attribute of specific color.

COLORED LIPS – 1) represents manner of expression conforms to specified color.

COLUMBINA - 1)[COMMEDIA DEL ARTE CHARACTER] 1) represents innocent and frivolous youthful maiden who falls in and out of love on a whim and does not take life seriously; 2) signifies one who can, through vulnerability, greatly alter the course of things.

COLUMBINE – [FLOWER] 1) hooded experience that draws inspiration for its past; 2) experience in life that is entirely based in past.

COLUMBINE –1) representative of relationship between past history and how present experiences are colored.

COLUMN – 1) represents necessary structure of support; 2) that which supports elevated structures for connection to divinity.

COMB – 1) represents that with which one organizes thoughts.

COMET – 1) movement of celestial event that is both commitment and obstacle; 2) fated event of celestial origins that is intersection of paths of potentially conflicting commitments on large scale; 3) dedicated commitment to fate, and facing what obstacles and conflicts may arise.

COMIC BOOK – 1) collected wisdom of vision and imagery.

COMMODE – 1) societal provision for changes that cleanse; 2) acknowledgment that one will always have need to grow through elimination of that which is unnecessary, no longer needed, and is practical to be rid of.

COMPETITOR – 1) represents one who strengthens opponents by opposing them.

COMPLEX HAIRDO – 1) highly organized and complex thoughts.

COMPOST – 1) waste, something you discard and throw off, that begins in a toxic state but will eventually provide nourishment if given ample time; 2) useful rot.

CONCENTRATE – [JUICE] 1) represents the essential residue of change or growth with flow removed in large part.

CONCERT – 1) represents society coming together creates beautiful and harmonious events.

CONCERT HALL – 1) place dedicated to communion with spirit in life by society; 2) society's venue for shared spiritual experiences; 3) regarding a common spiritual experience for society.

CONCH-SHELL - 1) mystery; 2) myth; 3) secrets to be unfolded through unraveling of codes embedded in nature like Fibonacci number sequence, etc.

CONCH-SHELL - 1) mystery; 2) myth; 3) secrets to be unfolded.

CONCRETE – 1) man-made barrier; 2) non-committal; 3) problems we make ourselves.

CONDITION OF ROOF – 1) represents quality of connection to spirit; 2) indicative of those elevated ideas and actions one relies upon to maintain conscious contact with spirit.

CONDOM – 1) elective barrier put up in moments of intimate vulnerability; 2) intervention of nature to avoid unwanted outcome.

CONDUCTOR – 1) medium; 2)

channel; 3) one who facilitates the delivery of spirit into the manifest.

CONDUCTOR'S BATON – 1) a necessary tool of **MEDIUMSHIP**; 2) necessary tool of channeling; 3) required ritual, tool, device or process that allows one to facilitate the delivery of spirit into the manifest.

CONFERENCE – 1) structured means of exchanging ideas, marketplace of ideas; 2) set agenda being actualized for specific purpose; 3) community coming together around something mutually beneficial.

CONFUCIUS – 1) countenance of Tao mastery; 2) ascending to elevated state of balanced mindfulness; 3) full acceptance of nature of all realities.

CONSTRUCTION PAPER – 1) represents a single, simplistic truth, *(exact meaning derived from specific color).*

CONVENTION – 1) traditional structured means of exchanging ideas, marketplace of ideas; 2) mutually agreed upon method, manner or organizational pattern; 3) imposed expectation.

COOKIE – 1) gift of nourishment that also brings pleasure.

COOKING POT – 1) represents a vehicle to put something through agitation so it becomes nourishment; 2) half commitment to prepare that which will nourish.

COOKING POT – 1) experience or possession that is designed to repress feelings for the purpose of internal change; 2) that which uses one's experiences and possessions to promote spiritual nourishment.

COPPERHEAD – 1) ability to beguile that will destroy if succumbed to; 2) beguilement that appears to promise illumination and delivery of light of spirit, but actually destroys all who in penetrates; 3) promise of change from enlightenment that actually destroys.

CORAL – 1) represents the material of a protective barrier that blends feeling with awareness.

CORAL REEF – 1) the slow building of a living organism of feeling and awareness that acts as a protective barrier from being overtaken by absolute change.

CORD – 1) represents a thought or idea that is resilient.

CORN – 1) represents the necessary intellectual nourishment that comes from taking in many highly organized commitments to ideas.

CORN FIELD – 1) practical origin of entire mini-society of related necessary collections of highly organized commitments to ideas, thoughts, conclusions and intellectual property *(e.g., a specifically themed library, an archive, collection of all laws passed by Congress from its inception; etc.)*.

CORNER – 1) represents a man-made structural element of one's spiritual home in the world.

CORRUPT – 1) that which is filled with decay; 2) that which has been caused to be in decline; 3) a state of debilitation illness; 4) any sort of malady that will ultimately, if it goes unchecked, spread and ruin the entire relative contextual location.

CORSAGE – 1) represents a particular or specific experience, that connects or protects the union between embrace of the world and actions in the world, that is prominently displayed for others to see.

COT – 1) temporary place in dwelling place of the soul for retreat and restoration of powers; 2) temporary or impromptu place for meditation in spiritual dwelling; 3) temporary location of restoring and recuperating rest.

COUCH – 1) shared moment in time; 2) a place for many to rest and repose; 3) several are still on their paths as their feet are on the ground; 4) a place to rest comfortably on belief systems and structures in life, designed to accommodate more than one; 5) a place to connect and share; 6) represents the need to come together and to connect with others; [VINYL COUCH] 7) a smooth place to rest *(not sleep)* on belief systems and structures in life that is desired by many people, a place to come together and to connect, rest and share; 8) this is not a place to change for with it there is a sense of stagnancy, of wasting time.

COUPLET – 1) expression that brings spirit; 2) balanced statement that is spiritual in nature but also memorable and entertaining; 3) spiritual expression for the many; 4) means by which one can express spiritual point of view or wisdom to all people.

COURT – [COURT OF LAW] 1) where justice and issues of legality within society are decided; [SPORTS] 2) location for competitive matching of skill in organized, pre-arranged and mutually agreed upon tests; [ROYAL] 3) the inner circle of the enactment of manifest destiny to rule and lead society; [RELATIONSHIP] 4) where and when one declares the intention in their heart, expresses their love, makes concerted effort to win affection of another.

COURT JESTER – 1) one who is in service to entertain, distract or divert with the entertainment skills; 2) being on call, to diffuse stress or great responsibility momentarily so that humor results; 3) represents state of selflessness in one who serves the pleasure of another without thought of self; 4) service at expense of self in society's view.

COURT OF LAW – 1) represents involvement of the persons, places or things where justice and issues of legality within society are decided; 2) suggests that an issue of societal legality needs to be determined.

COURTROOM – 1) where justice and issues of legality within society are decided; 2) represents the need to decide an issue in a larger arena than simply one's own mind.

COURTSHIP – 1) where and when one declares the intention in their heart, expresses their love, makes concerted effort to win affection of another.

COURTYARD – 1) nature that is found is in the center of the spiritual dwelling place of the soul in the manifest realm.

COUSIN – 1) peripheral and lateral association that is extremely close and in union with one; 2) signifies parallel familial lineage as relevant to one's specific moment in time.

COW – 1) primary provider of essence of life.

COWBOY HAT – 1) elective connection with, or protection from, divine is egotistical and meant to draw attention to the self and one's spiritual condition.

CRAB – 1) elements of the lower self, or base nature, each human being has *(e.g., lust, hunger, sex, eating, and greed)*; [CRAWLING UP OUT OF WATER ONTO THE SHORE] 2) something from the base-self is emerging; 3) a behavior of the lower self emerges and alters one's path.

CRAWLING INSECT - 1) highly evolved item or idea that intrudes, often in clandestine way to irritate or infiltrate; 2) that which takes away one's concentration and focus of what is going on in life; 3) the little things that eventually consume one.

CRAWLING INSECT – 1) things that one is bothered by; 2) things that take away one's concentration and take the focus off what is going on in one's life; 3) the little things that eventually consume one's time, attention, focus and serenity.

CRAYONS – 1) tools for communication through visual elements.

CREAM – 1) richest, fattest, part of essence of life; 2) divinity in manifest elements.

CREDIT CARD – 1) manifest societal tool for manipulating monetary flow *(color(s) are relevant as to nature, manner or means of that manipulation)*.

CRÈPE – 1) nourishment that is thin and is designed to carry a variety of sources of nourishment.

CRESCENT MOON - 1) deception is nearly complete; 2) cycle of self-deception has moved one to near total darkness yet one stays in denial.

CREST – 1) significant high point; 2) momentary elevation in life that allows brief feeling of uplift and the view that comes with it; 3) highest a particular path, activity or awareness can be.

CRIB – 1) society's first dictated decision of how a new life will rest; 2) social trend term for one's dwelling place of the soul in urban life.

CROCHET – 1) need to create belief system based on single, highly developed thought or idea is necessary for the individual to do; 2) repetitive pattern of belief system based on single, very developed idea, that creates depth and makes a design *(specific color(s) relevant when present)*.

CROCODILE – 1) descendent of ancient ancestral species being equally comfortable in spirit or manifest, and able to transition with agility from one state to the other; 2) antediluvian element of nature in which relationship between spirit and manifest in which only actions in manifest will nourish the soul.

CROISSANT – 1) spiritually based provider of life nourishment that is, of itself, a representation of the exponential curve, or Fibonacci sequence, of ever expanding life.

CROQUET – 1) the circular and anti-productive state in life when one simply plays with commitment as an exercise of practicality, rather than seriousness; 2) represents one who travels on one's path, playing with commitment, just for amusement of self; 3) disastrous waste of life when one does not take commitment seriously.

CROSS – RELIGION] 1) organized religion; [NON-RELIGIOUS SHAPE] 2) an intersection where manifest and spirit cohabit and give access to the psychically gifted for crossing over.

CROSSROAD – 1) where spirit and the manifest meet there is life; 2) a natural intersection where manifest and spirit cohabit and give access to the psychically gifted for crossing over, and therefore a prime location in which to perform rituals.

CROW – 1) solitary traveler who instinctively knows natural direction; 2) portent of death, ending or loss of direction; 3) dark inspiration.

CROWD – 1) represents a group within society.

CROWN – 1) responsibility to others by birthright; 2) inheritor of public trust; 3) imposed ego-centric stance; 4) born to role of domination.

CROWN CHAKRA – 1) represents one's connection to the divine.

CRUCIFIX – 1) structure of organized religion wherein the manifest and spirit intersect.

CRUMB – 1) represents a mere morsel of life.

CRUTCHES – 1) necessary means of aid to travel on the path.

CRYSTAL – 1) reflector of light; 2) has electric charge; 3) a living thing; 4) source of power, that which stores of power and information.

CUM - 1) life essence; 2) spirit essence.

CUP – 1) experiences, possessions; 2) cup of water that is rebirth of the spirit; 3) lesson learned, experience retained.

CUP OF TEA EMPTY – 1) potential to change and grow exists, but as yet there is no direction, objective or plan.

CUP OF TEA FULL – 1) potential growth remains impossible until one assimilates that change.

CUP OF TEA PARTIALLY FILLED – 1) potential to change has begun to present itself, or has been half way assimilated.

CUP POURING OUT BLOOD – 1) represents irretrievable loss; 2) suggests that one's show of feelings is making forfeit that which life has given one.

CUPCAKE – 1) small but special nourishment in celebration of an individual; 2) special solitary nourishment that is more celebratory of the self than substantial.

CURLY HAIR – 1) active thoughts; 2) active, circular or chaotic thoughts.

CURRY – 1) represents that which ads flavor to experience and makes it last regardless of contextual circumstances that might otherwise degrade or erode.

CURTAINS – 1) using a belief system to block view of alternative points of view; 2) use of a belief system to prevent light from entering one's spiritual dwelling place; 3) represents how easy it is to disregard opportunities to see things in a different way when one has a belief system that might block that view; 4) one's belief system can be used to entrap one with complacency.

CUT FLOWERS – 1) experiences that one has had; 2) past experiences one is holding onto, though they are dead and past.

CYBERSPACE – 1) imaginary or virtual place where individuals meet via electronic markers in self-created, self-directed social structure.

CYLINDER – 1) potential opportunity to take action that simultaneously involves commitment, necessity and extruding all one can from one's gifts; 2) momentary state in which taking an action will equally combine commitment, necessity and extruding all one can from one's gifts.

CYMBALS – 1) gift of sound that accentuates and celebrates.

D

DAFFODIL – 1) hooded, intellectual experience; 2) vibrant, mind-based experience that returns cyclically, and each time comes back stronger.

DAISY – 1) represents an experience that is intellectual or ego-based at its core, but yields a broad and consistent spiritual result in every direction.

DAM – 1) that which blocks flow; 2) societal means of containing and directing change, with primary objective of preventing change; 3) blockage of flow, growth or change due to predominant belief that these will cause destruction of social order.

DAMN – 1) to become aligned with darkness due to outside directive; 2) to wish to cause some person, place or thing to fall into darkness; 3) to willfully cause one (including one's self) to have one's connection with light severed.

DANCING – 1) one's body is being music, thus the body becomes the language of spirit; 2) manifestation of living spirit on one's path; 3) embodiment of spirit

DANGLING – 1) hanging on to inspiration even when it is dragging one down, but the outcome of letting go of the ideal or other inspiring thing is to be brought back to the path, which is ultimately good news.

DARE DEVIL – 1) one who only takes risks when the best positive outcome is merely ego-based laud and nothing more.

DARK CLOUDS – 1) presumption of nebulous coming darkness; 2) bad dreams; 3) dangerous, ego-based dreams or aspirations; 4) general paranoid state without firm basis; 5) dark outlook, foreboding, with no grounded basis.

DARK STAR – 1) dark, unique, isolated ideal; 2) distant source of light that promotes feelings of isolation, uniqueness, or stagnation; 3) concept, idea, belief, goal, or ideal about one's unique qualities, loneliness, isolation or stagnation that guides one through darkness; 4) those beliefs of uniqueness, isolation or stagnation which provide light in darkest moments of life, causing one to be able to make it through the darkness; 5) those beliefs of uniqueness, isolation or stagnation which sustains hope.

DART – 1) necessary means to target and attack something that must be addressed specifically and removed without harming anything at all connected to it.

DART BOARD – 1) place where one is able to effectively target and attack something that must be addressed specifically, yet can be later removed without harming anything at all connected to it.

DAUGHTER – 1) that which is brought to life that can, itself, then bring things to life; 2) a gift that keeps giving; 3) setting into motion something that will itself be a catalyst for more creation.

DAWN – 1) new beginning; 2) start of new journey; 3) one casts a long shadow, thus can see the horizon and the goal, yet you don't quite see the next step; 4) one sees the direction and the long term, but doesn't know how to get there.

DAY – 1) a specific journey within a life; [NEW DAY] 2) new beginning, start of new journey.

DAY BREAK – 1) new beginning; 2) start of new journey.

DAYDREAM – 1) a step away from conscious perception and into intuitive, meditative or non-rational vision state; 2) escape from reality; 3) disconnection.

DEATH – 1) inevitability; 2) highest thing at stake, and highest focus on what one needs to do in life; 3) ending of some element of our manifest life and opportunity to journey within; 4) cycle, reality.

DEBT – 1) aftermath requirements resulting from of past actions based on false flow, or projected future flow; 2) balancing effect in manifest; 3) duty coming from promise or commitment.

DEBUTANTE – 1) one entering society for the first time; 2) place of the beginner in pre-arranged societal role; 3) new beginning in social sense.

DECAY – 1) that which is waste, and is dismissed, will be that which will ultimately nourishes over time; 2) process of destruction in order to evolve into new intended and vital role.

DECORATION – 1) how one enhances one's dwelling place of the soul; 2) one's expression of one's soul's true habitat.

DEER – 1) gentle, shy, vulnerable, alert, quick, timid; 2) defense is awareness, fastness and alertness.

DENTAL FLOSS – 1) idea or thought that clarifies anger; 2) idea or thought that will remove lingering things which remain in one's expression after anger has been used to destroy.

DENTIST – 1) one who assists others to keep their anger in good condition, assuring nothing will make it deteriorate, and filling already deteriorated places with precious lasting replacement.

DENTURES – 1) false anger used after original and true anger has deteriorated, most often because anger has become a way of life.

DEODORANT – 1) assurance that the results of internal change do not have negative effect on the inspiration of others.

DESERT – 1) resource of ancient wisdom, 2) place where barriers that have been through everything that can be experienced have been reduced to nothing; 3) resource for all of life that appears devoid of life.

DESK – 1) where one prepares to interact with community; 2) a private place that allows for meetings and preparations that will bring something to fruition; 3) preparing to bring something to the community.

DETOUR – 1) augmented path when barrier renders original path forward impossible to follow.

DEVELOPMENT – 1) new intersection that is unplanned, but not necessarily unknown; 2) implementing what has come through imagination so that current progress can be augmented: 3) allowing, or assisting, the natural or planned progression to reach fruition.

DEVIL – 1) perversion of the mind and thought; 2) intellect's thought or belief regarding the spiritual self that makes one become one's own enemy; 3) self-destruction; 4) danger to self from within one's mind.

DIAMOND – 1) that which reflects and amplifies light of spirit in manifest; 2) that which allows spiritual light and intention to be broken into a variety of manifest forms; 3) that which can take variety of manifest forms of spiritual idea and refocus it as pure spirit; 4) the permanence of spiritual truth; 5) that which delivers spiritual light and truth; 6) awakening; 7) the grace of spirit presence; 8) generator and absorber of light energy.

DICTIONARY – 1) coming together of ideas from different cultures and matching them with like ideas of another culture or other cultures; 2) book of human wisdom that creates the possibility to communicate completely across manifest cultural boundaries.

DIETARY SUPPLEMENT CAPSULE – 1) commitment to assimilation that allows for better manifestation.

DIETARY SUPPLEMENT PILL – 1) gift that helps assimilation leading to better manifestation.

DIETARY SUPPLEMENT POWDER – 1) ancient wisdom that helps assimilation leading to better manifestation.

DIG IN EARTH WITH HANDS – 1) doing works that will nourish one's self or others.

DIGESTION CHAKRA - 1) see **ASSIMILATION CHAKRA**

DILAPIDATED – 1) has gone through so much in manifest that it no longer can function as originally intended; 2) nearing fulfillment of all paths through all obstacles and barriers to become wisdom.

DILETTANTE – 1) see **CHARLATAN** 1) one who professes knowledge or ability one does not have; 2) one who presumes to know better.

DIM SUM – 1) spiritual nourishment that is meant to share and that comes in little bites; 2) determined effort to get spiritual nourishment.

DINGY – 1) solitary means of navigating, enduring and working through change that requires inspiration.

DINOSAUR – 1) represents most ancient and primitive of human instincts; 2) irony in life that though something may be large, ferocious and powerful, before nature all is vulnerable; 3) as with the tower, representative of the fact that everything in the manifest is vulnerable regardless of size.

DIPLOMA – 1) manifest representation that one has completed a set of lessons that places them into a position of earned achievement, prominence and the responsibility for sharing what they have done.

DIPLOMAT – 1) one who has ability to be liaison between differing cultures, beliefs and systems.

DIRECTION – 1) path; 2) way forward.

DIRECTOR – 1) one who is tasked with leading forward through management and giving direction rather than more direct physical action.

DIRECTORY – 1) collection of wisdom that allows those who consult it to navigate, and find their way.

DIRT – [FROM THE EARTH] 1) nourishment resulting from decay.

DIRT FLOOR - 1) one's foundation is practical and potentially life giving.

DISAPPEAR – 1) transform from manifest to non-manifest; 2) no longer relevant to spiritual development on path; 3) move to another location in space-time; 4) become fulfilled.

DISASTER – 1) event in the manifest that serves as catalyst for widespread growth; 2) mass transition into another state; 3) collapse of current manifest alignment.

DISC – 1) gift, talent, or natural asset; 2) gift that is central to manifest purpose, so much so that it becomes one's fate; 3) gift that rises each day in one's life, as the sun does in the manifest, to which one must commit in order to be ultimately fulfilled.

DISCLAIMER – 1) dark statement of disassociation; 2) abandonment resulting from self-centered fear; 3) outward sign that one fears that others have the ability to so affect the self that by stating something it will change one, and so one feels compelled by this fear to declare to the world around that there is no association; 4) direct fear into repulsion.

DISEASE – 1) organism's way of balancing as over-abundance in some area of life by creating a matching deficit in another area; 2) impetus for movement toward health; 3) organic cry for help from the world around; 4) opportunity to others to be of selfless service; 5) catalyst for the stubborn to admit the need for help; 6) natural demonstration of need that sets the Law of Flow in motion.

DISENGAGED – 1) disconnected from something that was once, or is destined to be, connected; 2) divergence of paths once joined; 3) beginning of new direction and with it new associations; 4) refusal of closeness or interdependence; 5) prideful cutting off; 6) healthy distancing from something not right; 7) active decision to end association whether or not purpose of connection has been fulfilled.

DISH WASHER – [PERSON] 1) one who restores gifts to ready them for renewed use after they have just fulfilled a nourishing purpose; 2) one who performs selfless service for others so that their gifts may always continue to be of maximum service to the world; [MACHINE] 3) mechanism to automatically restore gifts to readiness for renewed purpose after episode of nourishing use; 4) attempt to automate that which is otherwise selfless service either to a} allow energy to be better spent, b} be certain gifts are always ready for new use, or c} avoid the need for selfless service.

DISINTEREST – 1) mind not able to embrace some thing; 2) lack of feeling of connection with something; 3) avoidance of something in one's path due to the opinion that the intellect knows better what should be in one's path than spirit; 4) construction of the mind to reinforce isolation; 5) attempt to avoid.

DISTANCE – 1) illusion of separation in time and/or space; 2) barrier created by space-time that serves as catalyst for spiritual growth opportunity; 3) test of durability of connection; 4) teacher of true importance of a connection.

DISTENDED – 1) pushed beyond a natural limitation to the point of distortion, discomfort, disease or collapse.

DISTRIBUTION POINT - 1) one or group who take advantage of a need that demands the transporting of that which is needed.

DISTRIBUTOR – 1) provider of needed goods or services; 2) one who assists in making connection available to wide array of situations; 3) generous one who shares with others; [IN COMMERCE] 4) one or group who take advantage of a need that demands the transporting of that which is needed.

DIVINE AXIS – 1) the crown and root chakras work together to complete the cycle of relationship between heaven and earth, which the human being represents.

DIVINING ROD – 1) power of the Great Y to find connection through divine grace; 2) bridging gap from bifurcated manifestation to spiritual unification; 3) using combination of spirit and manifest to find that which supports life, allows growth and change, and places one in connection with the flow of life.

DOCTOR – 1) one who has selflessly dedicated their life's path to the healing, health and wellness of all others; 2) trained healer; 3) imprimatur of legitimacy; 4) authority figure in matters of health and healing.

DOG – 1) represents natural companion; 2) in relationship through companionship; [LOST DOG] 3) a silent warning; [BARKING DOG] 4) active warning; [SLEEPING DOG 1] 5) companion available yet receiver of message is not open to companionship; [SLEEPING DOG 2] 6) a companion is not available at that moment but is there; [DOG ON LEASH] 7) guidance that one gets from or gives to companions *(depending who is leading)*; [DOG GUARDING HOUSE] 8) companion that protects dwelling place of the soul because of what the soul stands for; [GUARD DOG] 9) companion who is dedicated to providing one with protection; [SEEING EYE DOG] 10) familiar who serves as companion to one with vision or other spiritual gift so that they may maximize their gift of vision.

DOG GUARDING HOUSE - 1) companion that protects one's dwelling place of the soul because of what the soul stands for.

DOG ON LEASH - 1) represents guidance that one gets from or gives to companions.

DOILY – 1) inspired but ineffective spiritual protection; [LACE] 2) inspired but ineffective idea of spiritual protection, overly simplistic as entire network is based on a single thought or concept; [PAPER] 3) inspired but ineffective product of history in one's life, has not been adapted to suit present moment but is hopelessly lost in the past.

DOLL – 1) non-living representation of life for play; 2) false persona intended for amusement and fantasy.

DOLL HOUSE – 1) pretend or false dwelling place of the soul for play; 2) pretense of one with false persona that their pursuits are of a spiritual nature when they are actually for amusement or fantasy fulfillment.

DOLPHIN – 1) the knowing that guides instinctively through major change; 2) empathic messenger from spirit in times of growth, chaos, tumultuous change or evolution.

DOMINANT – 1) hierarchical relation dominance within Yang structure; 2) imposition of power over a situation, a group, a task, or another.

DOOR – 1) opening to a new path; 2) opportunity for something different *(might be a path, room, or abyss)*; [OPEN DOOR] 3) willingness; [LOCKING DOOR] 4) desire to control access of others to enter a new path, protection to have some means of determining who enters the new path; [LOCKED DOOR] 5) control over the portal to a specific path; [ROTTEN DOOR] 6) entry to a new path has been there for a long time and is disintegrating through lack of use.

DOOR CHIME – 1) need for direct use of harmonious spirit or spiritual harmony in manifest in order to gain access to new path that is available; 2) giving alert by means of spiritual harmony that there is a new path available.

DOORBELL – 1) need for direct use of spirit in manifest in order to gain access to new path that is available; 2) giving alert by spiritual means that there is a new path available.

DOORMAT – 1) protective measure so that when journey of new path begins it is free of any residue from prior paths; 2) reassurance that new path will begin fresh, without prejudice or baggage from earlier experiences; 3) guarantee of clean start on new path. *(in each case the specific color, construction material, imagery on, or words printed on the doormat give direct information as to precise meaning in each vision or dream in which the doormat appears).*

DOORWAY – 1) represents opening to, or avenue to, a new path.

DOPPLER EFFECT – 1) the moment to spiritually engage is when a thing is upon one; 2) hesitating or waiting one may engage but without the presence of spirit to grace the process; 3) an action of faith is the only way to properly engage; 4) when something in closest to one is the moment to engage it, do not wait.

DORSAL FIN – 1) one's past experiences will guide one through change.

DOUBLE CHIN – 1) has two distinct ways of entering a situation or event.

DOUBT – 1) ego's power of veto over the heart; 2) fear that disables forward movement on the path; 3) the faith killer.

DOVE - 1) manifest presence of the idea, concept, inspiration and opinion that is spirit.

DOWNWARD POINTING FINGER – 1) a message about earth and basis of life on earth.

DRACULA – 1) one who uses anger to remove feeling and heart knowing from another.

DRAGON – 1) ability to adapt easily between spirit and manifest, use inspiration as a means of mobility, and become actively passionate in the manifest realm; 2) vulnerable only to those spiritually strong; 3) symbol of amazing earthly power, untamable power on earth.

DRAGONFLY – 1) able to remain identified with abundance and preciousness while using inspiration to remain stable in times of great change, but still in connection with the change; 2) ability to remain actively engaged to changing path through use of inspiration.

DRAPES – 1) using a belief system to block view of alternative points of view; 2) use of a belief system to prevent light from entering one's spiritual dwelling place; 3) represents how easy it is to disregard opportunities to see things in a different way when one has a belief system that might block that view; 4) one's belief system can be used to entrap one with complacency.

DREAM – 1) of any possible combination among three elements: inner workings, precognition, or message from spirit; 2) means of self-healing *(through inner workings)*, and/or preparedness *(precognition)*, and/or divine guidance *(message from spirit)*.

DRESS UP - 1) trying on all different ways of appearing in the world.

DRINK – 1) self-determined, self-administered change in small and heavily controlled amounts.

DRIVING GLOVES – 1) activity that avoids path; 2) what one does in life to achieve goals without being on path of spiritual development; 3) how one interacts that aids in avoiding spiritual path.

DROUGHT – 1) lack of growth, change or development that kills one's spirit; 2) state in which if one does not change, one's life will die in spirit; 3) having forfeited everything due to stuborn unwillingness to change, grow, learn or develop.

DROWNING – 1) perishing due to absolute change; 2) changing from manifest to spirit, the ultimate change.

DROWNING IN MUD – 1) being completely altered by practicality; 2) practicality changes one's life entirely; 3) to completely change due to practicality.

DRUGSTORE – 1) manifest location where one can go for commitment to manifest presence on path; 2) gifts that help, through assimilation, to better or more effective manifestation on path, ancient wisdom that helps lead to better interaction with one's path, and every other aid for one's path.

DRUM – 1) instincts, essential nature of spirit in manifest form; <u>[DRUM BEAT]</u> 2) conveyance of information that informs anyone who hears it; 3) non-specific delivery of information.

DRUM BEAT - 1) conveyance of information that informs anyone who hears it; 2) non-specific delivery of information.

DUCK – 1) opinions that aren't well thought out, that are brusque and simple and enforced on people; 2) ability to use spirit, and spiritual opinions, so that one remains unaffected by change and unchanged though the world around has completely changed.

DUCKLING - **1)** new opinions that aren't well thought out, that are brusque and simple and enforced on people; 2) brand new ability to use spirit, and spiritual opinions, so that one remains unaffected by change and unchanged though the world around has completely changed.

DUCT TAPE – 1) belief system that is one-sided and binds anything, holding it immobile; 2) one-sided belief system that is falsely precious and creates stagnation.

DUKE – 1) **YANG** high position in life that comes with responsibility to care for those below but defer in all things to those above.

DUMP TRUCK – 1) powerful for removing and dumping unwanted things from one's path in accordance with one's will; 2) means of removing items from one's path so as to avoid actually interacting with one's journey on that path.

DUNE – 1) barrier found in ancient wisdom; 2) koan.

DUNE BUGGY – 1) means of avoiding ancient wisdom barriers, or traversing koans, without actually traveling on one's path, which results in an ironic aftermath of inspiration about the great truth found in ancient wisdom and its koans.

DUNGEON – 1) means of travel between manifest and spirit that will seem as entrapment, imprisonment or severe and cruel punishment unless encountered with actions of faith as a pathway to pure spirit.

DUSK – 1) the state in which one no longer sees the original goal and thus loses direction; 2) one does not remember the recent immediate past, yet one easily remembers the distant past and one's origins.

DUST – 1) image of mortality *(what the manifest body eventually becomes)*; 2) the temporal quality of life; 2) reminiscence bringing awareness that as one proceeds on one's path in human imperfection one will leave an imprint on the path as traveled.

DUST STORM – 1) when one is overcome by wisdom and blinded by it; 2) when forward movement, vision and everything else is stopped by a sudden all-consuming inspiration of ancient wisdom; 3) being overwhelmed by the high minded and absolute demands ancient wisdom place on one in life.

DUSTBIN – 1) combination of necessity and experience that assists in clearing one's path of unnecessary clutter and debris.

DYE – 1) change that is so complete the essential nature of the thing change has also been changed.

E

EAGLE - 1) ability to see clearly from afar, wisdom, opinion in wisdom, looks at the whole thing.

EAR – 1) what one hears and follows; 2) what one does with what one hears; 3) the interpretation one places on what one hears; 3) what literally enters one's head.

ears itching – 1) one must actively seek counsil, wisdom or advice.

ears tingling – 1) feeling the need to seek counsil, wisdom or advice.

EARTH – 1) symbol for abundance, for the bounty of nature; 2) commitment of all living organisms; 3) agreements and commitments of life forms to exist in an ever changing, cyclical, abundant and self-maintaining system; 4) for one to really embrace earth one must embrace being alive in a physical body; 5) foundation in manifest existence; 6) place of protection and isolation.

EARTH TURNING – 1) the unfoldment of one's life; 2) the whole of life.

EARTHQUAKE – 1) when one's grounding and foundation is upset, or put into sudden upheaval; 2) when one's nature makes is impossible to proceed on the established path; 3) that which unsettles everything one is connected to in reality.

EAST – 1) that which is the new beginning; 2) where one starts; 3) place from where things came into view and become real; 4) the origin, the new, the progression into the future.

EASTER – 1) Christian assimilation of Pagan celebration for political reasons, making it easier to convert Pagans; 2) spiritual renewal; 3) Pentacostal rebirth of the soul.

EASTER ISLAND – 1) earlier civilization that honored the African forefathers of the human race as the most superior beings.

EASTERN – 1) that which comes from the place of the new beginning; 2) also coming from where one started; 3) coming from the same place where things first came into view and becoame real; 4) from the place of origin, unto the progression toward the future.

EAT – 1) use anger to break down that which will ultimately nourish; 2) assimilation of world around in such a way as that it is absorbed and becomes part of one's manifest experience; 3) establishment of wisdom by taking in everything, particularly the things which cause anger, and making them part of you; 4) ultimate Yin connection and oneness with all, even through anger.

ECLIPSE – SOLAR] 1) when self-deception blocks the light of spirit; [LUNAR] 2) when the shadow self blocks one's view that they are self-deceived.

EDEN – 1) where mankind learned, and by learning were cast out of paradise, yet, through the irony of spirit, that learning that got mankind cast out of the Garden of Eden is the very thing that will allow mankind to re-enter that paradise; 2) memory of paradise that is how the mind is able to defeat the heart and cause mankind to self-destruct.

EDITOR – 1) person or agency of life that organizes one's wisdom before it is presented to the world.

EEL – 1) the ability of chi to traverse change with ease.

EFFERVESCENCE – 1) represents entertainment that is infused with hollow commitment to inspiration and deceives while it changes the host.

EFFICIENCY APARTMENT - **1)** one's dwelling place of the soul that is in a single cube within urban life where each individual has their own singular space within an **APARTMENT BUILDING.**

EGG – 1) commitment from which comes new life.

EGG SHELL – 1) represents spiritual commitment that contains the manifest blueprint of new life.

EGYPT – 1) symbol of ancient

wisdom; 2) origin of symbols of 22 Tenets of Spirituality.

EGYPTIAN – 1) infused with, of, or pertaining to ancient wisdom; 2) origin of current universal system of spirituality.

EIGHT – 1) represents the highest achievement of mankind in the manifest.

EJACULATE - 1) life essence; 2) spirit essence.

ELBOW – 1) the thing that articulates one's embrace of the world, allowing one to bring the thing embraced into one's heart.

ELECTION – 1) unification of collective voice to determine societal choice preferred by the majority; 2) collective use of individuals' expression of uniqueness taken together for the greater good.

ELECTRIC CHORD – 1) the manifestation of the idea that allows the artificial life force, ironically created by means of resistance and restriction of flow, to flow.

ELECTRIC FAN – 1) artificial source of inspiration.

ELECTRIC GENERATOR – 1) that which creates the artificial life force, ironically made by means of resistance and restriction of flow.

ELECTRIC HOLE PUNCH – 1) artificial means of penetrating one's results of wisdom and knowledge so that it can be contained in a collective but temporary resource.

ELECTRIC LIGHT BULB – 1) idea; 2) inspiration; 3) commitment that contains manifestation of light produced when an artificial life force is forced to encounter intentional restriction of flow such that the resistance itself generates heat and causes such an effect.

ELECTRIC LIGHT – 1) manifestation of light produced when an artificial life force is forced to encounter intentional restriction of flow such that the resistance itself generates heat and causes such an effect.

ELECTRIC SOCKET – 1) manifest source of artificial life force ironically created by means of resistance and restriction of flow.

ELECTRIC SWITCH – 1) the tool that controls the flow of artificial life force—ironically created by means of resistance and restriction of flow—that requires direct action to manipulate.

ELECTRIC TOOTHBRUSH – 1) artificial means of maintaining anger.

ELECTRIC TRAIN – 1) artificial means of transport on societal predetermined paths stripping individuals of their autonomy and unique individuality of path; 2) enforcement of singular path on the many.

ELECTRICAL CHARGER – 1) mechanism which resupplies artificial life force, ironically created by means of resistance and restriction of flow, to those things in life which rely on this source of force.

ELECTRICITY – 1) artificial life force ironically created by means of resistance and restriction of flow.

ELEMENT – 1) essential part or essential building block of manifest reality.

ELEPHANT – 1) commitment of purpose; 2) persistence of memory; 3) destructive force of both resentment s; 4) tendency toward blind greed.

elephant trunk – 1) function of memory.

ELEVATOR – 1) manifest structure that assists elevation, but is restricted to elevate only within the manifest world, and compounded restriction by the limits of what has already been created as structure within the manifest realm.

ELF – 1) the quality of humans to be magical; 2) the inexplicable effectiveness of humility; 3) that which is most aligned with light is considered least real in the manifest.

ELIXIR – 1) essence that nourishes body and soul; 2) nourishing change that refurbishes and rebuilds; 3) nourishment that entices, deludes and casts a spell over the mind.

ELOPE – 1) free expression of commitment to join together in love without being bound by societal traditions and strictures; 2) joining in love that is private and solely of and for the ones so joined; 3) denial of opportunity of others to celebrate a couple's love.

EMBASSY – 1) dwelling place of the spirit of communication, cooperation and common purpose between societal, organizational, military and governmental groupings of self-identified individuals working together.

EMBER – 1) remnants of destructive repression; 2) lingering destructive results of out of control inspiration and repressed feeling.

EMBLEM – 1) symbol or insignia indicating allegiance to, membership in, alignment with or loyalty to an established belief, societal structure, conceptual ideal, guiding principle or establish entity; 2) symbol that embodies precepts, goals, ideals and beliefs of larger body; 3) symbol that, when displayed, establishes connection with precepts, goals, ideals and beliefs of larger body; 4) visible marking indicating one who is faithful to lineage.

EMERALD – 1) represents the rarest agent in the manifest that brings abundance of spiritual light.

EMPIRE – 1) manifest joining of communities across a vast expanse of lands, unified under the might of one government with intention of conquering all known lands.

EMPLOYED – 1) one who is active in accordance with an agreement to exchange labor for compensation or provision in accordance with some pre-arranged scale.

EMPLOYEE – 1) one who is providing labor in exchange for compensation or provision in accordance with some pre-arranged scale.

EMPLOYER – 1) one who has agreed to give compensation or provision in accordance with a pre-arranged scale to those who provide labor.

EMPRESS – 1) spiritual tenet #3—the spiritual presence in the universe that has omniscient awareness of each manifest soul's life path and provides maximum opportunities to grow; 2) all that happens in all lives that gives all opportunity to grow comes from this spiritual power in the universe.

EMPTY CHAIR – 1) moment in time that is open and unfilled; 2) a promise; 3) another perspective, another moment in time.

EMPTY CUP OF TEA - 1) potential to change and grow exists, but as yet there is no direction, objective or plan.

ENDOSKELETON – 1) spiritual structure that supports manifest event yet is invisible from the outside; 2) that which lies at the core, gives structure from within, and is spiritual in nature.

ENEMY – 1) one locked in mutual strengthening process by opposition; 2) teacher by emotional and physical conflict; 3) the one who is most like one, but only in the ways one detests about one's self; 4) future friend and ally.

ENGAGEMENT RING – 1) perpetual, precious, ongoing union that brings spiritual light into the manifest.

ENGINE – 1) mechanism that causes and sustains forward motion and is powered by the joint efforts of the enterprise of mankind; 2) that which supplies constant energy so that a structure in the manifest may continue to function; 3) that essence-fueled thing that keeps a person, place, idea, pursuit or attempt in motion.

ENORMOUS – 1) of extreme mass, presence, size or importance.

ENTERING A ROOM FACING BACKWARD – 1) repeating an already traveled part of the path; 2) returning to the past but forfeiting knowledge gained from having progressed beyond that past; 3) traveling backward in time; 4) lack of forward momentum and impetus yet with forward vision.

ENTOURAGE – 1) group of followers or devotees; 2) those who surround a person of prominence; 3) those who wish to serve individuals in prominent positions due to their desire to benefit personally from such proximity.

ENTRANCE – 1) represents beginning of new path.

ENTREPRENEUR – 1) manifest conscious being who is a manipulator of ideas, resources, people and markets; 2) clever of manifest ways; 3) manifest magician; 4) non-spiritually aware being who is highly creative and by maintaining a highly productive life can progress in spiritual development and reach path goals so long as guided by the heart, and following morally and ethically sound and principled manner of enterprise.

ENVELOPE - 1) an idea that contains other ideas, concepts, and or philosophies.

ENVIRONMENT – 1) place; 2) unique combination of forces, presences, identities and cyclical processes that work as a singular construct.

ENZYME – 1) that which causes things to happen yet does not participate in the resulting actions; 2) one who remains unaffected and unmarked by that which they have caused to happen.

épaulets - 1) an acquired or elective state that pre-empts potential danger for those who feel vulnerable via an outward show of size, strength or evidence of importance of position in society.

EQUIPMENT – 1) those items or qualities, taken as a group, that are necessary to perform an entire complex function.

EQUIPMENT MANAGER – 1) one who manages all items or qualities, taken as a group, necessary to perform an entire complex function before, during and after *(in preparation for next function)* the enterprise is in action.

EQUIPPED – 1) to have all that is needed to perform an entire complex function.

ERASER – 1) condensed concentration of belief that will eliminate temporary ideas and communications; 2) the items created in the manifest realm that serve to eliminate temporary ideas and communications; 3) that which transforms anything from its manifest form into another, non-apparent or non-existent form.

ESCALATOR – 1) any system that, once engaged, will elevate one without the demand of action or expenditure of effort on the part of the one being elevated; 2) false elevation.

ESKIMO – 1) one who is adept at living as closely to spirit while still being alive as possible; 2) an avatar, ascended master, guru or spiritual being so advanced as to proceed in the manifest realm without the most common human needs and desires impeding the path.

ESSENCE – 1) conceptually essential element that causes something to manifest; 2) ejaculate; 3) that first, last and only thing that flows in manifest as the result of churlanta between og and warp.

ESSENTIAL – 1) the singular thing without which existence is impossible; 2) the thing that by its presence causes an entire manifestation to occur.

ESTUARY – 1) cumulative concordance of flow that results in a regularly appearing place of constant change for eons; 2) collective effect of joined flows; 3) pool of life being constantly replenished by that which flows into it.

ETHER – SPIRITUAL] 1) apparently non-manifest portions of existence within the astral but without taking recognizable or empirically discernable regular form; 2) place from which non-empirical spiritual influence is believed to come; 3) 19th and early 20th century term for spirit realm; [CHEMICAL] 4) gas that induces euphoria when inhaled, and makes the mind impervious to pain, believed at time of its discovery to promise a future without physical pain.

EUROPE – 1) the part of the universal commitment to manifest existence that includes the joining of tribes without each losing its unique cultural identity; 2) refinement of civilization in exchange for loss of spiritual bearing.

EVACUATION – 1) all living beings simultaneously leave a location; 2) mental exercise of contrast and comparison that produces useful result for particular specific use.

EVALUATOR – 1) one who examines and analyses for the purpose of making a determination that has been called for; 2) a standard or test that determines a sought for result.

EVANGELICAL – 1) one who so insecure that others must share exact belief and narrow interpretation in order to continue, usually calling for restrictive and punitive treatment for those who do not agree; 2) believer in a selected few simplistic truisms upon which a complex philosophy is built; 3) selective and restricted view that causes departure from awareness of true reality.

EVAPORATE – 1) to transform from state of change to state of inspiration.

EVE – RELATIONAL CONCEPT] 1) the onset of darkness that precedes new beginning; 2) on the brink of change or discovery that will shift paradigm; [RELIGIOUS OR MYTHICAL CONCEPT] 3) the first woman; 4) mother of the human race; 5) fashioned by god from the rib of Adam (see **BIBLE** genesis 2:18-25, also **ADAM**, **EDEN**, and **ADAM KADMON**); 6) eve, or "life," given after the transgression and its prophesied results, refers to first woman's function and destiny in the spiritual history or evolution of which she is the beginning.

EVEN KEEL – 1) to travel through change calmly and smoothly.

EVOLUTION – 1) generationally progressive change mandated by predisposition of all manifest things to be in constant state of change.

EXCREMENT – 1) the practicality of cleansing and discarding what is no longer useful; 2) waste that becomes fertile soil in cyclical environment of the manifest; 3) aspect of perfection of nature.

EXESSIVE YANG – 1) that which enforces division and domination; 2) stict controls on all things; 3) constant aggressive competition; 4) no possible peaceful coexistence; 5) lack of notion of equality among diversity.

EXCESSIVE YIN – 1) lack of boundaries, goals and definition; 2) vulnerable from being too passive and avoiding conflicts; 3) no willingness to stand for something and therefore will accept anything.

EXERCISE – 1) activity that promotes health and development of an organism; 2) to make use of a potential.

EXERT – 1) use of energy that causes something intentional to happen.

EXIT – 1) leave; 2) transition; 3) begin new endeavor not visible in the realm of current endeavor; 4) destination on society's path like graduation, marriage or giving birth.

EXODUS – 1) when an entire tribe, group, nation or community set off for another location by mutual agreement and universal consent.

EXOSKELETON – 1) external, rigid and protective commitment that contains living organisms and protects them in life; 2) commitment that protects from outside pressures.

EXPERIMENT – 1) a concerted and designed effort to see if hypothesized results do actually occur; 2) to try something out; 3) an isolated attempt to achieve something that, if successful, will then be applied on a less local environment, that has been selected with intention for similar purpose.

EXPRESSION CHAKRA – 1) being able to express in manifest for the truth of one's heart or spirit essence; 2) portal of chi flow through expression.

EYE - 1) window of the soul; 2) generator and absorber of light.

EYE LID – 1) represents one's ability to prevent others from seeing one's soul; 2) the way in which one might prevent light from entering.

EYE MAKE-UP – 1) decorative enhancement to enhance, draw attention to, or alter the look of the window of the soul; 2) presenting what one wants others to see when they look into your soul. *(color and detail attribute will contribute specific information about this process, its impetus, and its intention).*

EYEBROW – 1) over-arching thoughts how one views the world; 2) one's philosophical or higher minded thoughts about one's world view in the manifest.

EYEGLASSES – 1) how one elects to enhance or alter one's view of the world.

EYELASHES – 1) distinct and specific thoughts about that make up one's world view, or alter it by means of enhancement or embellishment.

EYELET – 1) incomplete parts of belief system that are an element of its design; 2) part of belief system that is designed to allow presence of anything that might be required to fill it by the individual; 3) belief system designed to allow and/or incorporate other beliefs.

EYELIDS - 1) how one controls the extent, or fact, of one's world view.

EYES – 1) see **EYE**.

EYESHADOW – 1) exercise of self-determination that allows one to show others how one chooses to view the world; 2) indicative of peripheral elements that color one's world view.

F

FABRIC – 1) belief system *(color and various elements and adornments give specifics)*; [WOVEN FABRIC] 2) belief system made up of intricate intersection and interrelationships between a great many different ideas and points of view coming together in time to form a solid network of thought; [KNITTED FABRIC] 3) a belief system based on a single idea that is twisted and turned back on itself in very meandering and convoluted ways so that it will appear to be far more intricate than it is; 4) simplistic belief system; [CLOTHING] 5) taking a belief system in life and with it creating protection, identity and/or personal expression.

FACE – 1) countenance, that which is presented; 2) that which is put forward as recognizable identity; 3) how one presents one's self to the world.

FACET – 1) one element of something far more complex; 2) a flat plane, or two dimensional aspect, that reflects and directs light.

FAITH – 1) taking an action because it is the right thing to do; 2) following the direction of the heart, ethical orientation, or spiritual construct with actions regardless of all else that may or may not support this action; 3) of doing the right thing no matter what, even when doubt and disbelief is in the way.

FALL – [SEASON] 1) maturity; [ACTION] 2) to loose movement on path and succumb to gravity; 3) involuntarily coming to ground.

FALLING STAR – 1) fleeting ideal; 2) distant source of light that traverses the darkness; 3) passing concept, idea, belief, goal, or ideal that can guide one through darkness; 4) that which momentarily provides light in darkest moments of life, causing one to be able to make it through the darkness; 5) that which gives a brief moment of hope.

FAMILY – 1) those with whom one is always connected; 2) national heritage; 3) those who guide, nurture, support and teach throughout one's life, even if unpleasant, abusive or contentious; 3) earthly physical connection to people.

FAN - 1)[HAND HELD] 1) perpetuating gossip by giving it inspiration; 2) determined effort; 3) to fuel the fire of stubbornness; [ADMIRER] 4) one who sees a person only as what they stand for, what function they serve, what duty they fulfill, rather than as who they actually are; 5) admirer of one's actions rather than one's self.

FANG – 1) hollow anger that can destroy without conscience; 2) represents state of heightened anger in which poison from within is directed to eliminate that which angers; 3) defensive and deadly invective that emerges in extreme states of anger and can completely destroy the target of that anger.

FARM – PLACE] 1) intentional organization of nature for the purpose of providing sustenance for a specific group of individuals; [ACTION] 2) to make use of earth with specific planned intention of producing sustenance for specific group of individuals.

FARM HOUSE – 1) dwelling place of the soul that is community minded and service oriented; 2) spiritual dwelling that is specifically used to feed and nourish a community.

FART – 1) unwanted, wasteful inspiration; 2) in cycle of nature, gaseous waste from digestion that serves as vital element of earth's atmosphere, fuel and overall balance.

FASCINATE – 1) to excite the mind and thereby disabling it from focus elsewhere; 2) manipulate the attention of others to ego-centric purpose.

FASCINATION – 1) to have one's mind excited and thereby disabled from focus elsewhere; 2) to have one's attention manipulated to another's ego-centric purpose.

FASHION – 1) societal trend that all, or most, follow.

FASHIONED OUT OF WOOD - 1) taking life and making it into something specific.

FATHER – 1) figure who brings one to life and bears the privilege and responsibility to educate, prepare, nurture, love and assist in the development of the emerging adult; 2) that which gives direction, sets boundaries, goals, etc. and is also supporter, provider, and authority designated to provide love and guidance throughout life but in particular in formative years; 3) lineage of yang, the yang in one; 4) that which gives one the gifts of yang *[i.e., ability to organize, prioritize, focus, recognize and make proper use of tools, etc.]*.

FATIGUES – 1) belief system used as protection, identity and advantage in fields of battle; 2) instinct bending to dark direction due to fear, presumed threat and sense of vulnerability whether or not it is actual; 3) advantageous direction on the path from defensive point of view.

FAUCET – 1) necessary and often precious means of applying controlled change to one's life.

FAUNA – 1) living organisms that make up vital part of balance of nature cycles.

FEATHER – 1) how opinion or gossip goes from one to another in an inspired way; [FEATHER IN THE AIR] 2) using speech to launch opinion or gossip and perpetuate its inspiration; [QUILL PEN] 3) using written word or publication to launch opinion or gossip and perpetuate its inspiration.

FEATHER ON HAT - 1) one claims information one received from elsewhere as one's own because it has become fully integrated it into one's being.

FEATHER WITHOUT BIRD - 1) one observes and believes what one has grown to stand for, it becomes one's own though later the observation comes that many people do it; 2) anything one figures out can be information, or become a new opinion.

FECES – 1) waste, something one has processed and then discards as toxic right now, will eventually nourish if given ample time; 2 [being soiled] one has processed something but will not let it go; it is no longer necessary and it can harm you if you don't let go.

FEEDING BIRDS BREAD CRUMBS – 1) using little bits of life to support one's own opinion; 2) knowing that all of life wouldn't support one's opinion, this represents a justification for keeping insubstantial opinions alive.

FEEL – 1) to experience an interaction with something that is not the self; [ACT OF TOUCH] 2) making the action of reaching out to connect with something outside of and other than self , one experiences the sensation of joining with other.

FEET – 1) the direction one goes on one's path.

feet itching – 1) one must actively change direction on one's path.

feet tingling – 1) feeling the need to change direction on one's path.

FELT – CLOTH] 1) a dense collection of small ideas, thoughts, opinions, facts, projections and observations brought together in a time of absolute change, followed by immense pressure to create a durable, flexible and very protective belief system; 2) a belief system that can be molded by necessity, along with passionately inspired, invasively forced change into whatever shape is happens to be forced into; [SENSATION] 3) an impression made by direct experience that is stored in one's memory for future reference.

FELT HAT – 1) a connection with the divine, and simultaneously a protection from naturally occurring intrusive change [see **RAIN**] , in the form of a belief system that is able to change to suit any circumstances, this belief system is made up of small ideas, thoughts, opinions, facts, projections and observations brought together in a time of absolute change, followed by immense pressure, which is at once durable, flexible and very protective.

FEMININITY – 1) societal designation of attributes, attitudes and actions that define one as being suitably female within that society only.

FENCE – PROTECTIVE BARRIER] 1) the meeting place of cultural differences in which each culture seeks to protect and keep pure its own cultural identity by constructing visible and practical, yet far more representative than prohibitive; 2) self created and enforced division from another; 3) practical, enforced separateness; [SPORT/DEFENSE] 4) opponents who have very strong feelings they are protecting, each with the desire to cut away all that is unnecessary from their world, i.e., each other.

FENCING – 1) the interaction between two opponents, with intensely strong feelings each is protecting, who each desire to cut away all that is unnecessary from their world, *(i.e., each other)*.

FERMENT – 1) a community-wide, or culture wide, proliferation of growth that is the result of the breaking down of cultural substance due to a combination of passion and an over abundant outward sweetness, this resulting growth is inspired and intoxicating, filled with chaotic and exponentially expanding hollow commitments that together form nothing exact, other than a further, self-fueled expansion of this transformation; 2) movement from pre-revolutionary to revolutionary state.

FERN – 1) a life state that produces many results but has little durable structure and no practical core; 2) a creative and prolific, but impractical life with no core strength that is highly responsive to light and darkness.

FERRET – 1) one who is drawn to flashy and glittery things, and very prone to secrecy and hiding.

FERRIS WHEEL – 1) ongoing and continuous fluctuation between manifest and divine, with no forward movement, and only for one's personal entertainment; 2) fate.

FERRY – 1) vehicle so that one can transverse necessary change that repeats over and over, without significant movement away from either shore.

FESTER – 1) self-destruction caused by unwillingness to allow inspiration or illumination to enter; 2) represents when a stagnant commitment becomes toxic when it goes unexpressed; 3) self-destructive power of unwillingness to express things one is truly and deeply committed to.

FESTIVAL – 1) annual, or regularly scheduled community celebration marking a milestone in the lives of people in the community; 2) coming together in spirit to celebrate a common event in community life.

FETID – 1) in state of decay that is beyond repair, and too toxic to become nourishment except after very long wait.

FETUS – 1) essence of an individual; 2) essence of manifestation of life; 3) deep, internal commitment to new life that by virtue of its presence fulfills that mission.

FIANCÉE – 1) one who is promised to another in anticipation of societal ritual of coupling.

FIELD – 1) natural setting that is open and offers promise of many possibilities.

FIG – 1) ripeness, things are ripe; 2) so ripe subject is ready to burst; 3) in late stage pregnancy, soon to give birth; 4) one in a state of knowing what simultaneously nourishes and fulfills.

FILM – MOTION PICTURE] 1) illusion that imitates life visible as a result of light traversing the film to create a projected image; [RESIDUE] 2) that which is left behind in the manifest as the result of an object having been physically present.

FILM DIRECTOR – 1) one who creates illusion that appears as life; 2) one who shapes and guides process of projecting illusion of life.

FILM PROJECTOR – 1) that which, in combination with spirit, will create illusion that appears as life; 2) mechanism that serves to create illusion of life; 3) that which creates visible illusion.

FILTH – 1) waste that is not discarded; 2) state when one has not completely let go of useless and unhealthy excess.

FINESSE – 1) flawless performance of one's duties in such a way that all goals were seemingly effortlessly achieved with great efficiency and poise.

FINGER – 1) solitary act of a person, yet falling short of the entire action; [FINGER POINTING DOWN] 2) about earth and basis of life on earth; [FINGER POINTING UPWARD] 3) represents acknowledgment of celestial; [ASTROLOGER, WIZARD FINGER UP] 4) points out significant planetary dance, and how it affects us on the earth; [AVERAGE PERSON FINGER DOWN] 5) regarding one's process of maintaining one's life in practical terms of their path; [AVERAGE PERSON FINGER UP] 6) celestial order coming into one's life, and need to become, or moment that one became, aware of it; [CHILD FINGER DOWN] 7) home, grounding, stability in life; [CHURCH-FIGURE FINGER DOWN] 8) attention on underworld and all the temptations; [CHURCH-FIGURE FINGER UP] 9) attention on divine, spirit, celestial; [FINGER POINTED INTO THE SEA] 10) attention on one's base nature *(hunt, kill, lust, defense)*; [INDEX FINGER] 11) guiding principle, specific act in life; [LEFT INDEX FINGER] 12) how the logical or linear process guides one's work; [RIGHT INDEX FINGER] 13) how the creative or non-linear process guides one's work.

FINGER POINTING TOWARD SEA – 1) indicating man's base nature (to hunt, kill, act on lust or in defense).

FINGERNAIL – 1) some specific action one takes; 2) furthest reach of some aspect of an action.

FINGERS – 1) see **FINGER.**

fingers itching – 1) one must perform action with far reaching effect.

fingers tingling – 1) feeling the need to perform action with far reaching effect.

FIR TREE – 1) everlasting life; 2) eternal life

FIR TREE – 1) everlasting life; 2) eternal life.

FIRE – 1) creative destruction; 2) inspired passion regarding a specific goal, direction, and/or belief.

FIRE ENGINE – 1) means of rushing to extinguish inspired passion that is not on a spiritual path; 2) societal means of intervention to suppress or extinguish inspired passion, particularly where viewed as destructive force.

FIRE SWALLOWING – 1) to take in and be nourished by inspired passion.

FIRE WALKING – 1) one's path is that of inspired passion.

FISH – 1) represents a message from spirit.

FISH HATCHERY – 1) place of change where messages are born and get started; 2) place of origin of messages that is watched over and manipulated by society.

FISH HOOK – 1) emotional means, maintained by a thought, idea or belief, that is able to find message in change; 2) following one's heart while in change to be able to find message available in that change.

FISHING ROD – 1) necessary means of finding message in change; [TO BE OFFERED A FISHING ROD] 2) the state of necessity to find message in change.

FIST – 1) works in life that are crude, destructive, brusque, and/or unrefined; 2) the state of lacking much control over actions; 3) determined but unrefined or crude action.

FIST - 1) actions in life crude, destructive, brusque, unrefined, and without much control.

FIVE – 1) represents the potential that exists whenever an element of the manifest is in the same place as an element of spirit.

FIVE-POINTED STAR – 1) perfect state of balance; 2) well balanced hunches, inspirations, dreams and thoughts that come from the mind in relation to the universe; 3) perfectly balanced ideal; 4) distant source of light that allows one to fall into perfect harmony; 3) concept, idea, belief, goal, or ideal of balance and harmony that can guide one through darkness; 4) that which provides light in darkest moments of life, causing one to be able to find balance and harmony in darkness; 5) vision, concept or belief in balance that sustains hope.

FLAG – 1) ego; 2) celebration of self; 3) dedication to self.

FLAME – 1) inspired passion that consumes; 2) inspired passion that takes over and transforms; 3) inspiration that allows passion to consume everything.

FLAN – 1) somewhat solid essence of life that nourishes the soul.

FLASH BULB – 1) sudden knowledge or realization that illuminates everything near or connected to it; 2) suddenly seeing things in a different context.

FLASHLIGHT – 1) that which is used when it is necessary to illuminates; 2) ability to be prophetic; 3) message that one must deal with spirituality; 4) when illumination is necessary to advance; 5) simultaneous need and ability to illuminate things in advance.

FLATULENCE – 1) unwanted, wasteful inspiration; 2) in cycle of nature, gaseous waste from digestion that serves as vital element of earth's atmosphere, fuel and overall balance.

FLIP FLOPS – 1) temporary and flexible connection to, or division from, one's path that is held in place by the concept of the Great Y.

FLIPPANT – 1) readily able to change mind; 2) may change mind just to provoke, rebel, irritate or disable a process.

FLOOD – 1) when sudden and unexpected change ends life as is has been known; 2) when one's path becomes impossible because everything suddenly changes.

FLOOR – 1) foundation; 2) that which supports one; 3) what one stands on; 4) foundational belief system; 5) the structure upon which one bases one's belief systems; [WOODEN] 6) cycle of life is what supports one; [SHINY WOODEN] 7) foundation of life reflects back to one' view their own foundation in life; 8) one's contact with one's own foundation; 9) the living of one's life is life itself; [STONE] 10) an obstacle or barrier that serves as one's foundation in life; [MARBLE] 11) one's foundation in life is such that it naturally cools any situation; [ICE] 12) one's foundation is change-based in its essence but stagnant, though close to pure spirit; [DIRT] 13) one's foundation is practical and potentially life giving.

FLORA – 1) living organisms that make up abundance of life in nature.

FLOSS – 1) idea or thought that clarifies anger; 2) idea or thought that will remove lingering things which remain in one's expression after anger has been used to destroy.

FLOTSAM – 1) unexpected occurrences or results coming from or in a time of change.

FLOWER – 1) experience; 2) complete sensory experience of activity in life; 3) youth; 4) [*wildflowers*] an abundance of chaotic experiences that are unexpected and unplanned for; 5) [*cut flowers*] past experiences one is holding onto, though they are dead and past.

FLOWER GARLAND - **1)** celebrating and showing off harvest, abundance and life experiences.

FLUORESCENT LIGHT –1) malleable idea that can be altered to take any shape; 2) convoluted or manipulated inspiration; 3) contrived commitment that contains manifestation of light produced when an artificial life force is forced to encounter intentional restriction of flow such that the resistance itself generates heat and causes such an effect.

FLUSTERED – 1) momentarily unable to find way of expressing one's self resulting from specific state or occurrence.

FLYING CARPET - 1) the foundation one rests on is taken into the realm of inspiration and used as a vehicle to give illusion of forward movement.

FLYING DINOSAUR – 1) represents inspired state of most ancient and primitive of human instincts; 2) inspired irony in life that though something may be large, ferocious and powerful, before nature all is vulnerable; 3) as with the tower, representative of the fact that inspiration in the manifest is vulnerable regardless of size, origin or ancient status.

FLYING INSECT – 1) the coming in of something; 2) a natural inspiration, like an idea that is good.

FLYING INSECT – 1) the coming in of something; 2) an inspiration, like an idea; 3) thing that is coming and is good.

FOG – 1) something that pretends to be spiritual or has a spiritual aspect in it, yet it prevents clear vision and clarity at the same time; 2) nebulous undercurrent in a religion that preaches or embodies prejudice against people of another religion; 3) a nebulous body or occurrence one thinks is spiritual, yet which removes one's clarity and vision.

FOLLICLE – 1) individual ideas, thoughts, and principles that participate in maintaining the health and cleanliness of an organism.

FOMENT – 1) to cause, or support the causing of, a change.

FOOD – 1) 1) that which nourishes.

FOOT – 1) see **FEET**.

FOOT STOOL – 1) illusion of

comfort when one is off of one's path.

FOOTBALL – 1) commitment that is practical, but only for entertainment.

FOOTBALL FIELD – 1) natural place where those who entertain themselves by making sport of practical commitment can do that.

FOOTWEAR - 1) how one connects to, or disconnects from, one's path.

FOREHEAD – 1) the source of vision in one's life; 2) represents the third eye and the vision it allows one.

FORENSIC – 1) study of the imprint of actions in life.

FOREST – 1) many lives united by geographical location or common purpose; 2) society that gathers naturally because of the involuntary nature of the geographical location.

FOREST FIRE – 1) inspiring passion that transforms and destroys a society.

FORK – 1) precious means of providing one's self with nourishment.

FORKED TONGUE – 1) that which divides speech into elemental contradiction; 2) that which causes the expression of ideas to become divisive, contradictory and lacking in credibility, yet is not detectable to those being communicated with.

FORNICATE – 1) to interact foundation to foundation to have maximum and profound effect on another.

FORTIFICATION – 1) protective boundary that is made stronger to avert intrusion or invasion.

FORTIFIED – 1) that which has a protective boundary that is made stronger to avert intrusion or invasion.

FORTRESS – 1) community that is fortified.

FOSSIL – 1) imprint of physical manifestation that has become obstacle or barrier in time.

FOUNDATION – 1) belief systems that serve as support structure for world view, outlook, and life itself.

FOUNDATION CHAKRA – *see* **MINERAL CHAKRA**] 1) represents one's foundation in life; 2) place that embodies health, security, ability to procreate and the sexual aspects of life, religious beliefs, shame, ethnics.

FOUNTAIN – 1) societal provision for growth, education, healing, change and advancement to citizens.

FOUR – 1) represents any work of man in the manifest.

FOX – 1) one who is sly; 2) one who strives to win; 3) one who strives to work one's way in.

FOYER - 1) place of possibility.

FRANKENSTEIN – 1) symbol for surprising and often misunderstood results of scientific exploration; 2) surprising and misunderstood results of intervention, creative or unconventional joining of unlikely parts; 3) making use of a variety of things from a dead past that, when they have heart, will serve great purpose.

FRANKINCENSE - 1) symbol of the divine name; 2) an emblem of prayer.

FRATERNITY – 1) a group that chooses to be exclusive; 2) a group united around common cause other than national identity.

FRAUD – 1) represents the intentional misrepresentation of the truth.

FRAYS - 1) overshadowing, yet not interfering.

FRENCH POODLE – 1) companion with thoughts that can be arranged in any number of decorative ways.

FREUD, SIGMUND – 1) psychologist and innovator who developed theories on the subconscious that revolutionized thinking and became used by his nephew, Mr. Bernais, in America to control and manipulate the population to support the greed of the few, and also used to create the basis of a form of dream analysis.

FRIAR – 1) one who has denounced earthly identity in favor of living a life of dedication to the ministry of spirit; 2) exclusive person of religion who serves in accordance with strict sets of rules for living; 3) warlock.

FRIEND – 1) one who stands by another.

FROG – 1) representation of an organism of nature that bridges the material and the spiritual.

FRONT - 1) what is happening in the moment that looks into the future.

FRONT OF HEAD - 1) what one thinks at that very moment.

FRONT TIRE – 1) that continuous, dark unfoldment in destiny that leads and directs one's vehicle of avoidance of one's path; 2) feature of destiny that causes one to avoid one's path while still embracing and racing toward one's goals.

FRUIT – 1) perfect nourishment, result from life, god's gift to us, we are meant by nature to eat fruit; 2) spirit commitment to nourish and heal.

FULL CUP OF TEA - 1) potential growth remains impossible until one assimilates that change.

FUNCTION – 1) specific use; 2) intended use.

FUNERAL – 1) honoring the life of the person who passed; 2) manifestation of a person's impact after they have passed from the manifest.

FURNITURE - 1) where you rest on your path.

G

GABRIEL – 1) the announcement or fanfare that immediately precedes presence of spirit.

GALAXY – 1) network of points of light that form a visual representation of a section of all that is in the manifest realm.

GALLERY, THE – 1) just after death, the manifest consciousness must transition to the new state of one's soul, and to do that is in a location that has three main features: the **GARDEN**, the **LIBRARY**, and the **GALLERY**. The Gallery is where every work of art, regardless of medium, exists as conceived without flaws that come from the interference, shortages, politics, compromises, influences, etc. on the creator in the manifest realm.

GALVANIZE – 1) state of being inundated with shakti and as a result having an enhanced experience in life; 2) state of enhanced positive health as a result of receiving shakti pad; 3) stimulated by shakti in sudden or unanticipated way that is unexpected and has disorienting effect; 4) to cause one to be surrounded by, and connected to, the world around due to activation of shakti; 5) God consciousness.

GAME – 1) structured network of activity for a temporal purpose that includes everyone, if each chooses to participate.

GANDHI, MAHATMA – 1) symbol of passive resistance.

GANJA – 1) state of repression and inspiration that distorts one's ability to think; 2) represents being in an inspired state of self-delusion mixed with fixation on self; 3) false sense of fascinating depth; 4) inspired state of inflated self-importance reflected in extreme paranoia.

GARAGE – 1) spiritual dwelling place for those vehicles in life that assist one in avoiding one's path.

GARAGE SALE – 1) market place, or place for exchange, right at the spiritual dwelling place of one's mechanisms of avoidance of path.

GARBAGE – 1) what is not valued, extraneous, or unused.

GARBAGE CAN – 1) 1) container for that which is not valued, extraneous, or unused.

GARBAGE COLLECTOR – 1) one who gathers and removes that which is not valued, extraneous, or unused.

GARBAGE TRUCK – 1) vehicle for removal of that which is not valued, extraneous, or unused, that assists in avoidance of path.

GARDEN – 1) earthly existence; [*spiritual garden*] 2) place where one's consciousness goes just after death of body; 3) where spiritual experiences happen at the end of the path.

GARDEN SHED - 1) a building that is a part of the dwelling place of the soul, where one finds tools and supplies to assist with productive interface with nature.

GARDEN, THE - 1) just after death, the manifest consciousness must transition to the new state of one's soul, and to do that is in a location that has three main features: the

GARDEN, the **LIBRARY**, and the **GALLERY**. The Garden is where all living things exist as their genetic code intends, free of deformities or distortions in the manifest that result from famine, drought, storms, malnutrition, injuries, diseases, etc.

GARLAND – 1) celebrating abundance; [WITH FRUIT AND FLOWERS] 2) celebrating and showing off harvest, abundance and life experiences.

GARLIC – 1) spiritual nurture that heals, fulfills, cleanses and gives nourishment.

GARNET – 1) source of spiritual light that comes from the dark places of earth and heart.

GAS – VAPOR] 1) ethereal and/or inspired state of all being; *(naturally produced organic methane)* 2) unwanted, wasteful inspiration; 3) in cycle of nature, gaseous waste from digestion that serves as vital element of earth's atmosphere, fuel and overall balance; [PETROLEUM BASED] 4) carbon based petroleum derivative that is easily combustible and can be used for engines, industrial processes and other things which serve mankind while destroying the planet.

GAS STATION – 1) location for purchasing carbon based petroleum derivative that is easily combustible and can be used for engines, industrial processes and other things which serve mankind while destroying the planet.

GASOLINE – 1) carbon based petroleum derivative that is easily combustible and can be used for engines, industrial processes and other things which serve mankind while destroying the planet.

GATE – 1) entry into the path is regulated; 2) you know what is coming because you see the new path; [OPEN GATE] 3) no judgment, no exclusion; 4) everybody can come in and enter this new path.

GEM STONE – 1) that which brings spiritual light into the manifest *(color, number and shape give specific attributes)*; 2) riches; 3) centerpiece of what is truly precious to one *(e.g. the idea behind the goal)*.

GENERATOR – 1) that which creates energy.

genitles itching – 1) one must actively influence the foundation of another; 2) one must actively interact in intimacy; 3) one must act on a sexual urge.

genitles tingling – 1) feeling the need to influence the foundation of another; 2) feeling the need to interact in intimacy; 3) sexual urge.

GEODE – 1) one must traverse a barrier to find spirit's message; 2) represents process by which one takes a barrier, breaks it into manageable pieces, then examines the pieces to find the living message of spirit within; 3) persistence until the truest gift within is discovered.

GEOMETRY – 1) laws of manifest sets of dimension *(either 2 dimensions or 3* *dimensions)*; 2) relationships in nature understood and codified by the mind.

GERANIUMS – 1) clustered experiences of heart and earth in abundant setting.

GHOST – 1) non-physical manifestation of a particular manifest consciousness.

GIANT – 1) overly large; 2) extreme manifestation.

GIBBOUS MOON - 1) state of self deception that has not yet taken one into dark phase; 2) one has just emerged from the dark phase and is more of light than darkness.

GIFT – 1) talent, calling or ability one finds as designed feature of manifest consciousness and physical body.

GIFTED – 1) to have a talent, calling or ability as designed feature of manifest consciousness and physical body.

GIGANTIC – 1) extremely large, far beyond expectations or presumptions.

GILDED – 1) preciousness of idea or intellectual relevance added to an otherwise ordinary thing.

GILT – 1) thing that adds concept of preciousness.

GIRAFFE – 1) state of being that is far more about expression than anything else, and has difficulty changing.

GISMO – 1) object of undefined function or purpose; 2) potentially useful once defined, but as yet undefined.

GLASS – see **CUP**] 1) potential of experience or possession of life yet filled; 2) experiences waiting for one to have.

GLASS – SUBSTANCE] 1) ancient wisdom that flows, and continues to evolve in current times; [RECEPTACLE] 2) reflects reality that ancient wisdom is constantly changing with each new experience of every individual; 3) there is no fixed standard or static state of wisdom.

GLASS CEILING – 1) presumed limit of potential elevated state; 2) established upward limit of elevation that is based on bias of collective wisdom of human kind is flexible and fluid, and evolves with each new experience in manifest realm.

GLASS HOUSE – 1) in view of ancient wisdom—the collective knowledge gathered from the cumulative experiences of all in the manifest—all spiritual dwelling places are clearly visible; 2) dwelling place of the soul that offers no privacy and is transparent.

GLASS WALL – 1) boundaries between all things that are invisible in the manifest, but clear from the point of view of ancient wisdom; 2) the uniqueness of each manifest being that both separates and unites.

GLASSES – 1) how one corrects, distorts or colors one's world view; [MIRRORED SUNGLASSES] 2) outside can't see inside, this world view makes others see themselves; [BLACK RIMMED GLASSES] 3) sees world framed in darkness; [BLUE RIMMED GLASSES] 4) world view framed with flow, growth or perpetual change; [RED RIMMED GLASSES] 5) world view framed with feeling or earthiness; [GLASSES IN HAIR] 6) world view avoided through elective focus on spirit; 7) seeking illumination, 8) sees world clearly but balances that view with integrated view of spirit; [SUNGLASSES] 9) elects to see the world as shaded or darkened *(specific color gives element that is shading view)*; 10) meant to alter or skew view of world; [SUNGLASSES IN HAIR] 11) has made decision to see world as it is, but block view of higher realms or spiritual point of view; [METAL RIMMED GLASSES] 12) frames world view with perpetual precious element, type of metal gives precise element.

GLASSES IN HAIR – 1) world view avoided through elective focus on spirit; 2) seeking illumination; 3) sees world clearly but balances that view with integrated view of spirit.

GLOBE – 1) commitment; [*also see* **SPHERE, ORB**].

GLOBE OF EARTH – 1) commitment from agreement between spirit and peoples' consciousness to have a place for learning, change, challenge, and development all serving spiritual growth.

GLOVES – 1) represents guarded activity; 2) what one does in life is done with caution and has protectiveness built in; 3) suggests one is very careful how one interacts with others.

GLUE – 1) change that binds things together.

GLUTEN – 1) nutrient that binds.

GOAD – 1) 1) purposely cause another to become angry, impassioned, violent.

GOAL – 1) overall spiritual purpose in life; 2) what one aims for in life; 3) basis for ambition.

GOAT – 1) tough nature; 2) stubborn; 3) will be nourished by anything at all; 4) likes the established order; 5) indiscriminate consumer.

GOATEE – 1) when one leads with thoughts upon first arriving.

GOD – 1) symbol of divinity, eternal spirit.

GODDESS – 1) pagan or yin-era deity; 2) divinity in birthing, and creation of new life; 3) divine state in which all is empty, where only the bringing birth of new life can fill it.

GODHEAD – 1) figurehead or symbol for divine presence in manifest form.

GOLD – 1) precious ideas, thoughts; 2) sees intellect as precious; 3) precious self-view; 4) precious thoughts or beliefs of lasting value.

GONG – 1) sound of the universe; 2) man's reality in the universe.

GOOD LUCK – 1) spirit presence manifesting in lives of those who take faithful actions.

GOOSE – 1) cyclical opinions that migrate depending on seasonal cycle; 2) opinions that give knowledge of where to go; when to go, and how to get there; 3) opinion of which way to go.

GOVERNMENT – 1) system that gives order to, protects and provides for community, group, nation or population.

GRADE – [RANK] 1) system of hierarchy; [INCLINE] 2) graduated amount of ascension or decent.

GRADIENT – 1) graduated change from one state to another.

GRADUAL – 1) subtle change over time.

GRAIN SILO – 1) monolithic and necessary place to store seed.

GRAND – 1) greatest of all on established scale.

GRANDEUR – 1) possessing character or characteristic of being greatest of all on established scale.

GRANDFATHER – 1) male ancestral figure; 2) yang presence through time.

GRANDMOTHER – 1) 2) female ancestral figure; 2) yin presence through time.

GRANITE – 1) obstacle or barrier that is spiritual; 2) [polished] obstacle or barrier that allows or promotes self-reflection.

GRANT – 1) allow.

GRAPEFRUIT – 1) commitment to natural intellectual thought or idea that gives nourishment.

GRAPES – 1) commitment to sensuality or pleasures of the body *(music, food, clothes, sex, lusciousness)*; 2) commitment to that which is sacred.

GRASS – 1) abundance and nourishment; [ONE BLADE OF GRASS] 2) one aspect of abundance and nourishment.

GRASSHOPPER – 1) natural abundance that is easily and suddenly inspired; 2) natural tendency to travel in bursts of inspiration on path; 3) abundance of spirit in nature.

GRATITUDE – 1) expression of acknowledgement of one's purposeful existence; 2) outward acceptance, and appreciation for, one's spiritual mission in the manifest.

GRAVITY – 1) inclination toward earthly path no matter how inspired; 2) enigma of existence and commitment to life path; 3) illusion that material things have weight, that they matter.

GRAY HOUSE – 1) neutrality is dwelling place of soul in manifest.

GRAY LIPS – 1) manner of expression is neutral.

GREAT Y – 1) mandate of all spiritual beings in the manifest to unite the divisions of the manifest world, and at the same time to bring into manifest the spiritual unity one represents; 2) duality becoming one, and one becoming duality; 3) represents the individual experience of living in life; 4) the voice of all wisdom gained from earthly experience.

GREEN – 1) abundance of nature; 2) flow of mind, which is constantly growing and changing; 3) changed mind; 4) awareness of movement, growth or flow.

GREEN HOUSE – 1) natural abundance is dwelling place of soul.

GREENHOUSE – 1) dwelling place of spirit that promotes natural abundance and allows perpetual growth.

GREENHOUSE EFFECT – 1) being enclosed in repressive barrier or container that causes inflammation of anger.

GREY – 1) state of balance between light and dark; 2) unity comes from separate parts being united either in harmony or conflict; 3) no commitment to, or not pertaining to considerations of light or dark; 4) undecided or indecisive.

GREY IRON BARS - 1) a solid but seen through barrier that is neutral on the question of light and dark; 2) spiritually neutral barrier; 3) confusion, spiritual apathy addressing the question of light and dark that causes a barrier; 4) not making a statement either way and, by so doing, creating a barrier.

GREY IRON BARS – 1) confining neutrality that is strong, durable and immobile but intermittent; 2) intermittent, but resilient and necessary, neutrality of spirit; 3) intermittent spiritual apathy addressing the question of light and dark; 4) regular and intermittent refusal to make a statement or take a stand, and stubbornly so.

GRILL – 1) place where repressed energy is used to provide nourishment for growth on the spiritual journey.

GRIME – 1) residue of waste that is not discarded; 2) tarnished state that results when one has not completely let go of useless and unhealthy excess.

GROCERIES – 1) abundance of natural bounty made available for nourishment.

GROUND – 1) stable manifest reality.

GROUNDED – 1) having solid base in manifest reality.

GROWING OLD – 1) transforming completely who one is; 2) unfolding of one's destiny; 3) becoming of what one is meant to be; 4) maturation process.

GUIDE – 1) one who is able to illuminate direction and immediate way forward on path.

GUIDE DOG – 1) 1) familiar who serves as companion to one with vision or other spiritual gift so that they may maximize their gift of vision.

GUITAR – 1) spiritual expression; 2) living spirit in the world.

GUST OF WIND – 1) sudden inspiration.

GUM – 1) useless substance that exercises anger; [BUBBLE GUM] 2) useless substance of feelings and spirit that exercises anger and occasionally forms into fleeting inspired, but hollow, commitments that immediately deflate.

GUN – 1) tool that is lasting, precious and dark with which one can penetrate and destroy the life of another being.

GURU – 1) manifest form of master; 2) being who serves as diamond in flesh by bringing light.

GYPSUM – 1) temporary spiritual change that soon becomes barrier that removes ability to embrace the world, take actions, travel on one's path or have any direction on one's path; 2) agency of spirit that has the ability to prevent or inhibit one's ability to embrace the world, take actions, travel on one's path or have any direction on one's path so that they can find spirit.

GYPSY – 1) spiritual ancestor who became lost and broke vows in order to serve self via use of vision and visionary skills ; 2) one with no defined path other than pursuit of enrichment of self in manifest terms.

H

HABIT – 1) automatic, repeated action that has become involuntary.

HAIL – 1) invasive natural change that is itself stagnant.

HAIR – 1) thoughts, ideas, opinions; [LONG HAIR] 2) well developed thoughts; [LONG HAIR ON BACK] 3) one who takes responsibility for thoughts and ideas, enduring thoughts; [LONG HAIR ON SHOULDER(S)] 4) one who's well developed thoughts influence the nature or substance of tasks taken on; [LONG HAIR IN BRAIDS] 5) one who avoids responsibility for thoughts and ideas and also does not take on tasks related to ideas by means of spiritual pattern used as excuse; [COMPLEX HAIRDO] 6) complex thoughts; [PONY TAIL] 7) thoughts organized in relation to past; [HAIR BROUGHT FORWARD OVER EYES] 8) thoughts focused on moment or future that are being looked at and considered; [CURLY HAIR] 9) active, circular or chaotic thoughts; [STRAIGHT HAIR] 10) well maintained, organized and clear thoughts and ideas.

HAIR BROUGHT FORWARD OVER EYES - 1) thoughts focused on moment or future that are being looked at and considered.

HAIR COLOR MISSING – 1) statement about pattern, development level and direction of thoughts with no indication of substance or nature of those thoughts.

HAIR COLORING – 1) specific color indicates substance and/or nature of thoughts.

hair itching – 1) one must think.

HAIR NET – 1) loose network of beliefs or ideas that inhibit thoughts or hold them in a particular, elective pattern or position.

hair tingling – 1) feeling the need to think.

HAIRBRUSH – 1) method of organizing thoughts that, when used, is necessary.

HAIRCUT – 1) intentional organization of thoughts, that stops them at a particular amount of development by inhibiting them, often with emotions.

HAIRLESS - 1) mind is organic and available; 2) without thought of any sort; 3) unable to use intellect; 4) incapable of intelligence; 5) inability to understand, remember or figure things out.

HAIRPIN – 1) precious means of inhibiting or directing one's own thoughts in specific pattern.

HALF – 1) in need of balance or completion; 2) destined to be joined with another; 3) incomplete.

HALLWAY – 1) a place from which one might enter into many new paths; 2) transitional part of the structure of the dwelling place of the soul that allows conveyance within that structure.

HALO – 1) partial aura; 2) aura of head; 3) visual designation of one who is of pure spirit in manifest world; 4) avatar.

HAMMER – 1) tool for necessary and unavoidable labor; 2) effort of determination; 3) actions performed with blind faith.

HAND – 1) actions in the world; 2) actions that connect one with things; 3) an action that motivates one to reaching for something; 4) nature of one's actions in life; 5) [cupped hands] actions of receiving or giving.

HAND IN HAND – 1) actions that are done together with another.

HAND WAVE – 1) one takes actions that are an inspiration in themselves; 2) a work of inspiration.

HANDKERCHIEF – 1) flag, thus an outward showing of self; 2) device for nurture and caring – 1) wipes tears, helps wounds; 3) surrender, a showing that you join the winning side; [WHITE HANDKERCHIEF IN HAND] 4) spirituality in the hand that is of service; 5) meaning outgoing action that conveys "I will help you, I will deliver to you".

HANDLE – 1) symbol of a wand connected with some sort of tool meaning that the action accomplished by the tool is essential and mandatory, though has no emotional or spiritual charge to the experience of it.

HANDS CLAPPING – 1) taking actions that, in themselves, show appreciation for what another has done.

hands itching – 1) one must take action.

hands tingling – 1) feeling the need to take action.

HANG GLIDER – 1) that which causes elevated state that is result of being suspended from inspiration; 2) mechanism activated by inspiration that carries one to elevation.

HANG GLIDING – 1) taking action that results in elevated state that is result of being suspended from inspiration; 2) act of using mechanism activated by inspiration that carries one to elevation.

HAPLESS – 1) without motivation or sense of purpose; 2) uninspired.

HAPPINESS – 1) state of wanting all that one has; 2) spiritual gratitude.

HARBOR – 1) place where others who have gone through major change have arrived in at the end of the change, that is also able to be utilized by others who have endured similar change; 2) safe place at end of major change; 3) goal of change.

HARD DRIVE – 1) manifestation, to be viewed as gift from spirit that duplicates functions of brain to store, sort and process.

HARD HAT – 1) purposeful barrier between one and divine that allows connection with spirit yet protects one from failed inspirations that cause a fall to gravity or depression *(color and other markings give specific information about nature and content)*.

HARE – 1) actively participating in material life; 2) erratic progression through life of earthliness; 3) human desires and instincts to procreate and to have fear; 4) nervousness; 5) ability to be inspired one moment and then go deep into darkness; 6) connected to development/origin of the Fibonacci number system.

HARLEQUIN – 1) represents state of selflessness in one who serves the pleasure of another without thought of self, and usually at expense of self in society's view.

HARLEQUINO – 1) archetype—representing the ability of each person that is the true state of selflessness in one who serves the pleasure of another without thought of self, and usually at expense of self in society's view—meant to inspire others to compassion, support and willingness to take such actions of faith.

HARNESS – 1) durable and adjustable belief system that provides means of controlling, guiding or restricting one's spiritual mission; 2) belief system that is illusion of safety so that actions of faith may be taken.

HARP – 1) ability to express pure spirit through music in the manifest that is derived from life and digestion of life's experiences.

HARPOON – 1) pointed emotional action that is intrusive and designed to penetrate the heart of one in the midst of change, that is also constantly connected to the one who deploys it by a strongly developed thought; 2) justified and self-serving means of taking advantage of one going through absolute change and attacking their heart.

HARPSICHORD – 1) tool that allows actions to bring pure spirit into the manifest realm.

HARPY – 1) being consumed by state of darkness in which ego is inspired and cannot cease its screaming; 2) relentless clamoring for ego satisfaction; 3) being overwhelmed and controlled by ego neediness.

HAT – 1) nature of connection to the divine, or conversely nature of disconnection from the divine; 2) relationship with the divine used to contain or control thoughts. *(color and other attributes denote content and context for a specific case)*.

HAT WITH FEATHER- 1) one claims information one received from elsewhere as one's own because it has become fully integrated it into one's connection with the divine.

HAVING CHEEK - 1) displayed lack of concern as to what a reaction may be, with the assumption of a predictable negative response.

HAWK – 1) ability to see clearly from afar; 2) opinion, as of predator animal, with sense of remove; 3) distant from something so one can achieve and/or maintain control; 4) needing distance to see clearly.

HDTV – 1) illusion of reality that appears very real, as if having three dimensions, yet is only flat and of two dimensions.

HE [HEBREW LETTER] - 1)ה– 1) expression, thought, speech; 2) content coming from **EXPRESSION CHAKRA**; 3) "take" (**HEI**) expresses revelation of self in the act of giving of oneself to another; 4) one giving to others in the form of self-expression is the ultimate gift of self.

HEAD – 1) that which gives origin to thoughts; [FRONT OF HEAD] 2) what one thinks at that very moment; [BACK OF HEAD] 3) what one used to think, old belief; [HEAD BENT DOWNWARD] 4) creating an internal cycle, harmony of self; 5) awareness of humble existence of all parts of self; 6) inward contemplation that is not expressed outwardly; 7) vision is directly related to focus on or contemplation of one's foundation; [INCLINED HEAD] 8) *(right)* mind's focus on creative; 9) *(left)* mind's focus on linear or logical.

HEAD BAND – 1) belief system that contains thoughts somewhat, but is built to change, and allows some inspiration; 2) represents complete openness in the area of an individual's connection with divinity.

HEAD BENT DOWNWARD - 1) creating an internal cycle, harmony of self; 2) awareness of humble existence of all parts of self; 3) inward contemplation that is not expressed outwardly; 4) vision is directly related to focus on or contemplation of one's foundation.

head itching - 1) one must actively think, or commit intellectually.

head of lettuce - 1) represents commitment to abundant, change-filled nourishment that satisfies and quells anger.

head tingling - 1) feeling the need to think, or commit intellectually.

HEADACHE – 1) compression of ability to think resulting from too little change, and too much demand, that is so uncomfortable that action, or change, becomes a necessity..

HEADDRESS – 1) nature or state of connection with divinity; 2) means by which one connects to the divine in a ritual or specific setting designed to accommodate such connection.

HEADLIGHTS – 1) vague reference to the sun as it is a light that illuminates the way forward on a path, except that it is in the darkness when there is no sun; 2) artificial "false" light in an atmosphere that the only naturally occurring lights are ideals and self-deception; 3) artificial light to illuminate the goal when in deep darkness, comes from false means forward without dealing with one's actual path; 4) man's imitation of that which spirit supplies; 5) illumination in the darkness, yet it is not truly light, though the false light makes it seem that the way is properly lit.

HEADPHONES – 1) in complete control of what one is hearing; 2) [black headphones] controlled connection to exclusive source of dark information.

HEADQUARTERS – 1) an effort's spiritual dwelling place that also supplies the thoughts, purpose, inhibitions, regulation and method for all who participate.

HEAL – 1) represents the return to a full state of health; 2) suggests that one should move toward better health.

HEALER – 1) one who has the gift of causing, facilitating, energizing and/or enabling the return to a full state of health.

HEALTH – 1) balance; 2) the intended maximum state of organic balance in flow in support of the divine plan for all parts of manifest reality.

HEAP – VERB] 1) to actively place things together in a designated location, but without order, structure, method or regard for outcome; [NOUN] 2) a pile or accumulation without order, structure, method or regard for outcome that is the result of the action to so locate these things in a previously designated location.

HEART – 1) one's intended guide throughout the journey through life on one's spiritual path; 2) the central vortex of the flow of all feelings in a manifest being; 3) where and how one holds things that are dear; 4) the quality of being fully infused with the divine knowledge of the intended guide through feelings.

HEART CHAKRA – 1) where the path of the heart emanates from; 2) where all feelings are alive and vibrantly transmitted through; 3) where all nurture, caring, support and challenge are felt as food to nourish the soul; 5) the location of both the non-compromising tempest of soul and greatest tranquility.

HEAT – 1) the result of a restricted flow of energy; 2) sure evidence that proper flow is forcibly resisted and restricted; 3) what occurs when passion and inspiration are greater than available capacity for and/or allowance of those things.

HEAT – 1) represents a state of repressed flow.

HEAVEN – 1) location within the astral—established in Taoist, Egyptian[3] and Hindu ancient texts and much later corroborated by the Bible—where the soul goes after a 'good' life; 2) blissful state.

HEBREW LETTERS – 1) mathematical system with 22 glyphs representing letters and concepts upon which is based a spoken and written language; 2) each of the 22 Hebrew letters is also associated with a number; 3) in the Kabbalah, there are 22 paths between balancing essences or elements that all must work through on the Tree of Life, each path is associated with one of the letter/numbers in the Hebrew system.

HEEL – 1) how one takes in chi.

HEI – Hebrew letter] 1) expresses revelation of self in the act of giving of oneself to another; 2) one giving to others in the form of self-expression is the ultimate gift of self.

HEIR – 1) first born who will inherit the wealth, holdings, position, power and responsibilities of their dominant parent, depending on the culture;[4] 2) he or she who bears the responsibility by station of birth to carry on the work of the ancestors through the descendants of the blood line.

HELICOPTER – 1) means of inspiration to elevation that does not need to travel in any direction, but may; 2) state of elevation from single element that generates inspiration.

HELL – 1) location within the astral—established in Taoist, Egyptian and Hindu[5] ancient texts

[3] According to Tibetan teachings on death, Heaven is fairly low down from the ultimate instantaneous absorption into the eternal light of all being initially offered in the first day of the first bardo. Since it has an opposite companion and balancing location that is Hell for the 'bad' life result, it is clearly within the astral, and within space-time, for such division and hierarchy is only a feature of space-time and mutually exclusive from the location of the eternal light of all being and love

[4] In patriarchal societies this is the eldest son, in Avuncular societies it is the eldest male kin, and in Matriarchal societies it is the eldest daughter

[5] According to Tibetan teachings on death, Hell is a lower point of division, and is merely a construction of the mind that once recognized vanishes, fairly low down from the ultimate instantaneous absorption into the eternal light of all being initially offered in the first day of the first bardo. Since it has an opposite companion and balancing location that is Heaven for the 'good' life result, it is clearly within the astral, and within space-time, for such division and hierarchy is only a feature of space-time and mutually exclusive from the location of the eternal light of all being and love.

and much later corroborated by the Bible—where the soul goes after a 'bad' life; 2) state of eternal damnation; 3) associated with eternal burning fires and tortures.

HELM – 1) the location from which one can navigate and steer in one's journey through extreme change; 2) place that offers some control over one's destiny in a time of extreme change.

HELMET – 1) protection for thoughts that is a hollow half commitment.

HELPFUL – 1) one who is of service for the highest good of his fellow, in the eyes of said fellow.

HELPING – 1) performing the actions of service for the highest good of a fellow, in the eyes of said fellow.

HELPLESS – 1) one who must rely on others in a state of desperation and turmoil; 2) a divine gift of opportunity to others so that they might fulfill their spiritual growth through actions of faith that serve the highest good of a fellow, in the eyes of said fellow.

HELSINKI – 1) represents a plan left unfulfilled[6].

HELTER SKELTER – 1) diabolical state of chaos; 2) state of madness, slaughter, and unimaginable depravity.

HEMISPHERE – 1) half of commitment, which is significant of attributes associated with relative half represented in vision.

HEPATITIS – 1) the term given to the state of imbalance of the body so that the liver takes on a disease to balance the whole health body.

HERB GARDEN – 1) organized and controlled abundance for the good of the community and general nourishment.

HERBS – 1) living organisms of abundant nature that serve as flavor, medicine, aroma and seasoning to enhance nutrition, health and overall wellness.

HERMIT – 1) paradoxical state of simultaneous ancient guiding wisdom and intentional withdrawal from the flow of life; 2) a state of healing and retreat; 3) a state of stagnancy and disconnection; 4) a state of connection to inner, ancestral and essential wisdom; 5) a state of being disenfranchised from one's spiritual purpose in manifest form.

HERO – 1) one who sacrifices self to save others.

HEROES – 1) group who have sacrificed self to save others.

HIBERNATION – 1) representative of the nature to find something, give one's self over to it, and then to hide in it; 2) cyclical retreat to heal, assimilate life's experiences, and maximize one's strength; 3) cyclical state of retreat to avoid life, protect self above other, and be utterly devoted to one's own survival and wellbeing.

[6] Largest city in Finland, first established as an intended trade route rival to Talinn, but never served in that capacity.

HIDE OUT – 1) location for avoiding, concealing, and deceiving; 2) a place to gain strategic advantage.

HIDING – 1) avoiding, concealing, deceiving; [HIDING IN ANOTHER PERSON'S ROOM] 2) to not be one's self so one might then become one's self.

HIGH – 1) state of repression and inspiration that distorts one's ability to think; 2) represents being in an inspired state of self-delusion mixed with fixation on self; 3) false sense of fascinating depth; 4) inspired state of inflated self-importance reflected in extreme paranoia.

HIGH BOOT – 1) heaviest connection to or protection from path when journey is anticipated to be filled with many dangers and trials.

HIGH HEELS – 1) connection to, or protection from, path that offers minimum inflow of chi, but maximum outflow of chi, and creates a state of lost vision of path.

HIGH SCHOOL – 1) training ground for social development and scholastic learning for those just on the cusp of young adulthood.

HIGH WIRE – 1) elevated concept that, should it become one's path, has extreme risks; 2) when following a life course based on an elevated concept or idea one can only be successful and not vulnerable to risks if one can remain perpetually inspired.

HIGH WIRE – 1) concept about traversing the void that represents a singular path that very few will be able to follow; 2) ascedic, mystical path of concentration that takes one through the void; 3) the 5th ring of strategy in which focus allows balanced and relaxed traversing of the boid.

HILL – 1) old barrier reduced to a mere obstacle; [LOW AND ROUNDED] 2) old barrier as been worn down by age and natural elements.

HILT – 1) how one manages ability to cut away that which is unnecessary in one's life when it is mandatory; 2) how one essentially controls the outward expression of emotions by turning them into actions in the manifest realm.

HINDU – 1) a rare religious faith where talk of and striving for mystic achievement is discussed and embraced at all levels; 2) religious faith of more than 4000 sects originating in ancient India, featuring many gods and perhaps the most intricate and confusing depiction of social order, religious service, cleansing atonement and rules for living of all systems of mankind.

HIP – ANATOMY] 1) the origin of impetus for movement on the path, which is an offshoot of the foundation; [STATUS] 2) superficial status that indicates one who acts outwardly in a manner found to be popular in social circles of the ego.

HIPPIE – 1) one who has some degree of allegiance to non-aggression, or devotion to medicating life's pains with drug-induced pleasures and ultimate oblivion.

HIPPOPOTAMUS – 1) ponderously large being with constant need for external change, whose excrement serves millennia living organisms and systems when its waste is united with change and becomes inspired.

HISTORY – 1) collection of opinions and memories that shape one's worldview of the past.

HITCH HIKING – 1) one who, in pursuit of their path, has a general but not specific direction to go in and so they adapt to somebody else's path; 2) to be connected to the path, or general direction, of another's journey without adopting their specific goal (e.g., a spouse will often take on the partner's path).

HIVE – 1) represents a collective societal pattern of living, where the community becomes a single organism, and its members highly specialized functionaries within that system.

HOAX – 1) intentional misrepresentation of facts that create the desired effect of response from a targeted population.

HOCKEY – 1) the group effort of combining their collective life actions for the purpose of gaining control over the whole communities single dark gift so that their sub-group might prevail—this is done for amusement of themselves and those who support their effort.

HOLES – 1) places where inspiration might enter an otherwise closed barrier.

HOLIDAY – 1) societal consensus agreement of a significant date on which all celebrate.

HOLOCAUST – 1) mass destruction that is the result of over-inspired passion that consumes all it encounters; 2) organized wave of destruction based on idealistic belief that can only prevail with mass extinction of those who the ideal holds up as the enemy.

HOLSTER – 1) means of carrying, and keeping ready, a tool that is lasting, precious and dark with which one can penetrate and destroy the life of another being.

HOLY GRAIL – 1) item assigned with maximum, and ultimate, significance, trumping all other artifacts, ideals, concepts, principles, or objects, in pursuit of which many generations will lose their lives.

HOME – 1) dwelling place of the soul; [CHILDHOOD HOME] 2) dwelling place of a child's soul; 3) pure connection with spirit; 4) not compromised by conditionings and the world.

HOMELESS – 1) soul has no place to dwell in the manifest world; 2) there is no place for spiritual centering; 3) no structure to house spiritual growth; 4) usually there is the seeking of structure represented by a **DOORWAY** or **WINDOW**.

HOMEOPATHY – 1) healing capacity in nature's abundance put to use through human ingenuity.

HOMEWORK – 1) action of development and growth that must be done within the sanctity of the dwelling place of the soul that is for application and to meet the demands of the manifest realm in which one participates.

HONEY – 1) result of industriousness and inspiration, and the benefit of cumulative exposure in life to a wide variety of different life experiences, that in nourishment for mind and body.

HONOR – 1) to participate in commitment by way of support, belief and respect for the purposes of the commitment.

HOOF – 1) simple and rigid connection to one's path; 2) simplistic path can only be successfully traveled based narrowly upon ones quest or one's animal instincts.

HOPE – 1) faith-filled expectation of new light, the power of spirit, and the bounty of abundance in the world that allows for action, inspiration and commitment to that which is yet achieved.

HOPELESS – 1) to act in a manner that demonstrates lack of faith-filled expectation of new light, the power of spirit, and the bounty of abundance in the world that allows for action, inspiration and commitment to that which is yet achieved.

HORIZON –1) the past or future, depending on relationship to point of view and sun/moon placement in sky.

HORIZONTAL STRIPES - 1) goes throughout being intermittently, 2) alternate states of being that change as one elevates.

HORIZONTAL STRIPES- 1) goes through being intermittently; 2) alternate states of being.

HORN – 1) spiritual warning (positive or negative) in the manifest; 2) electromagnetic connective flow structure that protects; 3) ability to attack displayed clearly.

HORNET – 1) means of inspired, intellectual goal or ideal in attacking that which challenges one and will, if not fended off, produce emotional devastation; 2) defensiveness with tendency to rage; 3) state of imagined vulnerability that compels one to attack anything within the proximity for fear of devastation through emotional compromise from within.

HOROSCOPE – 1) symbols of various states of being based on specific collective influence of ideals; 2) mark on the blueprint of the structure of one's psyche caused by combined gravitational pull at the moment of one's birth of all of the elements of the universe.

HORROR – 1) state of fear induced by events beyond one's imagination, but based on current knowledge or experience of phobia, pain, fear and vulnerability.

HORS D'OEUVRES – 1) that which prepares one to fully assimilate a lesson on the path; 2) nourishing elements that prepare one to fully assimilate the manifest world, but that come in advance of the substantial manifest world's offered experiences.

HORSE – 1) represents one's spiritual mission in life; 2) movement toward one's acknowledged goal; 3) athleticism in pursuit of one's quest; 4) that which carries one forward toward goals without changing or containing; [BROWN HORSE] 5) practicality of following one's quest in life; [REARING HORSE] 6) means of going forward may sometimes fail due to resistance in the path of a mission and/or a movement towards a goal.

HORSE AND BUGGY – 1) when one's designated quest is matched with means in the manifest of going smoothly forward, but eliminates actual connection with one's path.

HORSE SENSE – 1) intuitive sense based on one's conscious awareness of one's exact goals.

HORTICULTURE – 1) endeavor and actions that combine manifest actions with abundance of nature; 2) working with the processes of nature.

HOSPITAL – 1) where healing happens; 2) community joined in common goal of individual health; 3) respect for the perfection of each living thing and dedication unto that thing's health.

HOSPITALITY – 1) making another feel comfortable and welcome in one's spiritual dwelling place.

HOT – 1) repressed flow.

HOT AIR BALLOON – 1) being carried to elevated state based on inspiration that comes from commitment to repression; 2) commitment to inspiration leads to elevated state and expanded view.

HOT DOG – 1) practical nourishment that is necessary.

HOT OIL - 1) growth causing agent that works with some agitation or passion in the flow of the material world; 2) the agent of increased or agitated flow of things in the material world that changes how one presents one's self to the world.

HOT TUB – 1) change to attain relaxation and comfort.

HOTEL – 1) a comfortable temporary dwelling place for the soul when away from one's permanent spiritual dwelling place; 2) statement that our manifest reality is a temporary home for the soul; 3) illusion of a home.

HOTEL LOBBY – 1) where individuals can come through to get to the illusion of a home for the soul.

HOTEL LOBBY – 1) where people in transit and away from spiritual dwelling place come through to get to the illusion of a home.

HOUSE – [BLACK] 1) dwelling place of the soul that is remote or distant; 2) dwelling place of the soul that is stagnant, confining or absent of light; 3) dwelling place of the soul that is unique or different.

HOUSE – [GUARDED BY DOG] 1) companion that protects one's dwelling place of the soul because of what the soul stands for.

HOUSE – 1) dwelling place of the soul; 2) soul is embodiment of spiritual life; 3) houses spiritual growth, spiritual well-being, and spiritual centeredness; 4) where potential for fulfillment and growth can happen.

HOUSE [YELLOW] – 1) represents a person whose presence of spirit and soul is an intellectual process.

HOWL – 1) spiritual demonstration as prepared, and eager, to be a companion coming from within darkness.

HUGE BREASTS – 1) displaying in manifest world commitment to providing nurture; 2) [when blocking heart] commitment to provide nurture has become obsession and blocked one's own heart.

HUGE SOLID BOAT – 1) vehicle used to navigate, survive and manage change is solid and strong, can contain many

HULA – 1) interplay of foundation and actions that demonstrate alignment with spirit and nature.

HULA HOOP – 1) hollow, ongoing circumstance that is kept in motion by constantly shifting foundation.

HUMANITY – 1) manifest reflection of vastness, omnipresence of divine love and creativity.

HUMBLE – 1) outwardly honest; 2) lifestyle of selfless service; 3) truthful.

HUMILIATED – 1) having been abused by insecurity to create false sense of esteem.

HUMILITY – 1) honesty; 2) selflessly of service to others; 3) perpetually living in truth.

HUMOR – 1) communicating through inspiration for the purpose of making others laugh.

HUNT – 1) to pursue for the purpose of ending the life of another being for one's own benefit.

HUNTER – 1) one who pursues for the purpose of ending the life of another being for one's own benefit.

HURRICANE – 1) state of inspiration and nuance that creates order out of chaos and becomes enormously destructive; 2) power of nature that confuses state of inspiration into patterns of construction.

HURTFUL – 1) when one takes actions or expresses with the ultimate result of harming another.

HUSBANDRY – 1) combining one's abilities and gifts for the purpose of supporting and caring for animals.

HUSHED – 1) having been stopped by another from communicating with others.

HUSTLE – 1) to move more quickly, or to cause to move more quickly, on one's path; 2) to use rapid motion or communication to confuse another for the deliberate and intentional purpose to take advantage of that individual.

HUSTLER – 1) one who moves more quickly, or causes another to move more quickly, on one's path; 2) one who uses rapid motion or communication to confuse another for the deliberate and intentional purpose of taking advantage of that individual.

HYDRANGEA – 1) a partial aspect of life based on commitment to clusters of experience that are either spiritual, heart-based in spirit, or involving growth or change; 2) having one's life dwarfed or diminished by clusters of like experiences that evolve into an obsessive commitment.

HYDROFOIL – 1) vehicle for navigating and traversing change that is propelled by inspiration.

HYMN – 1) use of expression in purely spiritual way, joining with others in similar activity, for the ultimate purpose of great spiritual inspiration, simultaneously for those involved and the community.

HYMNAL – 1) collected wisdom that gives specific examples that can be used by a group to express in purely spiritual way for the ultimate purpose of great spiritual inspiration simultaneously for those involved and the community.

HYPER-EXTENDED – 1) natural state in which the ability to reverse articulation of means used to move on one's path or embrace the world is accentuated, and must be monitored so that this tendency to reversal does not cause one harm.

HYPNOTIST – 1) one who employs power of motion, repetition, communication or any other means to separate another from their conscious control over their subconscious mind.

HYPODERMIC – 1) tool for inflicting intrusive change into another by means of an abrupt emotional interaction.

I

ICE – 1) state of pure spirit, so much so that life ceases; 2) where growth and change are no longer possible.

ICE CREAM – 1) when spiritual change is no longer possible because the state of spirituality is such that life experiences no longer have an effect of change or growth.

ICE FLOOR - 1)one's foundation is change-based in its essence but stagnant, though close to pure spirit.

ICE RINK – 1) where state of pure spirit, so much so that life ceases, becomes one's path; 2) place where growth and change are no longer possible that becomes way of life.

ICE SKATES – 1) means by which to advance in place where state of pure spirit, so much so that life ceases, has become one's path; 2) way of traveling forward in the place where growth and change are no longer possible and has shaped one's way of life.

ICHTHEMOL – 1) dense, dark application of change that causes healing; 2) dense, dark means of causing one to eliminate things from their life that prevent them from health.

ICICLE – 1) change that is in process and hasn't completed itself; 2) change that never has been allowed to complete itself

ID – 1) foundation of one's identity in society; 2) internal foundation that makes one a member in society

IGUANA – 1) ability to adapt easily between spirit and manifest, use inspiration as a means of mobility; 2) vulnerable only to those spiritually strong.

ILL AT EASE – 1) state of stagnancy, where forward movement on path has stopped temporarily, in which one desires to keep moving but is not able to move effectively forward.

ILLNESS – 1) state of imbalance in an organism; 2) opportunity to balance one's life; 3) opportunity to be of service to another who has illness.

ILLUMINATE – 1) make visible due to interaction of spirit.

ILLUSTRIOUS – 1) state of being that is extreme and visible to others.

IMP – 1) humble and cute.

IMPECCABLE – 1) well ordered; 2) without mar or flaw; 3) well organized.

IMPERCEPTIBLE – 1) insufficient to be detected by available senses.

IMPLICATE – 1) take action that shows another is at fault to intentionally cause them a problem.

IMPLICATION – 1) action that shows another is at fault that is done intentionally to cause them a problem.

IMPRESS – 1) to blend with; 2) to merge together, unifying to become one; 3) actions that cause another to think more highly of one.

IMPRESSION – 1) the act of blending with; 2) the act of merging together, unifying to become one; 3) the way one's actions cause others to thinkof one.

IN BED TOGETHER – 1) indication that one shares one's spiritual dwelling place.

INCHWORM – 1) one who, in doing practical things, cannot move forward evenly, but slowly in a measured way that eventually achieves the goal; 2) practical and determined; 3) methodical.

INCLINED HEAD - 1)[RIGHT] 1)

mind's focus on creative; [LEFT] 2) mind's focus on linear or logical.

INDEX FINGER – 1) attention on guiding principle; 2) attention on specific act in life.

INDEX FINGER – 1) guiding principle; 2) specific act in life.

INDIGESTION – 1) indication that one has not been able to comfortably take in the world, or specific elements of one's world.

INDOORS – 1) within one's spiritual dwelling place.

INDUSTRY – 1) coordinated actions of a community for the purpose of production, or achieving a goal.

INFANT – 1) new life; 2) new action in life; 3) fresh start; 4) start of new project.

INFANTICIDE – 1) one who prevents new life; 2) one who precludes or prevents an action in life; 3) make a fresh start impossible; 4) to block the start of a new project.

INFORMANT – 1) one who uses opinion, observation, or idea to expose another and make them vulnerable to harsh or negative treatment; 2) to identify another as representing something, or being a participant in something, specific.

INFORMATION – 1) facts one has collected.

INFORMER – 1) one who shares information.

INGRATE – 1) one who does not appreciate what one has.

INK – 1) dark ability to cause change through communication of ideas or intellectual concepts.

INKJET – 1) use of dark change to cause action.

INLET – 1) narrow avenue through which change may enter one's life.

INNER BANK OF RIVER – 1) additive flow of life.

INNOCUOUS – 1) of little or no effect.

INOCULATE – 1) use sudden, intrusive emotional event to change another so that they are no longer vulnerable.

INQUISITION – 1) targeted and intentional interrogation designed to implicate another; 2) inflict a self-fulfilling interrogation upon one.

INSECT – 1) highly evolved item or idea that intrudes, often in clandestine way; [CRAWLING INSECT] 2) highly evolved item or idea that intrudes, often in clandestine way to irritate or infiltrate; 3) that which takes away one's concentration and focus of what is going on in life; 4) the little things that eventually consume one; [FLYING INSECT] 5) the coming in of something, an inspiration, like an idea that is good.

INSIDE OUT – 1) protects one as one goes into the world; 2) feeling protected in the world.

INSIDE OUT JACKET – 1) protects you as you go into the world, you feel protected in the world

INSIGNIA – 1) symbol or emblem indicating allegiance to, membership in, alignment with or loyalty to an established belief, societal structure, conceptual ideal, guiding principle or establish entity; 2) symbol that embodies precepts, goals, ideals and beliefs of larger body; 3) symbol that, when displayed, establishes connection with precepts, goals, ideals and beliefs of larger body; 4) visible marking indicating one who is faithful to lineage.

INSINUATE – 1) to intentionally manipulate through inspiration the minds of others so that a specific person, place or thing becomes suspect.

INSTANT – 1) represents synchronicity; 2) suggests that one allow what is meant to be to be.

INSTITUTE – VERB] 1) to bring about a thing due to it rallying around a single concept or idea; [NOUN] 2) a grouping that has formed around a single concept or idea.

INSTITUTION – 1) an established grouping that has formed around a single concept or idea; 2) an organization, tradition, practice, habit or other regularly occurring event that is known and anticipated as a mainstay of society or a community.

INSULT – 1) to cause harm, intentionally or not, to another through actions that creat inspiration toward that end.

INSURANCE – 1) the idea, concept, holding or status that, so long as it is in place or accessible, guarantees some kind of interrelationship to be sustained or achieved.

INTEGRATE – 1) to meld to multi-faceted things into one larger, single entity.

INTELLECTUAL – 1) solely of the mind.

INTELLIGENCE – 1) measure of one's intellectual ability.

INTELLIGENT – 1) one who relies solely on one's mind and achieves positive outcomes in the manifest.

INTERCONNECT – 1) to bring together without change anything relative in space-time through those common elements already in place, or that are integral to the participating entities.

INTERNAL COMBUSTION ENGINE – 1) mechanism that uses contained destructive rage to cause and sustain forward motion and is powered by the joint efforts of the enterprise of mankind; 2) that which uses contained, destructive rage to supply constant energy so that a structure in the manifest may continue to function; 3) that rage-fueled thing that keeps a person, place, idea, pursuit or attempt in motion.

INTERNET – 1) manmade structure of interconnection via electronics that gives the false illusion of being actually connected.

INTERROGATE – 1) targeted and intentional questioning designed to uncover the ways in which another is or is not involved with a particular event, person, place or thing; 2) inflict a targeted and intentional questioning designed to uncover the ways in which another is or is not involved with a particular event, person, place or thing upon one.

INTERROGATION – 1) the act, or event, of performing a targeted and intentional questioning designed to uncover the ways in which another is or is not involved with a particular event, person, place or thing; 2) the act, or event, of inflicting a targeted and intentional questioning designed to uncover the ways in which another is or is not involved with a particular event, person, place or thing upon one.

INTERROGATIVE – 1) the specific elements or questions in a targeted and intentional questioning designed to uncover the ways in which another is or is not involved with a particular event, person, place or thing.

INTERTWINE – 1) to combine two well-developed ideas or concepts into one interrelated and stronger idea or concept.

INTERVIEW – VERB] 1) to ask questions designed to elicit desired information about the suitability of the subject for a particular position; [NOUN] 2) the act of asking questions designed to elicit desired information about the suitability of the subject for a particular position.

INTESTINE – 1) specific spiritual means by which one takes in the world, or the events in one's life, so that it is assimilated into the manifest consciousness.

INTROVERT – 1) one who seeks within; 2) a spiritual seeker.

INVERTEBRATE – 1) one with strong constitution; 2) having confidence; 3) one who is not easily pursuaded.

INVISIBLE – 1) that which is undetectable in the manifest; 2) spiritual aspects that cannot be seen or experienced by those who are not also living a life of spirit.

IRON – METAL] 1) durable, somewhat precious dark neutrality that is very sturdy and can be structural or serve as foundation; [VERB] 2) using repression, strength and precious neutrality to correct or straighten out belief system.

IRON BARS – 1) a barrier of precious elements of necessity one can see through, yet they are a solid barrier; [GREY IRON BARS] 2) a solid but seen through barrier that is neutral on the question of light and dark; 3) spiritually neutral barrier; 4) confusion, spiritual apathy addressing the question of light and dark that causes a barrier; 5) not making a statement either way and, by so doing, creating a barrier.

IRS – 1) social control mechanism; 2) reference to numeric value (4); 3) that which tracks and controls flow.

ISLAND – 1) isolated and resolute with absolute change surrounding and encroaching; 2) using isolation to avoid change, holding out; 3) refusal to change even when everything around has changed completely.

ISTHMUS – 1) resolute determination to remain centered and balanced when opposing changes are imminent if one ventures away from center; 2) resistant to available opportunities to embrace spirit because they involve the risk of actions of faith; 3) obstinate clinging to Maya.

ITCH – 1) awareness through irritation of outward connection with most personal boundaries is initiated from the outside.

IVORY – 1) extremely long lasting anger that, over time, has become enormous; [CARVED IVORY] 2) ancient grudge that has been kept alive and animated by time, and any attempt to break it down or erode it only makes it more attractive and of greater value.

IVY – 1) austere, learned; 2) enterprise of learning through study of manmade and natural barriers, structures and obstacles that produces a multiplicity of results.

J

JACKET – 1) protection; 2) what one believes is needed for protection based on expectation derived from past experience, or projection of future expectation.

JACK-IN-THE-BOX – 1) manmade structure (4) that has a pre-planned surprise of unusual, flamboyant; 2) construct that is startling and entertaining belief systems on display when another falls into the temptation to explore the structure.

JACK-O-LANTERN – 1) dedication to natural passion that has been made incapable of duplicating or replicating itself; 2) commitment that brings forward the light of an individual's unique identity, vision or gifts.

JACKPOT – 1) enticement of ability to have exaggerated ability to flow in society gained through luck rather than work or true value.

JADE – [STONE] 1) abundant obstacle with inherent value; [CARVED JADE] 2) obstacle of abundance that has been used as an enhancement or element of decorative pleasure.

JAGUAR – 1) highly efficient, effective and agile spiritual state; 2) the power of spirit in one's life that enables quick development in forward movement on one's path.

JAIL – 1) state of being imprisoned in life by precious and mandatory elements of life; 2) state of being imprisoned in life by precious and mandatory elements of life that one has elected to have in life, often reflective of cumulative presence of necessary elements one has chosen in the past that now become so overwhelming that any forward movement on one's path is impossible; 3) becoming boxed in by one's choices in life.

JAIL-BATE – 1) temptation that, if succumbed to, will cause one to become imprisoned by obligation and repercussion.

JAILOR – 1) one who enforces imprisonment, even when conditions of imprisonment are self-inflicted.

JALOPY – 1) outdated means of attempting to reach goals without traveling on path; 2) holding on to one's obsession to avoid traveling on one's path through denial that things have changed.

JAM – VERB] 1) to force too many things into a small space; 2) to force something into a space that is too small to properly accommodate the item; [FOOD] 3) derivative of natural bounty to nourish that is condenced to provide essential nectar as nourishment.

JAMMER – 1) outside force that prevents flow in another system, environment or process.

JAMMING DEVICE – 1) device that issues outside force that prevents flow in another system, environment or process.

JAR – 1) reservoir and tool for change; 2) means of keeping reservoir and/or tool for change under one's control to apply as needed.

JAW – 1) how one is prepared to encounter resistance or criticism when facing the world; 2) the tough exterior one must present in advance when encountering the harshness of the world.

JAZZ – 1) essence of free spirited expression that inspires the like-minded; 2) exclusive free spirited and highly intellectual expression of spiritual principle that is only effective for those who are indoctrinated to that way of thinking.

JEALOUS – 1) simultaneous feeling of self-loathing due to feelings of inadequacy and desire to have what another has.

JEEP – 1) unrefined means of moving quickly toward goals without encountering one's actual spiritual path.

JEER – 1) one with world view or outlook that is judgmental, aggressive and intrusive; 2) a world view or outlook that causes desire to use that outlook to provoke others with imposed judgment.

JEHOVAH – 1) one with vision able to prophesize spiritual development for mankind; 2) spiritual oracle.

JELLO – 1) transparent source of nourishment that only builds the effectiveness of one's defenses; 2) opportunity to absorb and assimilate an essential element depicted by color and other attributes.

JESTER – 1) one who is in service to entertain, distract or divert with the entertainment skills; 2) being on call, to diffuse stress or great responsibility momentarily so that humor results; 3) represents state of selflessness in one who serves the pleasure of another without thought of self; 4) service at expense of self in society's view.

JESUS – 1) avatar embodying love, kindness and passive way of life; 2) manifest representation of deity embodying love and kindness as a means of forward movement on a spiritual path.

JET – 1) inspired passion that is repressed to build up pressure so that when released there is dramatic and sudden movement forward; 2) completely in inspired state, without actually being on one's path.

JET ENGINE – 1) mechanism that gathers and condenses inspiration and thus causes and sustains forward motion and is powered by the joint efforts of the enterprise of mankind; 2) that which supplies constant energy from pressurized inspiration so that a structure in the manifest may continue to function; 3) that inspiration-fueled thing that keeps a person, place, idea, pursuit or attempt in motion.

JET SKI – 1) inspiration mixed with the flow of change and growth enables rapid advancement of flow toward the goal; 2) being is state that allows easy survival through the process of change.

JETSAM – 1) stuff of life left behind in change, removed from one's being by the process of change itself.

JETTISON – 1) cause to be removed through sudden and unexpected inspiration.

JEWEL – 1) that which brings spiritual light into the manifest *(color, number and shape give specific attributes)*; 2) riches; 3) centerpiece of what is truly precious to one *(e.g. the idea behind the goal)*.

JEWELED BOX – 1) man's works in man's world that are precious and adorned with many elements which in themselves bring the light of spirit.

JEWELER – 1) one who through expertise adds adornment of elements which bring light of spirit; 2) one who is able to create the proper preciousness so that elements that bring the light of spirit are shown most prominently.

JEWELRY – 1) personal adornment of elements that bring the light of spirit and/or show the most precious things prominently.

JIGGLE – 1) action that causes movement in another, not for the purpose of aiding in movement on the path, but rather to end stagnation.

JIZM – 1) life essence; 2) spirit essence.

JOB – [OCCUPATION] 1) one's actions of labor in life; [BIBLICAL PERSONAGE] 2) persistence in devotion and dedication to spiritual way of living.

JOKE – 1) expression that causes others to find humor.

JOKER – 1) one who expresses so others will find humor; [COURT JESTER] 2) one who is in service to entertain, distract or divert with the entertainment skills; 3) being on call, to diffuse stress or great responsibility momentarily so that humor results; 4) represents state of selflessness in one who serves the pleasure of another without thought of self; 5) service at expense of self in society's view.

JOKESTER – 1) one whose actions are intended to cause others to falter in a way that may seem humorous to onlookers.

JOKING – 1) expressing or acting in a way that is not serious; 2) expressing or acting in a way that is intentionally aimed to misinform or mislead for the purpose of amusement.

JONQUIL – 1) hooded experience that is equal parts intellectual and spiritual; 2) vibrant, mind/spirit-based experience that returns cyclically, and each time comes back stronger.

JOSTLE – 1) sudden strong action that causes movement in another, not for the purpose of aiding in movement on the path, but rather to end stagnation.

JOURNAL – 1) record of one's achievements and product of living.

JOURNEY – 1) entirety of movement on one's path.

JUDAS – 1) one who will turn on a friend; 2) inability to escape destiny.

JUDGE – 1) one who bears responsibility to determine correct assessment and suitable outcome in terms of the laws of man's world and those who may have broken them; 2) responsibility to be true to one's innate spiritual orientation when asked to assess, condone or condemn in the manifest.

JUDGMENT – 1) one's actions are judged at the moment they take place; 2) one cannot defer results or implications of one's actions.

JUDICIOUS – 1) ability to see clearly ramifications and effects of the actions of others; 2) not prone to emotional, intellectual or reactionary responses; 3) inner calm when confronted with intrusive or invasive outside forces that attack the ego.

JUGGLE – 1) manner of dealing with too many commitments, so much so that they become mutually exclusive and must be dealt with in inspired state; 2) inspiration to alternate or rotate one's commitments so that they can all be continuously met.

JUGGLER – 1) one with too many mutually exclusive commitments, who must deal with them in an inspired state; 2) one with inspiration to alternate or rotate one's commitments so that they can all be continuously met.

JUGGLING – 1) dealing with many mutually exclusive commitments in an inspired state; 2) alternating or rotating one's commitments with inspiration to so that they can all be continuously met.

JUGULAR – 1) core flow of life force.

JUICE – 1) essence of change coming from life's most nurturing and nourishing commitments.

JUICER – 1) means of extracting essence of change coming from life's most nurturing and nourishing commitments.

JUMP ROPE – 1) idea that is cyclical and must be avoided, which one can only avoid in temporary state of inspiration.

JUMP SEAT – 1) place of presumed comfort that not only takes one off of one's path while attempting to reach goals without dealing directly with path.

JUMPER – 1) belief system that obscures origins of movement on one's path that is derived from tasks one tends toward in life.

JUMPING – 1) moving away from one's path in an inspired way; 2) self-induced elevated moment.

JUNGLE – 1) abundance of life; 2) crowded.

JUNGLE ROT – 1) such excessive abundance that unnecessary elements will be turned into soil rather than being used.

JUNIPER – 1) life that is un-developed and everlasting, filled with dark commitments.

JUNK – 1) excessive and unneeded elements of manifest reality that were perhaps once useful but are currently not.

JUNK MAIL – 1) excessive and unneeded messages from others sent indiscriminately to all, which might be useful to some but rarely are.

JUNKET – 1) journey or path with intention of introducing self or ideas to all met on the way.

JUPITER – 1) commitment to flexibility, expansion, growth, opportunity, and luck.

JURISDICTION – 1) range of responsibility.

JURISPRUDENCE – 1) range of governance of societal regulations, organizational demands, requirements or regimens.

JURY – 1) group who pool opinions to pass judgment.

JURY RIG – 1) quickly improvised solution to problem.

JUSTICE – 1) balance in universe that happens in direct response to actions taken that have had negative effect, generally.

JUSTIFICATION – 1) intellectual reasoning to account for going against one's heart's truth; 2) excuse.

JUSTIFY – 1) giving intellectual reasoning to account for going against one's heart's truth; 2) giving excuse.

K

KANGAROO – 1) one's pattern of movement on one's path is in the habit of pushing against the path so that one is propelled in inspiration for a brief time, but always comes back to it without having progressed much.

KAPPA – [ASSOCIATED WITH THE NUMERIC VALUE 20] 1) manifest completion; 2) fulfilling a projection, objective or task in the manifest

KARMA – 1) echo in life; 2) mirror of previous actions in current or future events due to limited and non-spiritual point of view; 3) result of spiritual fear when one clings to the manifest and is therefore haunted by past actions.

KAYAK – 1) singular or individual means of getting through change, requires constant action on all mandatory issues directly dealing with getting through the change.

KETCHUP – 1) flow of heart and earth events that makes any nourishing event easier to assimilate.

KEVLAR – 1) impenetrable belief system; 2) belief system that protects against any commitment another has to attack or harm one.

KEY – 1) willingness; [BOOK-LOCK-KEY] 2) one must use willingness as a way to get information, the willingness is there; [BIG CHURCH KEY] 3) spiritual willingness is the foundation of belief system, but one must act on it.

KEY RING – 1) indication that all means of willingness is precious; 2) one has ongoing way to keep all means of willingness available.

KEYNOTE – 1) the needed element for some planned event to begin; 2) *[keynote speech or address]* planned and called-for expression of self that, once made, puts a series of events and expressions in motion.

KEYSTONE - 1) idea on which things are based, central philosophy, world view.

KICK – 1) use combination of movement and direction on one's path to accomplish something next on the path.

KICK STAND – 1) returning to active movement on the path, but having precious means of resting one's conveyance of avoiding forward movement that has been previously used, and is still ready for use at any time.

KICKER – 1) one who uses combination of movement and direction on path to make commitments become inspired.

KID – [CHILD] 1) not gender specific, one who is still growing and learning; 2) an innocent or innocence itself; 3) accepting of one's fate, doing whatever is next;

4) someone in the beginning of an unfamiliar process; [VERB] 5) use expression to cause desired response in others; 6) create circumstances for others that cause amusement for onlookers; [BABY GOAT] 7) youth who is tough, stubborn, eats most anything and likes the established order and money; 8) young conservative, early success through determination; 9) from early in life shows to be rigid and unforgiving when others stand in their way; 10) immaturely moralistic and social, will always seek to ascend; 11) youth who takes up a profession of "law and order", (*i.e. doctor, lawyer, police, teacher*); 12) ignorant youth who likes to show off wealth.

KIDDER – 1) one who does not take life seriously, but is amusing to self and/or others.

KIDDING – 1) playfully misleading; 2) intentionally misleading in non-serious way to get a rise or response.

KIKE – FROM YIDDISH 'KIKKEL' OR 'CIRCLE'] 1) derogatory term for one of Jewish descent and/or faith; 2) means of identifying self as Jewish that is mocked by Christians *(on Ellis Island when Jewish immigrants could not write in Latin alphabet and were asked to sign their name, they placed a 'o' instead of the 'χ' used by Christians to distinguish themselves in their belief)*.

KILL – 1) an ultimate sign of a Tower Path, seeing one's self as equal to God; 2) take the life of another in literal or non-literal means.

KILLER – 1) one on a Tower Path, seeing one's self as equal to God; 2) one who takes the life of another in literal or non-literal means; 3) action, item or gesture that takes the spiritual life of another in literal or non-literal means.

KIN – 1) spirit relative.

KINDERGARTEN – 1) place for first spiritual lessons in life.

KINETIC – 1) motion on path.

KING – 1) creator of change; 2) someone who is in a position that has been given to them; it is earned; [TAROT KING] 3) creator and destroyer; 4) fully accomplished and established.

KING PIN – 1) primary figurehead; 2) primary target; 3) event, which when caused, then in turn sets off inevitable chain of events.

KINGDOM – 1) area of influence over which one holds power to create or destroy.

KINSHIP – 1) of a spiritual relationship or bond.

KIP – 1) the action that instantly causes one who has become stagnant on one's path to suddenly regain movement and direction; 2) to slip past something with intent to avoid; 3) small, but important and nourishing, message.

KIPPER – 1) an anointed message that has been dissected in an effort to prepare it to reach the largest group.

KISMET – 1) blessed and inevitable; 2) divine coincidence; 3) the belief or feeling that a heart connection is ordained as destiny.

KISS – 1) mutual expression of nurturing love; 2) the manner of expression one person makes specifically for taking or giving, and without regard for the other person; 3) affectionate manner of expression; 4) expressing affection instead of anger.

KITCHEN – 1) the part of one's spiritual dwelling place that provides spiritual nourishment, unity and warmth; 2) the aspect of one's soul that provides nourishment for self and/or other.

KLEENEX – 1) conclusions or ideas that are designed to capture, contain and prevent propulsion of inspiration; 2) that which stifles sudden inspiration; 3) inhibitor of inspiration.

KNEE – 1) aspect of forward movement that allows sudden extension to achieve greater range of movement.

KNEEL – 1) to cease movement on path because there is no means of extending motion other than that which is directly related to the foundation; 2) humbling effect in which one momentarily ceases forward movement; 3) to elect to show humility.

KNEELING – 1) experience of humility; 2) acceptance of greater power on path.

KNIFE – 1) immediate passion, emotion; 2) quick and efficient way of having devastating emotional impact on another.

KNIGHT – 1) quest; 2) mission; 3) ambition.

KNITTED CAP – 1) connection to the divine is by way of a belief system from a single, simplistic thought, which must be twisted, recoiled, reversed and meandering so as to appear substantial *(color and various elements and adornments give specifics).*

KNITTED FABRIC – 1) a belief system based on a single idea that is twisted and turned back on itself in very meandering and convoluted ways so that it will appear to be far more intricate than it is; 2) simplistic belief system.

KNITTING – 1) the action, with firm belief it is necessary and must define and exclude elements designated as 'other', of creating a belief system from a single, simplistic thought; 2) twisting, recoiling, reversing and meandering with a single thought so it appears substantial.

KNITTING NEEDLE - 1) a combination of wand and sword, it is the tool of the mind that has the ability to perform the action, with firm belief it is necessary and must define and exclude elements designated as 'other', of creating a belief system from a single, simplistic thought. *(color and attributes of this object in a vision further define it)*

KNOT – 1) use of major belief to hold something, or prevent it from moving, for as long as one chooses; 2) twist or doubling back of thought or belief that inhibits motion; 3) manipulation of a belief or thought so as to hold something in place, and thus prevent motion or distance.

KNOTTED – 1) twisting, or doubling back on itself, of a thought or belief so that it cannot be effective; 2) manipulation of thought or belief so as to render it ineffective; 3) to confuse one's thoughts so that they cannot progress.

KNOW – 1) to be spirit-inspired with certainty; 2) to be so closely joined as to become one with.

KNOWING – 1) state of spiritual vision such that comprehension of vision occurs without presence of vision; 2) when one suddenly is completely joined with another by means of spiritual intervention.

KNOWLEDGE – 1) state where intellect if properly functioning and can retain information for use later; 2) body of learning one carries at all times ready for access when needed or useful.

KRISHNA – 1) Hindu Godhead symbolizing various aspects: a god-child, a prankster, a model lover, a divine hero and the Supreme Being; 2) the use of flow, growth or change to bring one's unique gifts into their ultimate manifest form; 3) state of divine and mandatory inspiration that delivers one's gifts to their ultimate state; 4) being seduced by the powerful and moving beauty of one's own gifts.

KUNG FU – 1) use of one's body, in imitation of elements of nature, for protection.

L

LABOR - 1) the process when one's commitment and dedication in life becomes a life of its own.

LABOR CAMP – 1) place of societal entrapment where one's commitment and dedication in life is forced to dominate for the purpose of enslavement to another.

LABYRINTH – 1) koan; 2) mysterious and confounding progression on path that requires simultaneously absolute faith and clear-visioned patience.

LACE – 1) intricate illusion that is inspired but ineffective; 2) unnecessarily complex and pointless tradition; 3) convoluted plot.

LACE DOILY – 1) inspired but ineffective idea of spiritual protection; 2) an overly simplistic belief system because entire network is based on a single thought or concept.

LACE FAN – 1) actions that use

complex but ineffective belief systems for momentary inspiration.

LADDER – 1) means of ascending or becoming elevated; 2) making use of life itself to elevate on path.

LADY – 1) societal role for women based on prescribed set of actions and characteristics that are essentially limiting and out of step with reality.

LAKE - 1) A place of safe, comfortable and contained changes.

LAKE SHORE - 1)natural border to comfortable, natural and contained change.

LAMB – 1) gentleness; 2) willingness to be in a group; 3) one prone to have common experiences.

LAMP – 1) artificial means of illumination.

LAMP SHADE – 1) that which directs, difuses, focuses or blocks illumination coming from an artificial source.

LANCE – 1) mandatory or required action based on emotion with intention of piercing the boundaries of another.

LAND – 1) stability; 2) grounded; 3) manifest reality.

LANDING - 1) becoming grounded.

LANDSCAPING - 1) actively changing experiences in the life of the person.

LANDSLIDE – 1) when one's path suddenly shifts, disrupting things but not ending them.

LANTERN – 1) fixed idea; 2) self-unwillingness to change thinking.

LAP – 1) temporary place to hold things that is only available when one is not actively moving on one's path.

LAPIS LAZULI – 1) obstacle made of change that is present in life as obstacle but is also appreciated as adornment or decoration.

LARGE INTESTINE – 1) specific means of assimilating and taking in the world and its experiences.

LATIN AMERICA – 1) the part of the universal commitment to manifest life that represents the origin of the ancient gods; 2) Aztec, Mayan and Incan place of origin where gods Viracocha and Quetzalcoatl created some of the earliest civilizations on earth.

LATTUCE – 1) manmade grid in life that is intended to serve as a support structure for abundance in life; 2) support for potential abundant growth in life that serves as adornment by itself in the case that abundance is slow to materialize or fails to.

LAUGHTER – 1) expression of joy and celebration; 2) outflow of chi in celebration of life.

LAUNCHING PAD – 1) manifest creation from which vehicles of extreme inspiration and spiritual openness and exploration can be initiated; 2) creation of man that is designed to endure the most extremely destructive forces of passion and repression that are the catalyst for extreme inspiration and exploration of spiritual and celestial exploration and searching.

LAUNDROMAT – 1) societal system that allows individuals to develop, clarify, purify and clear their belief systems.

LAUNDRY – 1) belief systems that need to be developed, clarified, purified and cleared.

LAUREL – 1) result of life, or product of life, that shows celebratory appreciation for the accomplishments of another; 2) means of praising, noticing or recognizing others.

LAUREL WREATH – 1) receiving or being given praise; 2) being noticed by the community; 3) one's pride in self; 4) need to gracefully receive recognition from others.

LAVA – 1) reflects state when one's barriers no longer block forward movement because they have been transformed to fluidity; 2) transformation of barrier to flow.

LAW – 1) societal or social regulation designed to support orderly behavior, justice, fairness and restrictions; 2) guidelines of regulation and consequence for individuals who wish to live in society and are therefore bound to live within the boundaries of behavior represented therein.

LAWN – 1) artificial place of abundance that is contained and selectively or exclusively available for those pre-designated few to use as foundation in moments of seeing inspiration.

LAWYER – 1) one who studies and represents societal or social regulation designed to support orderly behavior, justice, fairness and restrictions; 2) one who uses guidelines of regulation and consequence for individuals who wish to live in society and are therefore bound to live within the boundaries of behavior represented therein.

LAY – 1) to stop moving on one's path in order to create tantric liaison with the path; 2) act of aligning one's chakras with path so that energetic movement may be restored.

LAYING ON BACK – 1) state of resting on and accepting who one is, and what one's path is, up to that moment in a solid place; 2) aligned with path, focused on heaven, but stagnant.

LAYING ON STOMACH – 1) aligned with one's path but in a complete state of vulnerability because such alignment is stagnant.

LEADER – 1) one who inspires and sets path forward; 2) one with vision who has gotten others to share, and follow, that vision; 3) one with responsibility for community or group who trust in them and their vision.

LEADERSHIP – 1) quality of one who inspires and sets path forward; 2) quality that places one with vision so that others to share, and follow, that vision; 3) possessing quality to take responsibility for community or group.

LEAF - 1) result from life.

LEAKING ROOF - 1) roof is not fulfilling its function, no protection, something is wrong.

LEAN - 1) to be without stable foundation; 2) not properly aligned with plane of path.

LEAN-TO – 1) temporary dwelling place of the soul in nature; 2) how one who is spiritually at home in nature can establish home whenever and wherever one chooses to take the action to create such establishment.

LEARN – 1) take in facts, memories, ideas, concepts, etc., of the mind and have them available for use when needed.

LEASH – 1) one's link to something one controls; 2) being linked to one who controls.

LEASHED DOG - 1) guidance that one gets from or gives to companions *(depending who is leading)*.

LEATHER – 1) natural boundary between being and world; 2) natural boundary that makes perfect allowance of and protection from change.

LEATHER BELT – 1) natural protection that is used to hold foundational belief system in place; 2) the natural sense of perfect allowance of change (not too little, not too much) that allows one to adopt a belief system that informs the foundational beliefs as basis of world view, and is with one throughout movement on one's path.

LEATHER GLOVES – 1) natural but protective activity; 2) what one does in life to protect one's self that is entirely natural to the person; 3) how one interacts to protect one's self and is natural.

LEAVING A ROOM BACKWARD – 1) retreating into the past while seeming present; 2) investigating how one arrived at the point where they are; 3) refusing to accept where one has arrived on one's path, and attempting to retreat to an earlier point.

LEDGE – 1) path that leads one along the boundary of challenge; 2) narrow boundary that can serve as a path that borders a boundary and is dangerous, risky and hard to proceed upon; 3) part of path bordering obstacle that requires one's entire focus and attention.

LEFT – [SIDE] 1) representative of linear nature; 2) that which is of structure, order, predictable sequence or linear organizational pattern; [HAVING DEPARTED FROM] 3) that which was, but no longer is, part of one's path; 4) thing, event, location, person or association no longer needed on path.

LEFT INDEX FINGER – 1) attention on how the logical or linear process guides one's work or path; 2) indicating the need for one to consider thing pointed to in linear, logical or organized fashion.

LEFT OVER RIGHT – 1) accepting standard, logical or traditional approach in situation; 2) traditional way to be the guiding principle.

LEGS - 1) means by which one moves along one's path.

legs itching – 1) one must actively move on one's path.

legs tingling – 1) feeling the need to move on one's path.

LEI – 1) ongoing cycle of experiences that, when shared, indicate another has equal place to celebrate these experiences.

LEMON TREE – 1) life dedicated to, and producing, commitment to intellectual or mind-based; 2) life in which intellectual commitment requires breaking down of commitment and blending with nourishing elements in order to be effective.

LEOPARD – 1) spiritual nature that moves one quickly on path; 2) willingness to pursue spiritual or occult connections in life; 2) following esoteric or mystical practices in order to achieve one's goals.

LETTER – 1) statement of one's wisdom, knowledge or results from life in lasting way that is accessible only to specific person or persons; 2) expression of one's ideas or conclusive results to an individual or a specific group; 3) means of making demand, petition, statement, supplication, exposition, ultimatum, conditions or giving information.

LEVEL OF SPHERES – 1) astral location where all commitments are visible; 2) the manifestation of all experiences of the relationships between things.

LIAISON – 1) agent of connection; 2) presence and effect of **YIN** that unites.

LIBERTY – 1) freedom from restrictive regulation.

LIBRA – 1) blind justice; 2) indicative of state of planning, waiting and analyzing information; 3) with subconscious goal to create a family based on balance and intellect; 4) one who negotiates a relationship first with the intention of a desired outcome already in mind; 5) one who is creative, idealistic and/or artistic.

LIBRARY – 1) structure or location where resource of mankind's knowledge is accessible.

LIBRARY, THE - 1)just after death, the manifest consciousness must transition to the new state of one's soul, and to do that is in a location that has three main features: the **GARDEN**, the **LIBRARY**, and the **GALLERY**. The Library is where all knowledge is found. One can go and learn every fact one wishes to know.

LICENSE – 1) having inherent permission; 2) societal indicator of one who has inherent permission to a specific sub-set of things.

LIE – 1) expression of non-truth.

LIFE – 1) one's spiritual path; 2) means of achieving spiritual growth.

LIFETIME – 1) opportunity to achieve spiritual growth; 2) limit in space-time that gives value to one's path in the manifest.

LIGHT-BULB – 1) idea; 2) inspiration; 3) commitment that contains manifestation of light produced when an artificial life force is forced to encounter intentional restriction of flow such that the resistance itself generates heat and causes such an effect.

LIGHTING A CANDLE – 1) action of bringing something to life; 2) to start the life of another person, event, experience, endeavor or path; 3) putting life into a new life.

LIGHTING A MATCH – 1) taking required action that brings inspiration to passion so that repressed anger may become active force.

LIGHTNING – 1) presence of light that breaks through even when it is opposed; 2) life force; 3) shakti-pad; 4) sudden influx or surge of divine energy...

LILY POND – 1) place of contained and peaceful change that has experiences that are celebrated and tranquil.

LIMOUSINE – 1) conveyance of convenience and luxury designed to deliver one to one's spiritual goals and yet avoid traveling the path toward those goals; 2) entitlement and sloth that lead one to believe spiritual goals can be reached without the challenges or discomfort of traveling the path, and while being catered to in the lap of luxury.

LINE – 1) idea, thought or continuous development of a concept; 2) border creating duality; 3) connection between things; 4) linear- or time-path.

LINE THAT CONNECTS THINGS – 1) idea; 2) concept.

LINGERIE – 1) innermost connection and choice; 2) [white lingerie] choosing on the deepest level that spirituality is the way.

LION – 1) strength; 2) symbol of the sphinx, its mysteries; 3) symbol of the lost library of mankind; 4) reminder that the biggest strength is to not have to use the strength; 5) psychic gift that has a sense of dignity and status about it; 6) supremacy; 7) regal quality, or kingliness.

LIPS – 1) manner in which one expresses or communicates; 2) how one communicates affection; 3) how one takes in nourishment, change; 4) the ability to use inspiration as an alternative to anger; 5) the ability to negotiate rather than fight.

lips itching – 1) one must actively change one's manner of expression.

lips tingling – 1) feeling the need to change one's manner of expression.

LIPSTICK – 1) mechanism to enforce choice of manner in which one expresses or communicates; 2) how one manifests one's choice of how to communicate expression; 3) method of indicating how one takes in nourishment, change; 4) means of shaping one's ability to use inspiration as an alternative to anger; 5) one's attempt to manipulate one's expression as a way to negotiate rather than fight.

LIQUOR – 1) change that destroys mind, confidence in one's self; 2) change that is destructive, delusional.

LISP – 1) inability to have clear manner of expression.

LIST – (LEAN) 1) to be without stable foundation; 2) not properly aligned with plane of path; (WRITTEN) 3) action of recording ideas, thoughts in essence form.

LIT CANDLE – 1) life in progress *(relative length of candle not yet burned indicates how much of life one has left)*.

LIT MATCH – 1) having taken action to be readied, and therefore to use the inspired passion of repressed anger as an active force.

LITTER – 1) discarded, no longer needed items left on paths of others.

LIVING ROOM – 1) place in one's spiritual home for community.

LIZARD – 1) ability to adapt easily between spirit and manifest, use inspiration as a means of mobility; 2) vulnerable only to those spiritually strong.

LLAMA – 1) thoughtful condition that is without motivation, and is not vulnerable to hostility or lack of reception in outside world.

LOAFERS – 1) means of connecting to or separating from path that is natural and temporary.

LOBBY – 1) where others first enter the spiritual dwelling place of another.

LOBBY OF HOTEL – 1) where people in transit and away from spiritual dwelling place come through to get to the illusion of a home.

LOBSTER – 1) lower world elements such as lust, hunger, sex, eating, and greed; 2) something from one's base-self is emerging.

LOCKED DOOR - 1) control over the portal to a specific path.

LOCKING DOOR – 1) *(action of...)* desire to have, or having control over access of others to enter a new path, protection to have some means of determining who enters the new path.

LOLLIPOP - 1) nourishment that is sweet and entices one, yet when one takes it in one is left with something that must be dealt with.

LONG BEARD – 1) one expresses

one's self in a manner that shows great, developed thoughtfulness.

LONG HAIR – 1) well developed thoughts.

LONG HAIR IN BRAIDS - 1)one who avoids responsibility for thoughts and ideas and also does not take on tasks related to ideas by means of spiritual pattern used as excuse.

LONG HAIR ON BACK – 1) one who takes responsibility for thoughts and ideas; 2) enduring thoughts; 3) taking responsibility for thoughts and ideas.

LONG HAIR ON SHOULDER(S) - 1)one who's well developed thoughts influence the nature or substance of tasks taken on.

LONG HANDLE – 1) the action accomplished by the tool, which is essential and mandatory and without emotional or spiritual charge, is easy to reach and easy to be in touch with.

LONG NECK – 1) indicates great distance between heart and head, significant of central role expression and its manner have in how the natural order is such that expression of the heart is meant to bypass the intellect; 2) nature of one's communications with others is keeping the heart's message clear and true.

LONG SLEEVE – 1) belief system that determines how one embraces the world.

LOOM – 1) mechanism by which ideas are combined so as to become belief system or thought pattern.

LOON – 1) opinion about or concerning inevitability of change that mocks those destined to change in that way.

LOOP – 1) idea or concept that is linear but circles back on itself and goes nowhere.

LOOPING BIRD - 1) opinions that are inspired but go nowhere.

LOPSIDED – 1) off balance; 2) out of sync with overall balance.

LOST DOG – 1) a displaced companion; 2) companion with specific destination or attachment that cannot find that connection.

LOTION – 1) spiritual change that works on boundaries and is present through one's own determined actions.

LOTS OF TREES – 1) many lives united by geographical location or common purpose; 2) society that gathers naturally because of the involuntary nature of the geographical location; 3) lots of life.

LOTUS – 1) divinity; 2) divine presence on earth; 3) life experiences that are about growth, change or flow.

LUAU – 1) festival of nourishment.

LUCIFER – 1) manifestation of source of self-loathing; 2) name given to that power which causes one to turn against one's self.

LUCK – 1) spirit presence manifesting in lives of individuals that is good or bad depending on presence of faithful actions or not.

LULL – 1) inner tranquility.

LULLABY – 1) spirit presence that allows inner tranquility and total peace.

LUNAR ECLIPSE - 1)when the shadow self blocks one's view that they are self-deceived.

LURK – 1) using pause or elected stagnancy on one's path for the purpose of hiding, searching or pursuing something the ego desires.

LYRE – 1) the ability through one's actions to bring spirit to any setting; 2) balance as result of action that brings spirit presence.

M

MACHETE – 1) emotional or strident opinion that is designed to remove, maim or eviscerate that which one deems as unnecessary; 2) tool for shaping the world into one's desired vision, particularly by removing what is unwanted.

MACHINE - 1) mechanism that causes and sustains action and is powered by the joint efforts of the enterprise of mankind; 2) system that ensures that a structure in the manifest may continue to function.

MACHINERY – 1) mechanisms in man's world that assist one; 2) resources with collective functions that allow one to do things otherwise impossible.

MACRAMÉ BELT – 1) narrow belief system constructed of very few actual concepts or ideas that are twisted, knotted and turned back on themselves in order to form a structure adequate to contain or control; 2) twisting facts and ideas into a form that then can be used to connect or disconnect assimilation from foundation in life.

MAGAZINE – [PERIODICAL] 1) temporary collection of results, ideas and expositions that are then distributed to society at large; 2) temporary collection of ideas; [AMMUNITION DEPOT] 3) storage place of commitments designed to ultimately cause destruction and death.

MAGIC – 1) putting to use everything in the manifest; 2) manipulation by ego in the manifest to bend nature to one's will; 3) utilizing power of nature to have desired effect on the manifest world.

MAGIC WAND – 1) necessary tool to redirect natural forces in manifest; 2) necessary tool of channeling nature's force in order to alter manifest reality to one's will; 3) required ritual, tool, device or process that allows one to facilitate the manipulation of forces the manifest.

MAGICIAN - 1) having available all one needs with which to do anything one chooses to do; 2)one who utilizes power of nature to have desired effect on the manifest world; 3) one who manipulates by force of one's ego in the manifest to bend nature to one's will; 4) one who puts to use everything in the manifest.

MAGNET – 1) that which has the precious ability to unite.

MAGNETIC TAPE – 1) invisible binding element of society that interrupts chi flow; 2) artificial concept that connects persons, places or things that, once they are connected, distorts chi flow to them, causing perpetuity of the false connection; 3) false connection through manipulation or distortion of chi and based on an artificial and manipulative concept of joining, togetherness or unity.

MAGNETISM – 1) force that unites.

MAID – 1) one who lives one's life in service to others; 2) function of restoring order in the world as means of service to others.

MAKING A MOVIE – 1) creating an illusion of life, in life.

MALE – 1) one of the nature to introduce spiritual change into foundation of another for purpose of creating new event, life, occurrence or situation; 2) potential to be father.

MALL – 1) natural seeming, though manufactured, area like a glen or pasture which is location where abundance serves as the foundation for inspiration; 2) designated area or marketplace for commercial enterprise and retail exchanges.

MAMMAL – 1) state of nature in which survival, procreation, defense and recreation are native.

MAN – 1) manifest lifetime experience; 2) housing for soul; 3) individual.

MANACLE – 1) precious and resilient perpetual restriction that makes taking action impossible; 2) anything considered precious to society that inhibits the actions of individual members of that society; 3) precious internal standard, conflict or restriction that does not allow one to take action, but is considered too precious and ongoing to discontinue.

MANAGER – 1) one who organizes, oversees and is accountable for designated activities often with fixed objective of results or effect.

MANGER – 1) spiritual home for all beings.

MANMADE LIGHT – 1) false light of spirit, though actual light in manifest; 2) non-naturally produced light demonstrates parallel of relative function between manifest consciousness and spirit; 3) all beings, manifest and spirit, possess the ability to create light, just as they possess creativity and love in unlimited amounts; 4) potential for man to do god's work in the manifest; 3) artificial life force is made to encounter orchestrated flow restrictions so that the resistance generates heat to causes light-effect.

MANNEQUIN – 1) imitation (not expression) of life; 2) phony surface.

MANSION - 1)beautiful and spacious soul or greater spirit and all of its manifestations in a life-time.

MANTILLA – 1) belief system that is intricate and inspired illusion ineffectively serving as temporary connection with (or division from) the divine yet is also on display for others; 2) unnecessarily complex and pointless belief system that is utilized for spiritual ritual; 3) convoluted plot belief system that serves used as dramatic display of one's connection with divinity.

MARBLE FLOOR - **1)**one's foundation in life is such that it naturally cools any situation.

MARBLES – 1) minor commitment suited to actions of self-amusement; 2) symbol for illusion in **MAYA** being aligned so that all commitments are sources of amusement and enjoyment if one takes action with such intention; 3) freedom from burden of commitment.

MARIJUANA – 1) state of repression and inspiration that distorts one's ability to think; 2) represents being in an inspired state of self-delusion mixed with fixation on self; 3) false sense of fascinating depth; 4) inspired state of inflated self-importance reflected in extreme paranoia.

MARIONETTE – 1) false individual supported by few ideas, only able to seem real or alive when manipulated; 2) state of being vulnerable, due to simplistic beliefs, to manipulation.

MARS – 1) natural tendency to war like behavior; 2) commitment to, or association with, energy, vitality, aggression and assertion.

MARY – 1) possessing message of peace, kindness, gentleness, forgiveness; 2) the **EMPRESS**, thus provides opportunities to grow; 3) originator, and benefactress, of all that happens in our lives that gives us opportunity to grow comes from her.

MASCULINITY – 1) societal designation of attributes, attitudes and actions that define one as being suitable male within that society only.

MASSAGE – 1) action of healing through manipulation of physical body; 2) actions that restore, resuscitate, heal, re-energize and calm.

MASTERPIECE – 1) work in manifest that is highest achievement of man and is universally recognized as wholly authentic; 2) one's highest achievement in this world; 3) truest representation of gift's manifestation.

MAT – 1) that which separates from,

protects, or makes more comfortable one's path.

MATCH – 1) a mandatory part of life that, should action be taken, brings inspiration to passion so that repressed anger may become active force.

MATHEMATICS – 1) intellectual study of numbers, their relationships, and the interrelationship of trends and effects within sets of numbers; 2) the way in which numeric intellectual concepts unfold, inter-react in a theoretical place of perfection not prone to outside or unexpected forces (i.e., nature, emotion, chance or divine intervention).

MAYA – 1) manifest realm; 2) man's world—including all physical, emotional, intellectual, spiritual, religious, legal and imagination based structures—that forms one's world view and the totality of one's experiences in life.

MEADOW – 1) element of lush vegetation represents an abundance in nature; 2) a reference to the ecosystem (plant → oxygen →oxygen breathing organism → carbon dioxide → plant); 3) the way in which the earth embraces human existence by giving life and asking nothing in return; 4) without barriers; 5) very welcoming.

MEASUREMENT – 1) means of determining size, distance, volume, weight, height, or other quantitative value in manifest form; 2) relevant distance between things in space-time; 3) volume of sphere representing extent of commitment.

MEAT – 1) basic element of physical mass of manifest being, without structure or fluid content; 2) strength available.

MECHANIC – 1) one who is adept at managing, creating, correcting and/or monitoring man-made things.

MECHANICAL – 1) man-made physical objects that perform a function, or assist in manipulation of the manifest world.

MEDICINE – 1) elements, essences, minerals, chemicals, plants or any other thing that has healing or curative properties; 2) body of knowledge of how to administer medicines (see definition 1) for the purpose of health, healing and having a curative effect.

MEDICINE MAN – 1) shaman; 2) one who knows how to administer elements, essences, minerals, chemicals, plants or any other thing that has healing or curative properties, or is used as a preventative to disease and/or means of sustaining good balanced health.

MEDITATION – 1) deep listening to spirit or inner truth of the heart; 2) practice of slowing the body and speeding the mind function so that one's state of consciousness is able to operate at a different level; 2) method of altering one's ability to perceive and therefore purposely alter one's consciousness.

MEMORIAL – 1) ritual to unite participant's hearts and intention in honor of predetermined specific event, individual or intention.

MENOPAUSE – 1) transition of one's state in life from creating to guiding; 2) inevitability of change; 3) evolution.

MERCURY – [METAL] 1) fluid preciousness that give fleeting view of self; [PLANET] 2) represents communication, particularly communication that honors the synthesis of content, context, and timing.

MERIDIAN – 1) main avenue of **CHI** flow in holistic system of the manifest body; 2) yin nature of being, indicative of how each organ of the manifest body serves the whole body.

MERMAID – 1) being of change that invites and seduces one to total change; 2) ability to be totally at home in spirit while still in manifest form.

MESS – 1) disarray in manifest; 2) results of lacking in control of one's environment in the manifest; 3) unplanned and excessive results of effort to achieve something entirely different.

METAL BOX – 1) precious, man-made creation that isolates, holds, reserves or contains.

METAL HAIRBRUSH – 1) precious method of organizing thoughts that, when used, is necessary.

METAL RIMMED GLASSES - 1) frames world view with perpetual precious element, type of metal gives precise element.

METALLIC WATCH – 1) preciousness of time; [ON LEFT WRIST] 2) linear and/or logical use of time to either connect embrace of the world with actions, or divide embrace of world from actions; 3) one for whom time very valuable in linear and/or logical ways; 4) one who makes linear and/or logical use of time. [ON RIGHT WRIST] 5) creative and/or emotional use of time to either connect embrace of the world with actions, or divide embrace of world from actions; 3) one for whom time very valuable in creative and/or emotional ways; 4) one who makes creative and/or emotional use of time.

META-MORPHING – 1) transforming completely who one is; 2) unfolding of one's destiny; 3) becoming of what one is meant to be; 4) maturation process.

METAMORPHOSIS – 1) transforming completely who one is; 2) unfolding of one's destiny; 3) becoming of what one is meant to be; 4) maturation process.

METAPHYSICS – 1) body of knowledge that combines manifest intellectual processes with spiritual, clairvoyant, psychic and/or mystic processes.

METEOR – 1) celestial commitment that comes from inspiration out of darkness into one's life; 2) intentional intrusion of spiritual commitment that comes from inspiration in darkness to one's life; 3) traveling shard of celestial object that had been both commitment and obstacle but is now broken down; 2) remnant of failed event of celestial origins that had been an intersection of paths of potentially conflicting commitments on large scale; 3) remnant of lost dedication or commitment to fate, that was lost when it was faced with obstacles and conflicts on its journey.

MICROPHONE – 1) necessary task to communicate to others about one's specific commitment; 2) commitment in form of action that is precious, mandatory and is connected by spirit to a very developed idea, precious at its core, and manifests as a conduit for one's expression.

MICROPHONE STAND – 1) precious and mandatory support for tasks of communication representing a conduit for expression.

MICROSCOPE – 1) one takes action to view manifest realm in elemental or essential way.

MIDDLE EAST – 1) the aspect of the universal commitment to manifest existence that represents the start of the human race; 2) the origin of the foundation for the major religions of the current era of human civilization since the last earth changes.

MIGRAINE – 1) intellectual capacity is disabled; 2) commitment to intellectuality that is debilitating; 3) when one's commitment to intellectual is disabled by presence of light or spiritual vibration.

MILE – 1) measure of distance in manifest; 2) significant or considerable distance in manifest.

MILITARY – 1) element in manifest prepared for defense; 2) recognition that there is the possibility of danger and being prepared for it; 3) being realistic about, and prepared for, the dangers, obstacles and trials of the manifest world.

MILK – 1) inheritance; 2) essence of life; 3) taking in the essence of life from spirit; 4) spiritual growth mechanism; 5) the essence of spiritual lesson in life.

MILK SHAKE – 1) sweet, nourishing inheritance; 2) pleasurable essence of life; 3) taking in the essence of life from spirit in ways that please, amuse and nourish; 4) pleasant spiritual growth mechanism; 5) the most nourishing and pleasant essence of spiritual lesson in life.

MIND – 1) intellectual capacity to remember, store, sort and access information; 2) resource that aids in managing one's interaction with one's path that, when used as a guide, becomes the enemy of the heart.

MINE – 1) to delve deep within a commitment, or break down a barrier so as to expose the precious benefit of that commitment and/or barrier in one's life.

MINERAL CHAKRA – ALSO SEE **FOUNDATION CHAKRA**]1) represents one's foundation in life; 2) place that embodies health, security, ability to procreate and the sexual aspects of life, religious beliefs, shame, ethnics; 3) foundations of life; 4) the sexual aspects of life; 5) religious beliefs; 6) origins of one's shame; 7) basis of one's world view.

MINIATURE – 1) the insignificance of the manifest; 2) manifest seen from point of view of spirit; 3) disorientation that occurs when one travels outside of space-time and then views the manifest realm from that perspective.

MINK – 1) unique and very practical ideas and thoughts that together protect one and signify a state of extraordinary advantage in the manifest; 2) the ability to look into out of the way, small places and as a result develop a wealth of unique, dark and practical thoughts that may be used for protection, though sometimes that use is the result of taking advantage of the vulnerability of the original state.

MINUTE – 1) basic unit of time; 2) short amount of time.

MIRACLE – 1) manifestation of divine will that defies logic and comprehension of physics and science at that time; 2) spirit intervention on manifest; 3) that which is not yet understood.

MIRROR – 1) psychological confrontation of self; 2) self-realization; 3) reflection of identity in the light

MIRRORED SUNGLASSES - 1) outside can't see inside, this world view makes others see themselves.

MISCHIEF – 1) characteristic of one who initiates actions that cause others to react for the sole purpose of amusing one's self.

MISSILE – 1) vehicle of extreme inspiration and spiritual openness that enable exploration; 2) creation of man that enable exploration of spiritual and celestial searching.

MISSING MOLARS - 1) one can get what one wants, can do things with it, but cannot assimilate or internalize the benefit.

MISSING TEETH AT SIDES - 1) one can get what one wants, but cannot do anything with it.

MISSING TEETH IN FRONT - 1) represents that one has no way to get what one needs.

MOAT – 1) use of ongoing, perpetual change manipulated out of practicality for protection of one's spiritual dwelling place; 2) symbol for amount of control one actually has in manifest; 3) change protects spiritual life.

MODEL – 1) representative of; 2) duplicate in visual aspect only; 3) imitation that appears accurate only is dwarfed or hollow.

MODEL AIRPLANE – 1) representative of vehicle that can take one to a new place through inspiration; 2) symbolic of that which allows inspiration without remaining on one's path; 3) imitation of inspired means to a goal that avoids actual path; 4) creating illusion of that which allows using inspiration to avoid work on path.

MOLECULE – 1) cluster of essential elements coming together to form unique essence.

MOLINE CROSS – 1) symbol of union of spirit and manifest; 2) symbol of the Greek Orthodox Church.

MONASTERY – 1) a place of prayer and connection to spirit removed from the world; 2) location where, through meditation and ritual, the purpose is to find the connection with spirit.

MONEY – 1) flow in manifest; 2) how man's world associates the distribution of abundance; 3) #4.

MONK – 1) one who has denounced earthly identity in favor of living a life of dedication to the ministry of spirit; 2) exclusive person of religion who serves in accordance with strict sets of rules for living; 3) warlock.

MONKEY – 1) adept at life; 2) highly socialized; 3) uninhibited and naturally at home in the world.

MONOCLE – 1) gift of wisdom that allows selectively clear view; 2) ancient wisdom put to use for current and future vision.

MONOCYCLE – 1) single, ongoing and perpetual cycle that falsely promises one to reach spiritual goals without being directly on one's path ; 2) vehicle that moves one forward in life, not quite connected to the path and with singular means of forward momentum is awkward; 3) an opportunity for illusion of movement on the path in which one can move forward only if one can find and maintain personal balance; 4) unity and singularity of purpose become illusion of forward movement but all focus and energy must be forever focused on maintaining balance, and so goal may fall from sight.

MONSIGNOR – 1) one who has denounced earthly identity in favor of living a life of dedication to the ministry of spirit, yet is relatively high in the religious hierarchy; 2) exclusive and esteemed person of religion who serves in accordance with strict sets of rules for living; 3) prime warlock.

MONSOON – 1) sudden change that is divinely inflicted on a community.

MONSTER – 1) representative of danger that is defined by attributes specific to vision in question; 2) representation of belief, idea, memory, emotion or element of life that poses extreme spiritual danger.

MOON – 1) self-deception; 2) being unaware that things have changed; 3) being deceived by self or other without knowledge of it until too late: 3) gift of sight or vision; 4) essence of female as a gender; [CELESTIAL BODY]

5) represents truth in vision; 6) authenticity of female manifestation; [full moon] 7) birth and death; 8) harvest; 9) insanity; [CRESCENT MOON] 10) deception is nearly complete; 11) cycle of self-deception has moved one to near total darkness yet one stays in denial; [GIBBOUS MOON] 12) state of self deception that has not yet taken one into dark phase; 13) one has just emerged from the dark phase and is more of light than darkness; [WAXING MOON] 14) growing delusions of grandeur as form of self-deception; [WANING MOON] 15) deceiving self by viewing self as less than what is accurate; [SHOWN WITH MULTIPLE FACES] 16) state of self-deception though oblivious to one's changing face.

MOON BUGGY – 1) means by which one believes a deluded state is one's actual path of light.

MOONSTONE – 1) represents ill omen of self-delusion; 2) a thing that brings illusion of light, connection, that is actually the reverse.

MOOR – 1) stagnant state in which there is no inspiration, passion or direction, that can kill one; 2) darkness that envelops and traps one and that changes one into all that is dark; 3) state of dark change that once one is in it one cannot get out; 4) permanent change to darkness; 5) spiritual stagnation.

MOP – [NOUN] 1) mandatory part of life in which one is required to use one's collected thoughts to make minor changes for the better to one's path; [VERB] 2) making mandatory changes to one's path, clearing it, through the use of one's collected thoughts.

MORNING – 1) new beginning; 2) start of new journey.

MORTAR BOARD – 1) connection with divine entirely through the works of man; 2) academic means of connection with divine, in which only the most moderate, reasonable and central ideas might be inspired.

MOTHER – 1) earth; 2) one who dedicates one's life to that which one has brought into the world, nurtured, nourished and protected; 3) aspect of the **EMPRESS** that signifies dedication, tenacity and commitment to what one has brought into the world; 4) the yin in you; 5) origins of one's yin aspects (i.e., experiences, events, people, things, etc.); 6) that which nurtures, feeds , protects and cares for one.

MOTHER OF GOD – 1) that which brings the message of peace, kindness, gentleness, forgiveness; 2) the **EMPRESS**, thus provides opportunities to grow; 3) originator, and benefactress, of all that happens in one's life and gives opportunity to grow.

MOTOR – 1) mechanism that causes and sustains forward motion and is powered by the joint efforts of the enterprise of mankind.

MOTOR BOAT – 1) mechanism that causes and sustains forward motion of the vehicle that carries one through change; 2) vehicle that carries one through change that is powered by the joint efforts of the enterprise of mankind.

MOTORCYCLE – 1) vehicle powered by the joint efforts of the enterprise of mankind that allows one to simultaneously feel inspiration as one rushes toward goals without being on actual path.

MOULI – 1) action that, with assistance of man's works in the world, breaks down nourishment; 2) actions that breaks down nourishment into fine bits so that it may be present in all one assimilates.

MOUNTAIN – 1) natural barrier; 2) opportunity to change everything about one's life if you cross a specific barrier; 3) barrier that, by crossing it, allows one to have expansive, divine view of life; 4) mystic challenge.

MOUNTAIN RANGE -1) natural barrier that is inescapable should one go forward in any direction on one's path; 2) inescapable and broad opportunity to change everything about one's life by crossing a barrier that exists no matter what direction one goes on one's path, so long as it is generally forward; 3) inescapable barrier that, by crossing it, allows one to have expansive, divine view of life; 4) inevitable mystic challenge; 5) denotes that one is destined to mysticism no matter how they proceed forward.

MOUNTAINTOP – 1) represents a barrier transcended; 2) when one faces no major barriers; 3) one has achieved divine vision of all of life by having transcended a significant barrier; 4) one has learned the lesson a barrier was designed to teach.

MOUSE – 1) secret investigator; 2) one who gets information from everywhere; 3) state of being equally at home in darkness and light; 4) instinctive urge to gather information other than the official story; 5) power of humility; 6) one who recognizes the treasures found in detailed observation and tenacious investigation.

MOUTH – 1) manner in which one expresses self; 2) openness to nourishment; 3) manner in which one consumes the events encountered in life; 4) attributes of mouth in vision (color, shape, etc.) represents kind of manifestations one's expression involves.

MOVIE – 1) illusion of life; 2) creating obstruction to light so that it appears to take on meaning not inherent in it; 3) illusion that imitates life visible as a result of intentionally warping light to project to others a desired image.

MOVIE CAMERA – 1) mechanism to capture images that will later become illusion of life; 2) that which records light reverse imprint so to then creates filter to obstruct light so that it appears to take on meaning not inherent in it.

MOVING ON WAVES – 1) represents failure in trying to be in balance through change, but being altered on one's path; 2) instability as one resists the events of change.

MUD - 1) practical state where stability and flow mix.

MUD SLIDE – 1) sudden and natural imposition of absolute state of practicality where stability and flow suddenly mix and are forced on one's path.

MULTI-FACED MOON – 1) indicates state of self-deception though oblivious to one's changing face.

MUSHROOM – 1) memory of all of the details of things deep in the past; 2) the human spirit that adapts and fights for existence regardless of circumstances; 3) the richness and benefit even in very dark, sterile and overly practical situations.

MUSIC – 1) eternal essence of spirit; 2) spirit presence; 3) spirit.

MUSIC STAND - 1) assists one in bringing spirit to life in one's world.

MUSICAL STAFF – 1) universal manifest agreement of societal organization of spiritual expression; 2) common means upon which expression of spiritual expression is based; 3) agreed upon way of homogenizing spiritual expression so all may participate.

MUSTACHE – 1) thoughts that govern manner in which one expresses self.

MUSTARD – 1) malleable thoughts used to enhance nourishment while assimilating life's nurture.

MYCELIUM – 1) yin; 2) that which connects things; 3) omnipresence of manifest life force in all things; 4) that which supports wholeness and completion yet does not seek to be recognized nor to reproduce itself; 5) that which allows life force to flow universally, but does not itself appear to be present; 6) undetectable mechanisms of life force flow; 7) that which allows the illusion of magic to appear.

MYRRH – 1) the medicinal quality of combing intellect, practicality, inspiration, and heart in earthly application; 2) the fact that healing often requires distasteful things; 3) reminder that healing can involve struggle, discomfort or even repugnant means.

MYSTERY – 1) presence of spirit in life that cannot be comprehended by the intellect; 2) that which allows one to make an action of faith; 3) man's inability to comprehend God; 4) spirit that defies description.

MYSTIC – 1) one who can consciously travel independently of space-time; 2) one who has given one's self entirely to the teachings and molding of spirit; 3) state in which one can communicate with spirit entirely.

MYTHOLOGY – 1) cultural truth; 2) encryption of societal truth that allows it to be passed intact to future generations.

N

NAIL – 1) emotionally unifying strength of yin; 2) those things, precious and mandatory, that connect; 3) representative of the fact that direct emotional connection is precious and necessary, but takes determined effort of action, dedication of task and focused embrace of its need to accomplish.

NAKED – 1) when one is completely natural in their own unique way; 2) vulnerability and beauty of being completely true to one's nature.

NANNY – 1) represents that one's work in life is to watch over a new path and thereby aid in establishment of a new life; 2) to step into a life in the role of a guide; 3) one's work in life is to protect, guide, teach and nurture.

NANO – 1) represents function of the unseen world; 2) the importance and effectiveness of tiny details, minute adjustments or changes, and minor functions.

NAPKIN – [CLOTH] 1) belief system, often of pure spirit, that assures that life's nourishment does not overreach its intended function; 2) use of a spiritual belief system to separate nourishment from manner of expression; [PAPER] 3) results of lifetime experiences and knowledge, often of pure spirit, that assures that life's nourishment does not overreach its intended function; 2) use of results of lifetime experiences and knowledge to separate nourishment from manner of expression.

NARROW – 1) representative of encroaching boundaries that leave little or no room for passage between; 2) closed to idea, concept or imagination; 3) change, growth or flow that is presented as near exclusive opportunity.

NATION – 1) societal association with an ideal, a principle or a treatise that binds a specific group of individuals; 2) bond resulting from shared sentiment that becomes established as self-defined union of identity.

NATIVE – 1) that which is, or one who is rightfully bound to a location-specific habitat; 2) one who is descended from aboriginal inhabitants of a land; 3) that which is completely natural to one.

NATURAL – 1) that which gives unique identity; 2) that which is habitual, unique, specific, identifying or associative attribute that defines a specific item by function or characteristic; 3) the overall state of manifest realm before imposition of the manmade.

NATURAL HISTORY – 1) prior path leading up to a moment in time that establishes uniqueness of identity;

2) record or memory of that which is habitual, unique, specific, identifying or associative attribute that defines a specific item by function or characteristic; 3) evidential record that shows the evolution of the state of manifest realm before imposition of the manmade.

NATURAL ILLUMINATION – 1) active presence of spirit; 2) solution to primary koan; 3) grace of spirit that allows all sight.

NATURE – 1) unique identity; 2) habitual, unique, specific, identifying or associative attribute that defines a specific item by function or characteristic; 3) state of manifest realm before imposition of the manmade.

NAVIGATION – 1) finding direction while en route; 2) leading the way for others in a time of change or growth by following established ideals.

NAVIGATOR – 1) one who can find direction while en route; 2) one who is able to lead the way for others in a time of change or growth by following established ideals.

NAVY – [MILITARY] 1) societal structure for overall protection during change; 2) coordinated grouping of vehicles to navigate and safely pass through profound change that serves an entire community in times of change; [COLOR] 3) dark change; 4) becoming unique, or growing into one's specific truth; 5) paradoxical state where there is movement, growth, change or development that is stagnant in spite of involving movement; 6) change, growth or fluid movement that leads to isolation, confrontation, rebellion or becoming stuck.

NAVY BLUE -1) dark change; 2) becoming unique, or growing into one's specific truth; 3) paradoxical state where there is movement, growth, change or development that is stagnant in spite of involving movement; 4) change, growth or fluid movement that leads to isolation, confrontation, rebellion or becoming stuck.

NAY-SAYER – 1) one who is in perpetually negative state and expresses negativity in a negative manner; 2) one who expresses dire and difficult outlook in life.

NAZI – 1) societal system that is imposed on inhabitants in often cruel, demeaning or abusive ways; 2) one who is abusive and punitive by nature; 3) imposition of strict, narrow, punitive, abusive or oppressive requirement of behavior.

NEANDERTHAL – 1) Celtic ancestry, inheritance or cultural attribute; 2) one who is basic, wild, uncivilized; 3) determined about task or path yet completely without intelligence.

NEAR – 1) available, close and ready for connection; 2) represents opportunity for interaction and therefore spiritual growth should one have willingness to take the action to connect; 3) holds potential for spiritual lesson.

NEARLY – 1) potential that did not manifest; 2) action to connect was not strong enough, or was not taken; 3) potential may still exist for connection and the lessons that would provide.

NECK – 1) represents and houses the origin and content of one's expression [**COMMUNICATION CHARKA**]; 2) link between origin and content of heart's expression and both mechanism of expression and consciousness thought; 3) shows natural flow of origin of expression, manner of expression and intellect; 4) (long neck) indicates great distance between heart and head, significant of central role expression and its manner have in how the natural order is such that expression of the heart is meant to bypass the intellect; 5) nature of one's communications with others is keeping the heart's message clear and true.

neck tie –1) that extended and central belief system that can be used to force a united expression or manner of expression among people, places or things; 2) that central imposed belief system that is used to complete forced unification of expression.

NEED – 1) demonstration to universe that brings into being the thing needed; 2) demonstration of need is first step in Law of Flow; 3) humble honesty.

NEEDLE – 1) ability to connect emotionally in a way that binds things together with an idea; 2) ability to deflate realization; 3) precious emotion that carries idea that connects; 4) ability to be direct and specific with clear emotional expression; 5) need to bind things together that must be dealt with; 6) precious emotional necessity that carries idea with it and can be applied in multipurpose fashion; 7) precious emotional necessity through which any idea can go; 8) **YIN** gift of the **EMPRESS** that allows one to connect things in the manifest, that is both precious and necessary.

NEGRO – 1) first man, origin of mankind; 2) state in which one absorbs all light so that only darkness is reflected back; 3) kingliness that bears with it responsibility for all others; 4) invitation to drop prejudice and embrace humanity.

NEON – 1) state of emptying one's self of ego so that the light within may shine forth; 2) essence that contains light producing life.

NEPTUNE – 1) represents commitment to inspiration as well as delusions; 2) illusions and deceptions.

NERVE – 1) electrical nature of **CHI**; 2) ability to experience **CHURLANTA**; 3) specific path of chi that allows one to experience manifest existence; 4) pathway to lessons of pain and pleasure; 5) mechanism to overcome when performing action of faith.

NERVOUS SYSTEM – 1) electrical system of being; 2) interrelationship of entire manifest being; 3) organism element that allows one to participate in visceral ways to empirical existence.

NEST – 1) nature is one's most essential dwelling place of the soul; 2) practical accommodation of manifest existence; 3) manifest half of one's commitment to existence.

NEST EGG – 1) provision for new future life that is the ultimate purpose of finding one's dwelling place of the soul in nature itself; 2) commitment to bring new life that is centerpiece of overall commitment of every manifest being.

NESTLE – 1) pleasure and comfort of connection; 2) admitting vulnerability of human condition in which each one needs another, yet connection only exists when one takes action with one's entire being; 3) demonstrate need for other.

NET – 1) loose network of ideas that can withstand flow, growth, change and inspiration; 2) open minded belief system that allows for all that is, yet is able to capture the most major elements; 3) network of ideas that is useful yet non-intrusive.

NETTLE – 1) represents practicality of coming into unexpected, somewhat emotional and sometimes painful connection with elements that would otherwise go unnoticed; 2) annoying inadvertent emotional connection one does not anticipate or even notice as it connects along the path.

NETWORK – 1) loose and open connections that are sustained through common idea, need, objective or element; 2) yin nature of interconnection of all things; 3) opportunities that exist only when in connection with others who share basic precepts.

NEW DAY – 1) new beginning; 2) start of new journey; establishment of new life.

NEWSPAPER – 1) collective, but temporary, knowledge that when shared is of benefit to all; 2) information from outside of the moment, usually in very recent past, that shapes the moment; 3) represents sharing ideas with all.

NIGHT – 1) part of cycle that is in darkness; 2) contemplation of one's mortality; 3) ultimate test of faith; 4) potential to fall into self-delusion.

NIGHT LIGHT – 1) artificial illusion of spirit presence to counter fears of the faithless as they face slumbering in darkness; 2) beacon of hope, either artificial or unsubstantiated promise, that helps those who do not know spirit as they slumber in the dark.

NINE – 1) Divine order.

nipples itching - 1) one must actively nurture.

nipples tingling - 1) feeling the need to nurture.

NIPPON – 1) of strict societal order and elegant simplicity; 2) represents highest standard of honor; 3) tradition and ritual as representative of sublime harmony and balance.

NIRVANA – 1) state of inner tranquility and outward elation; 2) withdrawn into state of inner bliss; 3) becoming one with universe and spirit at the expense of interacting with the manifest on one's path.

NO HAIR – 1) mind is organic and available; 2) without thought of any sort; 3) unable to use intellect; 4) incapable of intelligence; 5) inability to understand, remember or figure things out.

NOM DE PLUME – 1) self-identification when presenting product of one's life to public; 2) indication that one has divided one's self from one's occupation.

NON-ENTITY – 1) presence without essential function; 2) manifestation that has no spiritual core; 3) without relevance; 4) unimportant.

NONSENSE – 1) ineffective communication; 2) frivolous expression indicative of nothing; 3) freedom from need to be understood.

NOODLES – 1) spiritual elements (slogans, symbols, costume, rituals, etc.) that make one feel filled with spirit, yet do not nourish the soul; 2) spiritual filler that actually accomplishes nothing other than transient comfort or nurture.

NOON – 1) half way to goal; 2) one can see exactly where one has been and where one is going; 3) one sees equally the past and the direction toward the future goal.

NORDIC – 1) believer in power of **ODIN**; 2) believer in sea-faring spirits; 3) one who journeys toward **VALHALLA**.

NORSE – 1) of the tribe who are believers in power of **ODIN**; 2) attribute, artifact, ritual, design, myth or object coming from those who believe in sea-faring spirits; 3) the culture of those who journey toward **VALHALLA**.

NORTH – 1) the direction that the truth of the heart leads one toward; 2) having to do with, or representing, that which guides one; 3) the specific direction, goal, or ideal of an individual.

NORTH AMERICA – 1) part of the universal commitment to manifest existence that represents the enterprise, curiosity and creativity of human civilization, yet without regard to the effect on nature.

NORTHERN HEMISPHERE – 1) elevated half of commitment.

NORTHERN LIGHTS – 1) aura of a planet; 2) normally unseen energetic perimeter; 3) envisioning the entire scope of a commitment and how it impacts things even in normally unseen ways; 3) churlanta of chi with warp.

NOSE – 1) vehicle or mechanism that integrates inspiration; 2) represents ability to encounter the non-visible essence of something; 3) mechanism for sensing that something is there; 4) part of the early warning system of the existence of something.

NOT BLINKING – 1) keeping one's window always open; 2) state of openness that is also vulnerable to elements that might intrude with intent of doing harm; 3) being without any natural filter of protection; 4) constancy of gaze or perpetually in state of vision.

NOTE – 1) idea.

NOVEL – 1) collection of ideas, concepts and creative expressions; 2) allegorical or symbolic presentation of knowledge.

NOVELIST – 1) one who has presented a collection of ideas, concepts and creative expressions; 2) one who presents their knowledge and ideas in allegorical or symbolic expressions.

NUCLEAR ENERGY – 1) the energy expelled when one's essential core is divided; 2) the power of internal collapse as it effects the world around.

NUMBERS – 1) elemental, additive or geometric associations of essential interrelationships; 2) essential elements expressed as value functions of basic relational association.

NUN – 1) represents one who has denounced earthly identity in favor of living a life of dedication to spirit; 2) exclusive priestess who serves in accordance with strict sets of rules for living; 3) witch.

NUPTIALS – 1) ritual of joining paths and bodies in manifest life; 2) state of sharing all one is, has and will become with another; 3) celebration of love through outward presentation of ritual.

NURSING – [HEALTH CARE] 1) caring for the ill; 2) tending sick, dying, wounded and impaired through ministration of health-related service; 3) giving one's service to those who are undergoing treatment for illness; [BREAST FEEDING] 4) transmitting the spiritual essence of one's heart's path into a new life; 5) transmitting the genetic code of immuno-defense and antibodies to local agents one has been exposed to in life.

NUTCRACKER – 1) mechanism that causes inability to create new life; 2) means of taking destructive action that kills the possibility of a future.

NUTRIENT – 1) essential elements that nourish; 2) basic parts of something that is nourishing.

NUTS – 1) commitment of nourishment that is result of life and for the purpose of making new life; 2) new life that is independent of its source; [CHOPPED NUTS] 3) commitment to starting new life that has been broken, shattered and killed; 4) inability to create new life; 5) taking destructive action that kills the possibility of a future.

NUTSHELL – 1) practical commitments used to protect elements that cause new life.

O

OAR – 1) the means by which to work through change; 2) the mechanism of necessity and responsibility used by an individual in charge of working through change.

OARSMAN – 1) one who works through change; 2) one who takes on the practical mandatory tasks of responsibility when charged with working through change.

OASIS – 1) unexpected means of change that will save a life; 2) treasured access to change and cleansing that will save a life abandoned in the experiential wasteland of wisdom without actions.

OATMEAL – 1) gift of nourishment and nutrition; 2) applying growth and fluidity to one's gifts and then assimilating them so that they become part of one's life.

OCCUPATION – 1) one's actions of labor in life.

OCEAN – 1) catastrophic change, absolute change; 2) huge, vast, powerful, unstoppable, following cycles of change; 3) undergoing massive change, growth or flow; [bottom of the ocean] 4) change that creates the wisdom as it has put one through everything one might endure; 5) seeking the maximum of change to go to the bottom of the flow of life where there is everything and nothing; coming to the point to understand the void; crossing the ocean – 1) decision to make a major change (like divorce, move, school)

ODIN - 1) NORSE god; 2) god who rules over believers in sea-faring spirits; 3) god who rules over those who journey toward **VALHALLA**; 4) god who communicates through **RUNES**.

ODOR – 1) the inspired essence of a person, place or thing.

OFFICE – 1) the part of one's spiritual dwelling place in which one prepares for, organizes, analyzes and stores information about the necessary and productive interactions with others on one's spiritual path.

OGRE – 1) represents one who uses a fictitious monster to manipulate fear; 2) legendary fictitious creature that is hideous in exaggerated girth that is result of consuming human life; 3) ironic tool used to create fear of fictitious threat that is, indeed, the very image of one who would use such manipulation; 4) represents being manipulated into fear of the false by the actual threat itself.

OIL – 1) dark fluidity, growth or ability to change of the material world; 2) the exchange or flow of currency; 3) the blood of a society, that which keeps the manifestation of the business of living going; 4) the means of anointment or consecration, through the application of which things in the material world are blessed and made divine; [HOT OIL] 5) growth causing agent that works with some agitation/passion in the flow of the material world; 6) the agent of increased or agitated flow of things in the material world that changes how one presents one's self to the world.

OMELET – 1) nourishment that comes from commitment to new life; 2) ironic state in which the commitment to new life is killed in order to sustain life.

OMNIPOTENT – 1) state of limitless potential effect on all things; 2) ultimate acceptance of presence of divine characteristic, and therefore potential, in one; 3) ability to do anything that challenge one's sense of spiritual ethics and morality; 4) dilemma of having absolute power over another person, place or thing and thus having to decide how to use one's influence.

OMNISCIENT – 1) ability to forgive all because one knows all; 2) ability to connect with divine consciousness; 3) one who possesses ability to see through the eyes of divinity; 4) the profound wisdom, compassion, forgiveness, acceptance and vision that comes to those who forego ego and give self over to spirit.

ONE – 1) essential presence of being.

ONE FOOT ON GROUND, ONE FOOT IN WATER – 1) lost between manifest and spirit; 2) lost between real and fantasy.

ONION – 1) layered commitment; 2) complex commitment in life that requires great concentration and perusal to explore, but in the end yields nothing.

OOZE – 1) fetid excess that flows outward as result of process of corruption; 2) that which simultaneously proves both the need for healing and the healing itself.

OPAL – 1) barrier that, when broken down, holds mystery and illumination within; 2) obstacle that causes one to comprehend the various aspects of spiritual light in the world, and in particular those spiritual lessons to be learned in the process of dealing with the obstacle.

OPEN – 1) free access; 2) without restriction or boundary; 3) inability to distinguish.

OPEN DOOR – 1) opportunity to try new, different path; 2) willingness to go in new direction; 3) possibility of new beginning; 4) ability to escape something that is no longer suitable.

OPEN ELEVATOR – 1) opportunity in life to become elevated; 2) potential of endless cycle of available choices; 3) ability to see many different openings, at various levels of elevation on one's path.

OPEN GATE – 1) without judgment; 2) making no exception,; 3) excluding nothing; 4) equal opportunity to enter new path to anyone.

OPEN MOUTH – 1) free manner of expression; 2) ability to consume or take in anything; 3) lack of refined manner or expression.

OPEN WINDOW – 1) opportunity to consider or see new, different way; 2) willingness to open one's mind to new visions; 3) possibility of new approach to life; 4) ability to escape from current vision in life that is no longer suitable.

OPEN WOUND – 1) indicates that one is in vulnerable state and must seek help to contain the loss of emotional strength; 2) shows one has lost protection and may become changed in negative ways.

OPERA – 1) spiritual expression of one's heart, mind or ideas; 2) elevation of one's expression to that which is of essential spirit; 3) public exposure of one's spiritual and emotional plight.

OPERA SINGER – 1) one who makes spiritual expression of one's heart, mind or ideas; 2) one who elevates one's expression to that which is of essential spirit; 3) one who publically exposes one's spiritual and emotional plight.

OPERATOR – 1) one who makes something else work; 2) one who organizes system, readying it for active function; 3) one who facilitates connections, expressions, communications and sharing.

OPOSSUM – 1) potential to remain safe by disengaging; 2) one who avoids being considered or called. by removing one's self from the situation; 3) ceasing all movement on path under guise of having reached spiritual fulfillment; 4) using spirituality to avoid life.

OPPORTUNIST – 1) one who always considers self first and will always take actions on behalf of self; 2) represents self-centered vision that always sees how self might benefit first; 3) those who are so spiritually empoverished within that they must illegitimately take to feel assured that they will be provided for; 4) faithlessness.

OPPORTUNITY – 1) spiritual lesson being presented, awaiting recognition and action; 2) anything that one comes into contact with; 3) where one is represents how one will grow.

OPTIMISM – 1) always seeing potential; 2) forever expecting best outcome; 3) active state of living in gratitude.

OPTIMIST – 1) one who always sees potential; 2) one who forever expects best outcome; 3) one who lives in active state of gratitude.

OPUS – 1) any creation; 2) result of action; 3) achievement.

ORACLE – 1) medium who answers direct questions with riddles; 2) source of spirit message that is both for the individual and the society;

3) remote mystical resource that is mysterious, cryptic and illusory.

ORAL – 1) origin of essence of outward expression; 2) having to do with openness to nourishment; 3) means by which consumes all that is encountered in life.

ORANGE – 1) commitment to passion that nourishes and replenishes; 2) commitment to passion with origin in light; [COLOR] 3) passion; 4) when idea and feeling are one.

ORATION – 1) art of public expression of one's message; 2) having to do with shaping and delivering message.

ORATORIO – 1) art of public expression of direct spirit message; 2) having to do with shaping and delivering pure spiritual messages.

ORB – [*also see* **SPHERE, GLOBE**] 1) spiritual commitment to reign; 2) represents that the ruler is the spiritual leader of the realm and/or world; 3) represents spiritual domain and responsibility; 4) public indication of spiritual commitment to agreement of responsibility, devotion and dominion.

ORCHESTRA – 1) community that is unified for the purpose of universal expression of pure spiritual presence; 2) those who come together, each using his or her native gift, to participate in the presence of pure spirit.

ORCHESTRAL SCORE – 1) musical staff which carries the complete blueprint from which each community member that is able to participate in the universal expression of pure spiritual presence; 2) that which guides those who come together, each using his or her native gift, to participate in the presence of pure spirit.

ORCHID – 1) pure symbol of the ultimate experience of sex.

ORGAN – [biological] 1) essential and vital commitment to a very specific part of life; 2) absolute commitment to function; 3) devotion to one's unique nature; [musical instrument] 4) represents taking inspired action on all of one's gifts, extruding from them the maximum, in order to fulfill one's mandate in life to bring spirit to all; 5) flawless coordination of one's actions, making full use of one's gifts, with the result of spiritual inspiration for all.

ORIENT – 1) having found the truth of one's heart, to then proceed to follow it; 2) acknowledgement via one's actions that one's gifts are one's truth; 3) the place of unique truth that is both exotic and fascinating to all who behold.

ORIENTAL – 1) the outward look of one who has found the truth of heart; 2) attributes, rituals, fashions and other stylistic indicators that one has found the truth of one's heart; 3) the place where one may go to find the truth of one's heart.

ORIENTATION – 1) amount one is aligned with one's spiritual purpose in life; 2) knowing what one's spiritual purpose is and maintaining one's commitment to it regardless of distractions or difficulties.

ORIENTED – 1) how one leads their life vis a vis their spiritual growth potential; 2) being willing to go to any length to live in accordance with one's spiritual mission.

ORION – 1) represents persistence of mission, and ability to succeed in hunting; 2) one who hunts; 3) symbol for the inevitability of an outcome or event.

ORNAMENTS – 1) something decorative or valued, yet not precious; 2) items that serve to project the image one wants to project; 3) things one is invested in moment to moment; 4) the small things in one's life that are valued.

ORPHAN – 1) one who is completely alone because others have left them; 2) state of being without lineage or predecessor; 3) one without a past.

ORPHANAGE – 1) where those who are completely abandoned and alone may gather; 2) stage of development between having been abandoned and establishing one's self anew.

OSCAR – 1) achievement of highest accolade of society; 2) recognition of highest achievement in creating fantasy illusions that the general public prefer.

OSCILLATE – 1) that which changes between opposites automatically; 2) self-contained state of balance due to shifting between opposites.

OSPREY – 1) rumor or opinion that kills; 2) one who, due to their opinion, sets out to overtake, overpower or eliminate the focal point of that opinion; 3) deadly bias; 4) opinion that represents a self-fulfilling prophesy of doom for its direct object.

OSTRICH – 1) denial; 2) opinion or gossip that is too dense to become inspired or take flight in the imagination of others.

OUIJA BOARD – 1) object that serves as medium; 2) system of divination in the manifest.

OUT HOUSE – 1) spiritual dwelling place for life's mistakes, excesses and waste; 2) one who divides spiritual dwelling, relegating disseminating excess and waste to a different and remote spiritual state than the rest of one's life; 3) spiritual double standard.

OUTER BANK OF RIVER - 1) destructive flow of life.

OUTLAW – 1) one who has rejected or acted against societal regulation yet wishes to remain independent; 2) one who has rejected, by acting against. societal regulation and yet wishes to still reap benefits from that very system.

OUTSKIRTS OF CITY - 1) something that is not part of normal social structures and social behavior.

OVEN – 1) represents that things in life are produced by repression of flow and refusal to express one's feelings; 2) birth that is result of repression; 3) womb; 4) sustainer of life of a resentment.

OVERCAST – 1) bad omen; 2) dubious and unclear connection with divinity; 3) when one's inspiration falls into the shadow of change; 4) indication that a rift with one's spiritual connection to the divine is coming.

OVIPAROUS – 1) when one establishes commitment with little thought or preparation; 2) one who easily commits.

OVOVIVIPAROUS – 1) when one commits internally and allows the commitment to develop completely before making the commitment public; 2) one who does not commit in flippant way; 3) one who seriously considers things in depth before making commitment known.

OVUM – 1) internal commitment to new life; 2) that which is within a person that can hold and develop the new; 3) ability to create what is new; 4) conditions within one's self that are perfect for creating new life, yet will only do so when all circumstances come together to form commitment to that new life.

OX – 1) strength; 2) determination

OZ – 1) place of perfect abundance; 2) fantasy state of an ideal place where there is nothing lacking; 3) constructed or promoted fantasy of perfect place.

OZONE LAYER – 1) highest form of inspiration; 2) high-minded and elevated state of inspiration that protects and envelops; 3) spirit's commitment to manifest existence.

P

PACIFIER – 1) person, place or thing that causes unity and promotes harmony; 2) that which unites opposites that are currently in contention; 3) that which diverts the energy of conflict and transforms it into the energy of union; 4) that which separate, unifies.

PACK – [verb] 1) to force into confined close proximity; 2) to organize elements into efficient occupancy of common space; [group] 3) group of like-minded who become unified into a singular force by instinct; 4) the survival instinct that unites a group into a singular, self-protecting entity; [backpack] 5) the structure which allows one to take full responsibility for any number of things; 6) sense of responsibility that will carry a diversity of causes; 7) that which takes on a burden for which responsibility is taken; 8) that which allows one to carry a heavy load from the past being brought forward into the present reality.

PAD – [ANATOMY] 1) natural element that provides softening of impact during movement on one's path or when taking direct action; 2) the escalating numbing, soporific effect when one avoids direct action and movement on one's path; [COSTUME/FASHION] 3) inflated under-structure of one's belief system that protects believers; 4) the artificial enhancement of size of a specific part of one's character *(i.e., ability to nurture, foundational world view, ability to influence the foundations of others, etc.)*; [EPAULETS]5) an acquired or elective state that pre-empts potential danger for those who feel vulnerable via an outward show of size, strength or evidence of importance of position in society; [SPORTS/UNIFORMS] 6) strengthening and building up of one's ability to take on tasks; 7) hidden but visible protection as outward signal that one can perform without risk of injury, or normal vulnerability to the intrusions of others.

PAGAN – 1) of or belonging to society or group that focuses ritual, belief and structure of spirituality on belief that the power of nature and all that is natural is divinity; 2) any person, place or thing that seeks to align with the seen and unseen powers of nature to better proceed with life.

PAGE - [OF A BOOK] 1) a single, individual idea of wisdom; 2) record of one's thoughts, beliefs and outlook; [STATION IN SOCIETY/STAGE OF DEVELOPMENT] 3) one who is servile in all ways to others who are older, of higher station, or in charge; 4) pre-pubescence; 5) innocence; 6) one's basic nature before being honed on the forge of life.

PAIL – 1) experiences, possessions, lessons and changes one can have always at the ready but requires constant action for that readiness; 2) way to keep available lessons and ability to change.

PAINT CAN – 1) that which provides potential to be different; 2) the soul is about to take on a different importance or mission; 3) represents being prepared to demonstrate an entirely new direction or stage of life.

PAJAMAS – 1) belief system which allows direct communication with spirit; 2) appropriate protection when one intends to commune with spirit; 3) ritual performed while one is in connection with spirit

PALM – [of hand] 1) vision portal; 2) vision gained through action; 3) represents that one is about to gain in wisdom and enhanced vision; [of tree] 4) lush results from life that has been surrounded by change; 5) represents that the more one is in contact with, or goes through, change, the richer the results of life and the more likely those results will inspire others.

palm itching – 1) one must actively take direct action to assure money is coming one's way.

palm tingling – 1) indication that money is coming one's way.

PALM TREE – 1) life of change that is lush with results; 2) vibrant and inspiring response to continuous warmth; 3) indicative of one with luscious and productive life who then serves all around them; 4) state of life that is endless and constantly changing.

PALMISTRY – 1) one's actions are able to lead one to interact with the truth of another through vision; 2) belief in vision accessible through one's interactions with the manifest realm.

PAN – 1) precious experience of using one's repressed feelings to create that which nourishes; 2) way to transform change into inspiration.

PANCAKES – 1) the offering of many gifts that will nourish one's soul if they are assimilated; 2) spiritual gifts are the tangible results of putting one's repressed feelings to practical use.

PANDA – 1) state of spiritual polarization in which one is extremely spiritual, yet all points of direct contact or integration with the material world are markedly dark; 2) when one is consumed with conflicting thoughts between purely spiritual and completely dark; 3) final stage of life, just before death, when central spiritual self is vibrant, but connection with the world and your manifest life is severed.

PANNIER – 1) to make one's foundation seem far more substantial than it is; 2) to have one's foundation expanded by inspiration but is actually mostly hollow.

PANT POCKETS – 1) adding to one's foundation that which is most needed to enhance one's movement on the path.

PANTS – 1) signifies condition of one's movement on path; 2) when one's movement on path is entirely dominated and defined by one's foundational belief system; [TIGHT AROUND ANKLE] 3) movement separate from direction of path; [ONLY TOES SHOWING] 4) just direction is seen, not the path; [RED PANTS] 5) earthly events cause one to move on path; 6) one's movement on one's path is emotional; [BLACK PANTS] 7) one's reasons move on one's path are dark; 8) when one has stopped moving on path; 9) represents having a very unique path that necessitates a solitary or lonely path in life; [BLUE PANTS] 10) when one's path has completely changed; 11) being suddenly beset by disease, catastrophes or major changes.

PANTS WITH ONLY TOES SHOWING – 1) just direction is seen, not the path.

PAPER - 1) ideas, unformed ideas, not wisdom yet; they are your own ideas.

PAPER DOILY - 1) inspired but ineffective product of history in one's life, has not been adapted to suit present moment but is hopelessly lost in the past.

PAPER NAPKIN - 1) results of lifetime experiences and knowledge, often of pure spirit, that assures that life's nourishment does not overreach its intended function; 2) use of results of lifetime experiences and knowledge to separate nourishment from manner of expression.

PARACHUTE – 1) belief system that allows one to remain inspired for a prolonged time, and will gradually allow a return to normal without sudden let down.

PARADE – 1) when a specific path in shared by many, and all who are on this path are of great interest to the general public; 2) the path that is for prominent people.

PARADE FLOAT - 1) the display of promised goals shared by many, encouraging that all who join on this path are participants in that which is of great interest to the general public; 2) the promise made to those who find themselves on a path that is for prominent people.

park – [area] 1) organized place of abundance for the benefit of members of the society; 2) area specifically set aside for activities and events surrounding a central idea or theme; [verb] 3) to come to rest and cease forward movement on one's path; 4) to cause the vehicle one uses to advance on one's path to stop moving, and to leave it where stopped.

PARSON – 1) one who has denounced earthly identity in favor of living a life of dedication to the ministry of spirit; 2) exclusive person of religion who serves in accordance with strict sets of rules for living; 3) warlock.

PARTIALLY FILLED CUP OF TEA - 1) potential to change has begun to present itself, or has been half way assimilated.

PARTNER – 1) person one shares one's life with; 2) each of a group of individuals that, collectively, are unified for a specific common purpose.

PARTRIDGE – 1) self-fulfilling prophesy that is told to a child therefore preventing them from development in life; 2) opinion that stops any future potential before it can take hold; 3) opinion, or bit of gossip, that stays in a local area and has no effectiveness elsewhere.

PARTY - 1) social gathering, coming together for the purpose to commune and be together.

PASSPORT – 1) record or document that proves that one is a member of a larger group; 2) means of establishing one's identity that is recognized by other groups and allows passage between territories.

PASTA – 1) spiritual nourishment; 2) nourishment for the soul that is only accessible once one has undergone change while one is repressing feelings.

PASTOR – 1) one who has denounced earthly identity in favor of living a life of dedication to the ministry of spirit; 2) exclusive person of religion who serves in accordance with strict sets of rules for living; 3) warlock.

PASTRY – 1) inspired life that is particularly enjoyable; 2) mainstay of life that is considered the most delightful and special part.

PASTURE - **1)** intentionally created element of lush vegetation represents an abundance in nature; 2) a reference to a man-made ecosystem that participates in or replicates a natural ecosystem (plant → oxygen →oxygen breathing organism → carbon dioxide → plant); 3) manmade structure that emulates the way in which the earth embraces human existence by giving life and asking nothing in return; 4) intentional illusion of being without barriers; 5) that which is made to appear very welcoming.

PATÉ – 1) combination of the very best basic elements of manifest being, used for highest ritual of nourishment; 2) that which provides the entire spectrum of strength.

PATENT – 1) manifestation of one's gift that is unique and widely recognized; 2) creative and original manifestation of one's gift.

PATH – 1) one's spiritual mission; 2) one's personal journey in life; [CROSSING OF TWO PATHS] 3) represents destiny created by chance intersection of paths; 4) wheel of fortune; 5) meeting destined by spirit; [RUNNING ON PATH] 6) represents that in life one is focused only on the goal; 7) not really present for one's journey; 8) working hard to escape one's path; 9) getting away from one's duties, responsibilities and destiny.

PATIENCE – 1) spiritual action that demonstrates one's faith by accepting life on life's terms; 2) represents that one has accepted one's path, gifts, challenges and destiny; 3) alignment with spiritual mission without question or hesitation.

PATIENT – 1) one who has aligned with the inadequacies of one's life, and the subsequent need for healing; 2) one who is ready and willing to improve; 3) represents admitting the need for assistance and allowing it.

PATIO – 1) where the dwelling place of the soul integrates with nature.

PATRIOT – 1) one who is loyal to one's society; 2) accepting one's connection to and responsibility for one's community.

PAVEMENT – 1) the foundation of societal paths, usually dark.

PAW – 1) base instinct to move forward on one's path; 2) manmade structure that allows one to move forward; 3) structure that awakens and allows one to follow one's instincts.

PEACE – 1) harmonious state of alignment between unlikely, and historically disparate, allies; 2) unification of parties in a conflict; 3) state of balance and calm when conflict has been resolved.

PEACOCK – 1) gossip and/or rumor that is meant to boost one's image suddenly and in a spectacular way; 2) showing off to others for the purpose of aggrandizing self as if a sudden change has occurred though it is planned; 3) manipulation of others through sudden rumor that will inspire.

PEARL – 1) wisdom that grows slowly over time, and is based on fulfillment due to having completely overcome a barrier; 2) commitment to spiritual wisdom.

PEARL EARRING – 1) ear for wisdom; 2) one who will listen when the speaker has prevailed over barrier; 3) one who hears wisdom as they listen to those who have overcome barriers.

PEAS – 1) commitment to abundance; 2) abundance that nourishes.

PEBBLES – 1) boundaries that have been broken down to very manageable obstacles.

PELVIS – 1) the foundation of one's world view, and the basis of one's shame.

pelvis itching – 1) one must take direct action on one's foundation's relevance; 2) one must actively rethink, question or address one's foundation.

pelvis tingling – 1) feeling that one's foundation is particularly relevant; 2) feeling the need to rethink, question or address one's foundation.

PEN - 1) personal belief that is indelible; 2) the fact that one's philosophical belief is visible to others who merely observe; 3) means of communicating ideas, beliefs and philosophies.

PENCIL – 1) personal belief that is strongly felt but temporary; 2) trying out one's philosophical belief on others; 3) means of communicating ideas, beliefs and philosophies that are temporary.

PENDULUM – 1) need to resolve longstanding problem; 2) indicates it is time to deal with a problem that has appeared over and over, but is always pushed out of the way so as to avoid it; 3) opportunity to put to rest a problem or uncertainty that repeatedly plagues one inside.

PENGUIN – 1) strict opinion that only resides in purely spiritual setting; 2) fluctuation between pure spirit and absolute darkness that is unrealistic.

PENIS – 1) foundational principle that must be acted upon, and when acted upon releases the soul; 2) means of joining, influencing or intruding upon another's most basic foundational beliefs.

PENNY – 1) singular gift of precious passion; 2) one's gift is the basis of how one integrates with the world.

PENTACLE – 1) gift, talent, ability to think, creativity; 2) the five-pointed star was, and still is, considered to be a symbol of the spirit in; 3) communion of the manifest with the four elements of earth, air, fire and water; 4) represents the "endless knot" of the five-pointed star denotes "eternity" as there is no beginning and no end.

PENTAGON – 1) manifest structures that embody potential; 2) systems of learning, permutation, chance and initiation; 3) structure that plans reactions to a wide variety of unforeseen circumstances, creation and enacting contingency plans, creative accommodation of diverse needs and any other response that must be specifically crafted.

PEOPLE – 1) society; 2) community within society.

PERIODICAL - 1) temporary collection of results, ideas and expositions that are then distributed to society at large; 2) temporary collection of ideas.

PETAL – 1) part of an experience that can stand alone; 2) unique part of larger experience that is remembered independently; 3) detail of something larger that is significant because it has qualities that stand out.

PEWTER – 1) precious but unobtrusive; 2) detached neutrality.

PHARAOH – 1) God-man mandated by birth to rule in the manifest; 2) mastor of change who divinely rules the manifest.

PHOBIA – 1) deeply rooted beliefs that make one mortally vulnerable; 2) the power and persistence of the ego to create believable illusion based in fear; 3) basis of one's personal progression of Bardos in Tibetan belief in how the non-spiritual will face reality of their own death; 3) manifestation of the extent to which the mind is the enemy of the heart.

PHONOGRAPH – 1) mechanism that assists in bringing one's unique gifts into the world; 2) that which turns one's unique gifts into inspiration for others.

PHOTO – 1) binary illusion that represents one's manifest self inadequately; 2) reverse image of a shadow of an illusion of self.

PHOTO ALBUM – 1) attempt to capture memories; 2) represents that memories are not real; 3) inescapability from remnants of the past; 4) inaccuracy of memories, and unreliability of history.

PHYSICS – 1) laws of nature in the manifest based on observation, challenges to hypotheses, and commonality among analyses; 2) the intricacies of the intersection of space, time, manifestation and spiritual need; 3) inability of human intellect to comprehend the balance between macro and micro.

PIANO – 1) that which allows spirit to enter manifest; 2) represents magic of compatibility when manifest and spirit combine; 3) represents actions in life that encompass light and dark and create spirit presence; 4) signifies that harmony is created out of life; 5) community coming together in harmony.

PICK POCKET – 1) one who's actions surreptitiously violate another's foundational belief system at a point of lateral vulnerability for the purpose of taking what is precious; 2) one who has no regard for the sanctity of one's foundational belief system.

PICTURE – 1) one's view of what should be; 2) two-dimensional things that one holds in esteem; 3) projection of the imagination that can either inspire, guide or blind; 4) the power of projection over reality.

PIE –1) nourishing gift one's actions can provide; 2) nourishing gift that can come from life's result s; 3) spirit commitment to nourish and heal that is its greatest gift.

PIG – 1) material wealth, 2) indulgence.

PIGEON – 1) common gossip, often neutral, that neither helps nor hinders, but annoys; 2) petty rumors and gossip that occupy the lonely, old, alienated and those who sincerely love nature.

PILE – 1) gradual build up that eventually becomes significant; 2) clutter and accumulated items that can become an obstacle.

PILGRIM – 1) represents that one is on a spiritual quest; 2) action of faith in which one's path is given to pursuit of one's spiritual goal.

PILLAR – 1) represents barrier that may seem decorative or authoritative, but instead is simply indicative of the actual barrier-an ideal; 2) that which supports and upholds the ideals of society.

PILLOW – 1) provision of support and comfort for the intellect; 2) that which allows one to take a break from the intellect.

PILOT – 1) one who inspires others with promise of reaching an elevated destination; 2) one who guides others on false pretense; 3) represents false prophet.

PIN – 1) minor emotional attachment; 2) emotional attack that can destroy illusions that have come from commitment to inspiration.

PINE TREE – 1) immortality;

PING PONG BALL – 1) minor, hollow spiritual commitment only used for entertainment and play; 2) spiritual commitment enjoined by two people who play with the commitment temporarily.

PING PONG PADDLE – 1) mandatory action, both practical and abundant, that allows one to toy with hollow spiritual commitments for amusement, competition or entertainment.

PINK LIPS – 1) manner of expressing one's self is combination of feeling and spirituality.

PIPE – 1) represents diverse sides coming to an agreement; 2) pact or treaty between would be allies or competitors; 3) establishment of a contract; 4) way to use inspiration and repressed energy to unite yin and yang in a balance.

PIRATE – 1) one who attacks those going through change for the purpose of destroying or acquiring their vehicle for enduring the change; 2) those perpetually lost in change who lose their bond with their own humanity; 3) symbol for how devastating change can be to one's soul.

PIZZA – 1) gift that allows each person to find nourishment as they wish.

PLAID – 1) belief system that takes distinct ideas or doctrines and combines them in a harmony that is in itself distinctive.

PLAIN – 1) no barriers; 2) no direction; 3) no goal.

PLAN – 1) the structure the intellect creates as expected future; 2) way the mind sees coming events in advance; 3) projection of probability or desirability that is illusion; 4) projection of probability or desirability that is guide.

PLANET - 1) each planet represents an element or group of elements of reality that exist as a shared commitment; 2) community, familial, societal or global commitment.

PLANT – 1) sign of life in general, particularly significant of both the fragility and precious abundance of life; 2) symbol of coordination between elements of biodiversity in natural cycles.

PLAQUE – 1) dark residue left over from expressions of anger; 2) resentment that comes from anger that when expressed only grows stronger.

PLASTER CAST – 1) temporary spiritual change that soon becomes barrier that removes ability to embrace the world, take actions, travel on one's path or have any direction on one's path; 2) agency of spirit that has the ability to prevent or inhibit one's ability to embrace the world, take actions, travel on one's path or have any direction on one's path so that they can find spirit.

PLASTIC – 1) symbol of both ingenuity and illusion of mankind; 2) malleable substance able to be used for any number of applications.

PLATE – 1) represents that one's gift can be used for any number of applications, all designed to serve others; 2) the source of nourishment in life.

PLATINUM – 1) precious spiritual neutrality that allows self-reflection.

PLATYPUS – 1) represents a person who is most at home in the instability and chaos of constant change, who tends to make commitments without preparation of thought; and who can and will attack with venomous intent on a whim; 2) the type of person who is territorial and mercurial.

PLAY – 1) to pretend at real life for entertainment; 2) to enact arranged scenes that have an underlying message.

PLEIADES – 1) celestial or divine intelligence brings change with illumination; 2) abundance of possibilities in the universe for different means of existence; 3) location for survival lies in determination and strength.

PLOT – 1) main thread that carries story forward; 2) plan or projection that is intended to be followed; 3) step by step view of past, present or future event.

PLUTO – 1) **EMPEROR** nature to create or destroy; 2) represents dismantling that which is outgrown and false-to-fact; 3) power to renovate or restore that which is actual and true.

POCKETS – 1) the ability of one's belief system to allow one to add that which may be necessary and carry; [SHIRT POCKETS] 2) actions that help the heart to achieve goals; [PANT POCKETS] 3) adding to one's foundation that which is most needed to enhance one's movement on the path.

PODIUM – 1) societal focal point from which messages, directives, instructions and announcements are made; 2) one who is in a position of responsibility to lead and govern; 3) prestige that gives one opportunity, prestige and responsibility for others; 4) the symbol of the test in life of a **TOWER** path.

POEM – 1) pure spiritual message brought into manifest by power of music fused with conception of words; 2) organizing speech into a form that speaks from the heart and to the heart.

POET – 1) one who is able to deliver pure spiritual message brought into manifest by power of music fused with conception of words; 2) one who organizes speech into a form that speaks from the heart and to the heart.

POETRY – 1) that which contains pure spiritual message brought into manifest by power of music fused with conception of words; 2) that which organizes speech into a form that speaks from the heart and to the heart.

POINTING TOWARD SEA – 1) indicating man's base nature *(to hunt, kill, act on lust or in defense)*.

POISON ARROW - 1) emotional statement that have intent to harm or kill; 2) action that shows desire to affect others in extremely negative and destructive ways; 3) idea or thought that goes outward for the sake of absolute destruction of the target, then takes on a life of its own; 4) action with an intended purpose to destroy its target, yet once done cannot be controlled, nor can one know the ultimate outcome.

POLICE – 1) outside societal voice that establishes meaning and law; 2) those charged with enforcing societal rules and guarding, protecting and aiding those within that society.

POLTERGEIST – 1) non-physical manifestation of a manifest presence by causing movement of objects or creation of sounds; 2) restless residue of a life that cannot assimilate and in its search for resolution uses movement and noise to indicate its presence.

POMEGRANATE – 1) commitment of perfect nourishment to life; 2) commitment to one's gifts from god that insures result of fulfillment from life; 3) spirit commitment to nourish and heal.

POND – 1) small, natural place of safe, comfortable and contained changes.

PONY – 1) one's quest when it is first imagined; 2) quest when it is revealed to the heart, certain and destined, yet to which one has yet to commit.

PONY TAIL – 1) thoughts organized and held in relation to past.

POODLE – 1) companion with easily manipulated, but not very logical thoughts; 2) companion in life that is more for outward show than benefit of true connection.

POPE – 1) one with direct communication with God; 2) man who represents god; 3) "god incarnate"

PORCELAIN – 1) delicate; 2) vulnerable; 3) fragile; 4) pure of essence.

PORCH – 1) structural place where one's soul meets the outside world; 2) where the outside world may come up and enter into a peripheral part of the structure of one's soul's dwelling place.

PORTAL – 1) where the worlds connect; 2) how one can pass between worlds due to a point of connection.

POST – [verb] 1) to present one's ideas, thoughts and conclusions to the public; 2) the act of making one's thoughts public; [noun] 3) the requirements in one's life that have become part of the path itself; 4) mandatory choices that become one's actual life.

POST IT NOTE – 1) brief, temporary and cryptic expression of one's immediate thoughts for whoever might pass by; 2) represents when one adds information or comment that is extraneous but important.

POST OFFICE – 1) societal facilitation of communication between individuals that cannot easily reach each other; 2) societal structure responsible for assuring communication between its citizens.

POSTCARD – 1) semi-private communication that is brief and most likely shallow; 2) quick and accessible means of expressing one's self to another that is not totally private.

POT – [cooking pot] 1) experience or possession that is designed to repress feelings for the purpose of internal change; 2) that which uses one's experiences and possessions to promote spiritual nourishment; [marijuana] 3) state of repression and inspiration that distorts one's ability to think; 4) represents being in an inspired state of self-delusion mixed with fixation on self; 5) false sense of fascinating depth; 6) inspired state of inflated self-importance reflected in extreme paranoia.

POT HEAD – 1) one who is often in a state of repression and inspiration that distorts one's ability to think; 2) represents always being in an inspired state of self-delusion mixed with fixation on self; 3) one who has false sense of fascinating depth; 4) normally in an inspired state of inflated self-importance reflected in extreme paranoia.

POTATO –1) practical commitment to spirit; 2) represents the fact that one's entire earthly experience provides the spiritual substance one needs.

POTTERS' WHEEL – 1) one who uses the provision of earth itself to create whatever one wishes, limited only by one's own imagination and facility; 2) one who make whatever one wants out of living on earth.

POTTERY – 1) creations made from earth itself in variety of forms and functions; 2) represents that the stuff of life is so limitlessly flexible that one is limited only by one's own imagination and facility.

POUCH – 1) represents the crude and natural tools and abilities one has at one's fingertips in anticipation of what life will demand.

POUNDING FIST(S) – 1) crude, destructive, brusque, and/or unrefined attempt at action.

POWER – 1) chi; 2) one's personal energy; 3) one's natural ability.

PRAYER – [HANDS IN PRAYER] 1) Actions of faith; 2) speaking to spirit.

PRAYER WHEEL – 1) that which comes into life unexpectedly; 2) fate; 3) the earth as the location for everything that can happen; 4) once one enters into it, it becomes one's fate; 5) commitment to that which is at once eternal, specific to the individual, exists in perpetuity so long as one lives and gives contextual continuity to one's life.

PREGNANCY – 1) ready to start a new life, path or commitment; 2) prepared to give birth and at the point that one becomes dedicated to something not solely under one's control.

PRESIDENT – 1) one who is entrusted with the welfare of a group, usually by the consent of that group; 2) having ultimate responsibility.

PRICE – 1) established societal value of a person's actions, a place or a thing; 2) the element, or amount of an element, that balances an action, possession or transaction.

PRIE DIEU – 1) place of ritual supplication to spirit; 2) mechanism that assists one in demonstrating humility before divinity.

PRIEST –1) one who has denounced earthly identity in favor of living a life of dedication to the ministry of spirit; 2) exclusive person of religion who serves in accordance with strict sets of rules for living; 3) warlock.

PRIESTESS – 1) represents one who has denounced earthly identity in favor of living a life of dedication to spirit; 2) exclusive woman of religious order who serves in accordance with strict sets of rules for living; 3) witch.

PRINT – [ON FABRIC] 1) personal statement based upon one's belief system; 2) personal statement from the heart.

PRINTING PRESS – 1) means of expressing one's self widely; 2) represents process of duplication of message for distribution to the general public.

PRISON – 1) self-constructed prison that is cumulative total of long range commitments; 2) enforced societal dwelling place of the soul assigned to those who have broken the required code of conduct; 3) place of confinement, restriction and imprisonment in society designed to punish those who disobey societal rules; 4) location designed with the hope of breaking occupants' resistance to conformity through rehabilitation to societal code.

PRISON CELL – 1) enforced societal dwelling place of the soul assigned to those who have broken the required code of conduct; 2) place of confinement, restriction and imprisonment in society designed to punish those who disobey societal rules, and with hope of breaking occupants' resistance to conformity through rehabilitation to societal code.

PRIZE – 1) unexpected reward for accomplishment; 2) award for successful completion of competitive contest.

PROFESSIONAL NAME – 1) self-identification when presenting product of one's life to public; 2) indication that one has divided one's self from one's occupation.

PROFESSOR – 1) person consigned to instruct at an establishment of learning; 2) wise person, or elder, who is responsible for passing that wisdom on to the next generation.

PROMISE – 1) expression of intended commitment in the cast that certain conditions be met; 2) spoken oath of guaranteed intention; 3) one's personal vow.

PROOF – 1) conclusive demonstration that case previously stated is indeed true.

PSYCHIATRY – 1) the emerging science of the mechanics of personality and brain function in relation to feelings; 2) the art and study of healing the mind, emotional body and feelings.

PSYCHIC – 1) communication that comes from a purely spiritual source; 2) the phenomenon in which information, energetic presence, initiation of flow or other input comes from outside of space-time; 3) any practice, event or item that has its origin from beyond the manifest; 4) practice of bringing messages from spirit into the manifest realm .

PSYCHOLOGY – 1) study of emotions, mood, state of mind; 2) seeking to establish motive, origin of internal impetus; 3) why one feels how one feels.

PSYCHOSIS – 1) when one's mood, emotional process, emotional state, psychological evolution, or motives for actions goes against established societal norms; 2) state of Devil, when one's internal workings turn against one's own highest good; 3) the state in which one will turn against loved ones, self, community or society itself in often self-destructive ways that also have negative impact on others or the natural flow of events.

PUBLIC PERSONA – 1) self-identification when presenting product of one's life to public; 2) indication that one has divided one's self from one's occupation.

PUDDLE OF WATER - 1) even in an area where things are stable and certain there are spots that are uncertain

PULSE – 1) cyclic and repetitive evidence of flowing life-force; 2) result of heart beat; 3) regarding the truth of self; 4) current state of affairs, conditions, events or attitudes in society.

PUMICE – 1) wisdom that comes from having completely exhausted all lessons learned from the repression of nature to the point of nature having countered with complete regeneration ; 2) the erosive effect of natural wisdom on unnatural, artificial or reactionary protections.

PUMP – 1) that which accelerates, perpetuates or initiates enduring change; 2) actions resulting in the delivery of flow or growth through societal channels; 3) repetitive actions taken with the intention of causing societal change from within society's structures.

PUMPKIN –1) natural, passionate commitment; 2) dedication to natural passion that has been made incapable of duplicating or replicating itself.

PUMPS – 1) those things which accelerate, perpetuate or initiate enduring change; 2) those actions resulting in the delivery of flow or growth through societal channels; 3) mechanisms that cause repetitive actions taken with the intention of causing societal change from within societies structures.

PUNCH AND JUDY – 1) dramatic presentation of common entertainment that represents the nature of mankind to settle issues with violence and conflict.

PUNISHMENT – 1) negative consequence imposed on those who violate societal rules, regulations, laws and traditions; 2) a means of exacting revenge or comeuppance on those who violate fixed boundaries.

PUPPET – 1) that which one manipulates through actions; 2) a person, place or thing that is used as a pawn, per preconceived design, to accomplish a specific plan.

PURPLE – 1) the blending of feelings and flow.

PURPOSE – 1) the path to one's goals.

PURSE – 1) preparedness; 2) what one uses to hold tools one anticipates the need to use; 3) container for emergency tools from the past that one perceives will be needed to meet future situations; 4) represents preparedness for future needs, yet there is an element of fear.

PUSS – 1) the spiritual growth that results from disease.

PYRAMID – 1) ancient wisdom; 2) the ability to direct chi flow in compliance with the directives of ancient wisdom; 3) represents that ancient wisdom enables the connection between **EARTH** and **HEAVEN**.

Q

QUALITY – 1) spiritual integrity of a person, place or thing.

QUANTUM – 1) absolute essence of a thing; 2) the most minimal element of anything; 3) that miniscule thing or force that causes a thing to occur in the manifest.

QUART – 1) mechanism of containment that is if minimal size but large enough to contain that which is adequate for the job.

QUARTZ CRYSTAL – 1) that which is common and readily accessible that will allow the light of spirit to enter one's life.

QUASAR – 1) origin or source of chi; 2) source of pure energy that puts into action the entire electromagnetic force that orchestrates mankind and all of the manifest.

QUEEN – 1) giver of opportunity; 2) one born with responsibility to care for and protect others.

QUEER – 1) the thing that makes one unique; 2) one's greatest gift.

QUEUE – 1) the necessary path in the manifest that one must go through to achieve one's goal.

QUICK – 1) the element of sensitivity that is the origin of all structures; 2) efficiency; 3) unrestricted flow.

QUIET – 1) acting in accordance with the humble acceptance that all things are as they should be; 2) peace that precedes and follows all manifest events.

QUILL (PEN) – 1) idea that can inspire once expressed; 2) using written word or publication to launch opinion or gossip and perpetuate its inspiration.

QUILT – 1) the true nature of one's belief system that it is never of one single philosophy, but a combination of many; 2) the fact that comfort in the manifest requires combining a great number of smaller beliefs and philosophies; 3) comfort and security comes only when one has crafted one's beliefs so that they are exactly true to one's deep knowing.

QUINCE – 1) amalgam of various elements that together nurture.

QUINTESSENTIAL – 1) the element of truth that is at the base and core of a thing.

QUIP – 1) appropriate use of one's intellect to create good will, cooperation and lighthearted feeling.

R

RABBIT – 1) actively participating in material life; 2) erratic progression through life of earthliness; 3) human desires and instincts to procreate and to have fear; 4) nervousness; 5) ability to be inspired one moment and then go deep into darkness; 6) connected to development/origin of the Fibonacci number system.

RABBIT FOOT – 1) that which represents the assistance of unseen or spiritual forces working in favor of one's best interest; 2) belief that there are forces beyond the manifest to which one can turn for assurance that all will go well.

RACCOON - 1) dark vision.

RACE CAR – 1) the mechanism that is equipped to get one to one's spiritual goal in a very quickly; 2) mechanism that support one to achieve one's goals that is focused on challenge and overcoming challenge.

RACE TRACK – 1) societal structure that allows fast movement on path, but a path that goes nowhere.

RACKET (SOUND) – 1) cacophony of inspiration; 2) the forces of the universe without the structure of the manifest.

RACKET (TENNIS) – 1) combination of mandatory elements one's life with one's structure of beliefs and thoughts that allows one to interact with commitment to spirit with the potential of success.

RADIO – 1) represents flow of chi in the manifest, in particular the ability of one to intercept and make use of it.

RAFTERS – 1) practical protective structure of the dwelling place of the soul; 2) practicality and structure of the wand.

RAILING – 1) a support that one has to deal with; 2) those mandatory things one must use for support as one either elevates or descends in the manifest path to one's spiritual goals.

RAIN – 1) change that comes upon one naturally *(puberty, falling in love...)*; 2) naturally occurring intrusive change.

RAIN FOREST – 1) lush abundant life that springs from the natural changes in the manifest; 2) resources of abundance in life that can provide everything one may need.

RAINBOW – 1) bounty, abundance, fulfillment; 2) symbol for how spirituality represents itself in life where variety of colors embody elements of spirit in the manifest; 3) how spiritual light shines through the prism of life and is represented by the vast diversity of the manifest.

RAKE – 1) the mandatory responsibility to gather every result from life one can find; 2) represents all one must do to maintain the abundance in one's life.

RAM – 1) the determination to go forward as one is designed to in the manifest regardless of what opposition one may encounter.

RAMP – 1) smooth regress or progress; 2) elevation on the way to achieving.

RANCH – 1) one's spiritual dwelling place that is vast and includes abundance.

RAPTURE – 1) a state of complete awe and wonder; 2) a mystic state that is not permanent.

RAT – 1) secret investigator of the lower elements of being in one's life; 2) one who gets information from everywhere but shares it to undermine others; 3) state of being equally at home in darkness; 4) instinctive urge to gather information other than the official story for the purpose of causing trouble for others.

RATTAN – 1) the systemic integration of abundance put to practical use; 2) when one reaps the benefits of abundance, and then keeps hold of it, in time it can be used for support and even structures.

RATTLESNAKE – 1) one who beguiles others who are vulnerable being distracted by obstacles for the purpose of destroying them; 2) one who warns those about to be attacked and destroyed just before the attack.

RAZOR – 1) precious device for preventing thoughts before they develop but also divides, cuts and harms.

REALITY – 1) the manifest realm.

REAR TIRE – 1) that continuous, dark unfoldment in destiny that follows and assists one's vehicle of avoidance of one's path; 2) feature of destiny that sustains one to avoid one's path while still embracing and racing toward one's goals.

REARING HORSE - 1) means of going forward may sometimes fail due to resistance in the path of a mission and/or a movement towards a goal.

RECTUM – 1) one's internal commitment to discarding waste; 2) ability to get rid of all unnecessary excesses.

RED – 1) emotions, and elements of the earth; 2) mechanics of earthy living, shelter, food, clothing, and companionship; 3) any dealings with mother earth that lead to matters of the heart; 4) refers to the fact that dealing with things of manifest reality specifically related to living on earth are the things about which manifest beings care about the most.

RED DWARF STAR – 1) the powerful ideal of the heart's truth that, though small, is most powerful; 2) distant-seeming source of light that reflects the truth of the heart and is actually small rather than distant; 3) concept, idea, belief, goal, or ideal in the heart that is small but powerful and can guide one through darkness; 4) those powerful ideas of the heart which are small but provide light in darkest moments of life, causing one to be able to make it through the darkness; 5) the heart's small truth which sustains hope.

RED HOUSE – 1) spiritual dwelling place is the heart; 2) one's truest dwelling place for the soul is the manifest realm.

RED LIPS – 1) one's manner of expressing one's self is through emotions; 2) one expresses everything through references to rites of passage, traditions and conditions of earthly living.

RED RIMMED GLASSES – 1) world view framed with feeling or earthiness; 2) issues too emotional to want to be seen.

RED SOCKS – 1) the direction on the path is based on feelings, events of earthly existence, or worldly achievements; 2) emotions are what keep one going in direction on path; 3) when decisions must be made about one's direction on the path, they are made based on feelings, and considerations of earthly life.

REFEREE – 1) one who judges in manifest realm; 2) color is significant of basis for judgment.

REGGAE – 1) an element of looseness, relaxation of strict detail or easing of personal standards that comes when one is isolated by change; 2) the battered, weather worn state one is in when life is completely consumed by change, with no let up in sight.

REIN – 1) means of controlling one's mission; 2) the ability one has through action to increase or decrease one's movement towards a manifest life-goal.

REINCARNATION – 1) close spiritual relative; 2) the ultimate result for those who cannot readily see themselves as pure and part of god upon their death; 3) reference to the Bardo Thodol[7] which

[7] Tibetan text that details the structure of one's journey after death meaning "The Great Liberation upon Hearing in the Intermediate State" and wrongly translated in English as "Tibetan Book of the Dead". A discussion of the Bardo Thodol is found in Mystic Apprentice Volume 5: Psychic Skills by Ken Ludden

illuminates the entire journey of the soul after the moment of death, in which each step of the way there are contingencies should the person not be able to accept the loss of their own identity as they take their rightful place as part of god.

REMODELING – 1) changing the dwelling place of the soul; 2) being satisfied with the basic structure of the dwelling place of one's soul, but not happy with the more superficial elements of it.

REMOTE – 1) that which is not easily achieved; 2) something difficult to understand or relate to; 3) distance across which one may reach or communicate that is too far to do so in physical form; 4) represents one's ability or mechanism for reaching across gap or distance.

RENTING – 1) you recognize that the state you are in is not permanent; 2) the manifestation of spirit state is temporary.

REPTILE – 1) of base nature; 2) that which relies on the external world, and elements of it, for connection, warmth and other human elements of life.

RESORT - 1) a place to experience the illusion of a comfortable home in a community of like-minded people.

REST – 1) to temporarily halt progress on one's path; 2) that which restores one's energy and resolve for forward movement on the path.

RESTAURANT – 1) place where one is nourished and fed; 2) a place that people go for nourishment.

RESURRECTION – 1) rebirth that leads to possibility of total fulfillment; 2) manifest event that gave Christ credibility; 3) represents that one's potential is materialized; 4) being reborn into that which will ultimately fulfill one.

REVOLUTION – 1) when one feels compelled from one's heart, or impassioned by a thought or idea to upset the status quo and break down the established order; 2) social movement that seeks to upset the societal rule and establish a new one.

RHYTHM – 1) the structure that is relied upon by spirit to be expressed in manifest; 2) the heartbeat of spiritual expression.

RIBBON – 1) belief that serves to embellish; 2) belief with which one can organize one's thoughts; 3) way to use a belief to draw attention to something or complete public presentation of a creation.

RICE – 1) spiritual nourishment that comes in small bits and no matter if you only get a very small amount, it is pure spirit and will be of maximum benefit.

RICKSHAW – 1) path of service to others by helping them along their way; 2) way of helping someone that actually takes them off of their path, though with the illusion of going forward more quickly to one's goals; 3) being of service even when the service doesn't actually help, but knowing that sometimes mistakes are the best way forward.

RIFLE – 1) the means for either protecting one's self or attacking a foe by imposing one's commitments in such a way as to stop any intrusions or attacks; 2) dealing with something in a permanent way; 3) being industrious as one creates a commitment that destroys things.

RIGHT – [SIDE] 1) representative of creative part of nature, non-linear, or emotional; 2) that which is of spontaneity, unobstructed flow, lacks inhibition from rule or organizational pattern; [CORRECT] 3) in alignment with one's nature; 4) in alignment with spiritual intention, spiritual progress and unencumbered growth or development.

RIGHT – 1) practicality, pragmatic part of nature, intellectual side, old; 2) *[left over right]* accepting the new, moving on; 3) *[right over left]* traditional.

RIGHT EYE – 1) logical, linear and practical view of life.

RIGHT INDEX FINGER – 1) attention on how the creative process is guides one's work or path; 2) indicating the need for one to consider the thing being pointed to in creative, emotional, flowing or organic fashion.

RIGHT INDEX FINGER – 1) attention on how the creative or non-linear process guides one's work.

RIGHT OVER LEFT – 1) accepting the creative, new, organic or emotional approach in situation; 2) needs all to be guided by principles of moving on, accepting the new.

RIGHT SIDE OUT - 1)a barrier that protects.

RING – 1) life, singular purpose, cycles of life, commitment; 2) complete cycle, continuum; 3) cycle of love or belief or commitment, can't tell whether it is the beginning or the ending; 4) perpetual, everlasting, a cycle that keeps repeating.

RINGING IN EARS – 1) hearing something that is not here; 2) could be mistaken for connection with spirit; 3) malfunction of the ear.

RISING SUN – 1) new beginning; 2) start of new journey.

RIVER – 1) flow of life; 2) *(outer bank of river)* destructive flow of life; 3) *(inner bank of river)* additive flow of life.

RIVER BANK - 1) natural border to fluid change; 2) place where one can experience the flow of life.

ROAD – 1) journey, life, path; 2) not a personal path, yet not as common a path as a street; (windy road) 3) your path is not goal oriented and straight-forward, it changes direction often; 4) easiest and most natural way to get through a natural landscape; 5) a process that is complex by nature.

ROBE – 1) belief system one has dealing with a specific part of one's life.

ROBOT – 1) manmade mechanism that performs actions for people; 2) imitation effort in life.

ROCKING CHAIR – 1) single moment in time where one stays awhile; 2) one makes one's life work by connecting to the path; 3) considering one's path in a way that restores one's resolve; 4) cyclical.

ROCKS – 1) obstacles; 2) minor set backs; 3) interruptions in progress; 4) elements from life that burden.

ROCKY MOUNTAINS - 1) brand new barriers; 2) barriers presented to one by the **EMPEROR** that, by the difficult task of crossing them, will utterly transform one's entire life and world view.

ROLLER BLADES – 1) method of going forward toward one's spiritual goals, in contact with the path, but not really traveling on it.

ROLLER COASTER RIDE – 1) entertainment of a predetermined course; 2) moving through challenges for the purpose of moving through challenges; 3) intentional.

ROLLING HILLS – 1) old barriers that are no longer difficult to transcend, but also have lost the benefit of providing expanded divine view of all of life; 2) remnant of pervious barriers crossed by ancestors; 3) species knowledge that comes from previous barriers crossed by early ancestors.

ROOF – 1) connection of person's soul to spirit; [COLOR OF ROOF] 2) quality of connection to spirit; [CONDITION OF ROOF] 3) quality of connection to spirit; [LEAKING ROOF] 4) roof is not fulfilling its function, no protection, something is wrong.

ROOM – 1) one aspect of the dwelling place of the soul; 2) a view of one in this manifest reality.

ROOSTER – 1) serving as a guide by being a herald; 2) leader, king of harem; 3) opinion that is impotent as it goes nowhere; 4) that which gets one going or gets things started, yet leads to nothing in terms of real life.

ROOT CHAKRA – 1) connection to the manifest.

ROPE – 1) complex idea that binds by bringing things together that would normally fall separately; 2) essence of what brings something together, idea, concept.

ROSARY – 1) prolonged ritual built of individual commitments to commune with spirit regularly in prayer or meditation, often with a specific target in place; 2) talisman of belief.

ROSE – 1) experience of love; 2) very emotional and meaningful experience in life.

ROTISSERIE – 1) mechanism for using one's passion and inspiration to create nourishment for many.

ROTTEN DOOR - 1) entry to a new path has been there for a long time and is disintegrating through lack of use.

ROWBOAT – 1) working through change.

ROYAL COURT – 1) those who, through the enactment of manifest destiny at birth, are called to rule and lead society.

ROYAL CREST – 1) symbol or insignia indicating presence of those personages who represent, through station of birth, what others have membership in, alignment with or loyalty to, and who represent societal structure, conceptual ideal, guiding principle or establish entity; 2) symbol that embodies precepts, goals, ideals and beliefs of the royal leaders of a society; 3) symbol that, when displayed, establishes presence of those members of family born to leadership; 4) visible marking indicating one who is of royal lineage.

RUBBER – 1) spiritual essence of life that is malleable, flexible and serves nearly any purpose one can imagine; 2) represents that spirit can serve any purpose, is useful in any circumstance and is never rigid..

RUBY – 1) spiritual light comes from feelings; 2) one's heart leads the way to spiritual truth for each person.

RUG – 1) the rich, warm, and beautiful network of ideas and beliefs that makes one's path easier to travel; 2) the way one can use belief and ideas to ease one's journey; 3) represents the fact that one can ease one's journey on their path via any network of thoughts and beliefs one wishes.

RULER – 1) established agreement in manifest against which things are compared to establish their place, prominence, importance or size; 2) that which dominates all hierarchy; 3) system of determining relative importance.

RUNNER – 1) one who is agile and swift on their path; 2) one who acts as liaison, is the bringer of news, or a messenger; 3) progressing quickly on one's path.

RUNNING SHOES - 1) one chooses to move forward on one's path very quickly, yet still connected to the path.

RUNWAY – [airport] 1) societal path that allows for vehicles to provide opportunity to achieve quick elevation through inspiration; 2) promises, campaigns, promotions and guarantees for avenue in life that will deliver quick elevation through inspiration; 3) false promise of reaching goals through elevation; [modeling] 4) elevated societal path for promotion of beauty and exposure of new and original belief systems; 5) avenue for exposure and fame.

RYE – 1) abundance available to all that provides nourishment; 2) common commitment that can provide nourishment or delusion.

S

SABER – 1) emotion that comes quickly and indirectly that will almost certainly cause loss, death and destruction; 2) deadly emotional weapon that is normally concealed until the moment of use; 3) secretive emotional strategy that seeks revenge or to inflict pain; 4) emotional tool that is easily hidden in belief system, and will be used suddenly and without warning to cut deeply.

SADDLE – 1) how one connects through one's foundation to the mission; 2) needed natural protection that filters changes in one's connection with the manifest; 3) natural foundation; 4) means that it is wise for one to have this mission.

SADDLE SHOES – 1) connection to path that begins and ends with spirit, but in its center is either darkness or practicality; 2) way of protecting one's self from path that appears, and is remembered, as spiritual, but is actually either dark or practical.

SAGE – 1) spiritual calling of one who has great, deep human wisdom that they share with all who seek it in order to be of service to the highest good; 2) a wise man or woman; 3) inherited thoughts, feelings, patterns or opinions passed down through many generations; 4) ancestral wisdom.

SAGITTARIUS – 1) refers to one on an ego mission from which one cannot free one's self; 2) represents that one's path in life has become an all-consuming mission; 3) when ego has become obsession; 4) one who survives by being able to mutate or change in social ways; 5) one who wants to reform society; 6) crusader who promotes quest with abandon and cannot be subtle or strategic.

SAIL – 1) spiritual belief system that allows one to become easily inspired.

SAILBOAT – 1) one's soul in life; 2) able to remain inspired and thus can survive and successfully navigate change.

SAILFISH – 1) message that very major change is coming but will be survived.

SAILOR – 1) one adept at navigating change.

SAINT – 1) one who is outwardly spiritual in the manifest world, often possessing special qualities and attributes of spirituality; 2) those who have achieved the highest status of spirituality within organized religion, but who are not necessarily clergy.

SALAMANDER - 1) unique ability to regenerate what is lost; 2) of a nature that is extremely adaptable.

SALE – 1) to exchange good or service for currency; 2) to offer a special, reduced, rate of exchange for services or goods.

SALESMAN – 1) one who exchanges goods or services for currency; 2) one who can easily convince others to need things they previously were not aware of; 3) one who will promote reduced rate of exchange for goods or services.

SALIVA – 1) the ability to transform what one has broken down with anger so that it can be easily assimilated; 2) ease in changing persons, places or things so they can be assimilated.

SALT – 1) natural purifier; 2) that which enhances lessons and often comes with change; 3) spiritual essence that can create barrier to evil or ill intended energies; 4) things essential to life but only in small quantities.

SALVAGE – 1) that which is discovered to remain after something has been destroyed; 2) searching for valuable remaining attributes left over after a devastating event.

SAND – SUBSTANCE] 1) ancient wisdom; 2) represents that natural barriers (mountains) have gone through everything possible and been broken down into dust, therefore represents having had every possible experience; 3) a symbol of the universe; 4) represents everything nothing; [COLOR] 5) spirituality is practical when one has vast experience; 6) represents significance of earth experience to spiritual being.

SANDALS – 1) natural barrier that protects against too much change when one's direction on path is natural; 2) natural way of connecting to one's path when the direction is natural.

SAND-DOLLAR – 1) gift one has as a result of coming from different culture; 2) gift that comes from exposure to diverse cultures.

SANDWICH – 1) symbol that life sustains life regardless of what is in that life.

SAPPHIRE – 1) memory, wisdom; 2) change, growth or development that brings light and promotes flow.

SATIRE – 1) use of humor in mocking a society to teach that society; 2) symbol of how ironic it is that one learns best by mocking or laughing at one's own flaws.

SATURN – 1) commitment to use of discipline and acknowledgement of one's limits and boundaries; 2) one who teaches; 3) one who is committed to taking that which is out of balance and restoring its balance. saw - 1)divisive, incendiary

SCALES – 1) balance; 2) justice; 3) dedicated to restoring equality when things have gone out of balance.

scalp itching – 1) one must actively connect with divinity.

scalp tingling – 1) feeling the need to connect with divinity.

SCEPTER – 1) equity and mercy; 2) mandatory responsibility to protect and govern members of a society; 3) indicates that one has been entrusted with the power to command people, defense systems and to govern.

SCHOOL – 1) one's spiritual path of developing in manifest; 2) place of learning.

SCHOOL BUS – 1) means by which students are placed together by society to avoid actually interacting with their own paths and forced to follow the predetermined journey toward society's stated goals of attitudinal or informational; 2) societal provision of illusion of mass progress to educational goals that actually detracts individuals from their own development on their paths.

SCIENCE – 1) study of the natural manifest world for the purpose of determining how it works; 2) man's attempt to marshal the powers of nature through intellectual understanding, codification and manipulation.

SCISSORS – 1) action in the manifest that separates, cuts and breaks into parts; 2) the power of one's emotions to divide.

SCRIPTURE – 1) record of ancient wisdom.

SCROLL – 1) reference to gifts from the high priestess that contain the true curiosity and certainty upon which every spiritual journey in life are based; 2) to know is to do; 3) represents that the moment one receives the message from spirit one must begin to take action; 4) word or message from spirit.

SCULPTURE – 1) creation of physical, three dimensional expression; 2) the manifest forms made by the hands of man that express the visions, emotions and truths of mankind.

SEA CREATURES – 1) one's base nature, instincts; 2) lower world elements such as lust, hunger, sex, eating, and greed; 3) represents that something from the base-self is emerging.

SEA HORSE SKELETON – 1) essence of a spiritual message lingers; 2) represents that at one point the spirit was present.

SEA TURTLE – 1) one who is at one with the soul, and is therefore able to exist in constant change with ease; 2) one who bridges the material and the spiritual, and has great patience of purpose.

SEAGULL – 1) represents that one has spiritual opinions regarding change; 2) one who possesses individual wisdom as a result of seeing the whole picture from a place of elevation and inspiration; 3) one who balances the natural state of elevation and inspiration with mundane knowledge of things.

SEA-HORSE – 1) represents a genderless spirit-being; 2) is an **ANGEL** bringing a message.

SEAL – 1) ascended spiritual being still alive in the manifest; 2) perfectly suited to absolute states and at ease with death so much so that the experience of passing over will almost go unnoticed; 3) being at home with absolute change and the state of pure spirit.

SEAM RIPPER – 1) instrument with which one can expose and take apart belief systems that are a combination of different ones; 2) cutting the thread of thought or concept that joins unlike things that have previously passed as a united whole; 3) knowing, and exposing, the subtle differences between things attempting to pull off appearing as one.

SEAT BELT – 1) the element of one's foundation that makes one un able to move forward on one's path; 2) that which protects one from becoming suddenly, and dangerously, inspired thus giving the feel safety; 3) that which inhibits too rapid progression on one's path.

SECOND – 1) that which comes after the first; 2) to take the place of, or sit in attendance to.

SECOND COUSIN – 1) distant association that is relatively close and in loose union with one; 2) signifies distant familial lineage as relevant to one's specific moment in time.

SEED – 1) the element containing a spark of life that, with change and illumination, will emerge as an independent, unique and vital thing; 2) commitment to new life; 3) essence of being from which another being can emerge.

SEEING EYE DOG - 1)familiar who serves as companion to one with vision or other spiritual gift so that they may maximize their gift of vision.

SEGMENT – 1) smaller part of a whole; 2) one part that can stand alone or be part of a whole.

SEGUE – 1) element that serves only to connect and cannot stand alone; 2) means of getting from one place to another that is neither a destination nor a resting place on its own; 3) that which intuitively knows the way.

SELF-CENTERED – 1) ego-centric; 2) self-assured and self-focused in a way that the world around is of no consequence, nor have any impact; 3) unaware of others and not at all spiritual in life.

SELFISHNESS – 1) the action of being dedicated to self; 2) uncaring about others.

SELFLESSNESS – 1) the action of being dedicated to other; 2) spiritual living.

SEMEN – 1) life essence; 2) spirit essence.

SENSIBILITY – 1) one's ability to use every manifest means to connect with the world around; 2) all of the ways in which one integrates with the manifest world.

SEQUEL – 1) off shoot of a work; 2) the subsequent work that is created when an original creation is so well received that another like it is desired.

SERVANT – 1) one who makes their living by being of service to others; 2) one who is positioned in a societal station below others.

SERVICE STATION – 1) a fixed location where one can go to receive essence.

SEVEN – 1) abundance.

SEXUAL ABUSE - 1) seeking to attack and alter the foundation/core beliefs of another person.

SHADOW – 1) that which is unclear; 2) the sense that darkness is falling over something, but without clear sense of what it is.

SHAKTI PAD – 1) divine energy transfer; 2) presence of light that breaks through even when it is opposed; 3) life force.

SHARK – 1) message from the lower realms of humanity that is dedicated to destruction; 2) those messages that encourage gluttony from the point of avarice.

SHAWL – 1) belief system that gives temporary comfort; 2) belief that can be applied at will when one has discomfort.

SHEATH – 1) the perfect place to keep an emotion when not in use, designed to exactly accommodate it.

SHEEP – 1) the faith-filled; 2) those members of a faith who work together and are united by their ideas; 3) *[black sheep]* faithlessness; 4) *[brown sheep]* practical kind of faith.

SHEERS – 1) that which, in the manifest, cuts ideas short; 2) emotions that terminate or prematurely stop thoughts from developing.

SHEET – 1) belief system that surrounds those who seek to commune with spirit directly.

SHELL – 1) secret derived from, or occurring during change; [1/2 SHELL] 2) secret revealed; 3) answer found; 4) treasure discovered; [CONCH-SHELL] 5) mystery; 6) myth; 7) secrets to be unfolded.

SHIELD – 1) that which protects; 2) precious ability to protect against assault, attack or attempt to murder.

SHINY – 1) thing that reflects the light of spirit; 2) evidence of something true, yet it will give a false impression.

SHIP – 1) in the process of change, represents means of survival; 2) way of dealing with change; 3) vehicle of getting through change; 4) a half commitment to a particular vehicle to survive change; 5) vehicle used to navigate, survive and manage change is solid and strong, can contain many.

SHIPSHAPE – 1) everything is ready to encounter whatever change may occur; 2) being entirely prepared to navigate, survive and learn from change.

SHIRT – 1) belief system that is close to heart and digestion; 2) those beliefs that are most dear and represent how one takes in the world

SHIRT POCKETS - 1) way of carrying with one those things which support actions that help the heart to achieve goals.

SHOE – 1) what connects or disconnects one from one's path; 2) vehicle one chooses to carry one forward.

SHOE LACE – 1) primary belief that enables one to maintain connection with or disconnection from one's path; 2) way one remains connected to vehicle one chooses to carry one forward on one's path.

SHOE RACK – 1) organized place for keeping one's options for various ways of connecting to or protecting one from one's path.

SHOOTING STAR – 1) fleeting ideal, belief of hope; 2) distant source of light that traverses the darkness; 3) passing concept, idea, belief, goal, or ideal that can guide one through darkness; 4) that which momentarily provides light in darkest moments of life, causing one to be able to make it through the darkness; 5) that which gives a brief moment of hope.

SHOPPING BAG – 1) means by which one can make preparations for nourishing one's self.

SHOPPING MALL - **1)**designated area or marketplace for commercial enterprise and retail exchanges.

SHORT SLEEVE – 1) belief system that initiates one's embrace of the world, but allows the embrace itself to be completely natural.

SHOULDER – 1) the type of tasks one will take on2) what one takes on; 3) those tasks one is prone to take on.

shoulder pads – 1) strengthening and building up of one's ability to take on tasks; 2) hidden but visible protection as outward signal that one can perform without risk of injury, or normal vulnerability to the intrusions of others.

shounders itching – 1) one must actively take on a task.

shounders tingling – 1) feeling the need to take on a task.

SHOWER – 1) self-imposed change designed to cleanse and free one; 2) that which changes one internally; 3) that which allows one to feel newly cleansed and in a state of understanding one's self.

SHREDDER – 1) that which destroys the ideas and proclamations others have put forth into the world that are no longer wanted or needed.

SHUTTLECOCK – 1) element of amusement that is spiritual in essence, and can—when inspired from the actions of others—lead to a successful spiritual outcome.

SIGNIFIER – 1) talisman that represents the subject of a ritual, reading or divination ceremony.

SILENCE – 1) the void; 2) the nothingness that holds everything.

SILK – 1) soft and strong; 2) that which is most resilient.

SILO – 1) space, extruded from one's gifts, that holds all that nourishes.

SILVER – 1) precious neutrality that allows self-reflection.

SILVER DOLLAR – 1) precious neutrality; 2) neutral wealth that is valued highly and that will last.

SILVERWARE – 1) precious, but neutral, means by which one can nourish one's self.

SINGING – 1) using one's own ability to inspire with which to bring spirit into the world.

SINGLES BAR – 1) location for exchange in which individuals seek to satisfy their specific manifest urges and needs; 2) resource for self delusion in which one seeks to find those things that will placate urgent desires; 4) location one goes alone for hiding from reality.

SINK – 1) device or location in which one manipulates and controls change, putting it to various uses.

SISTER – 1) fellow mystic or fellow member of one's spiritual community who is in the same place as you; 2) person with whom one's shares one's spiritual dwelling place; 3) another with whom one feels an absolute yin connection.

SITTING - 1) resting on one's foundation while taking a break from one's journey on the path.

SITTING ON STOOL – 1) learning one's craft; 2) state of being a student.

SIX – 1) fulfillment that comes from complete union between spirit and manifest.

SKATEBOARD – 1) portion of life that allows one to advance more quickly on one's path, while still partially connected to it; 2) time in one's youth of impatience and desire for life to move very quickly toward goals.

SKATER – 1) one who advances more quickly on one's path while still partially connected to it; 2) the eagerness of youth.

SKATING – 1) attempting to advance more quickly on one's path while still partially connected to it; 2) one who has the eagerness of youth.

SKATING RINK – 1) where state of pure spirit, so much so that life ceases, becomes one's path; 2) place where growth and change are no longer possible that becomes way of life.

SKEIN OF YARN – 1) single and very developed thought or idea that can be made into simplistic belief systems; 2) commitment to making simplistic belief systems.

SKELETON – 1) enduring structure that supports spirit; 2) essence of being.

SKELETON KEY - 1) foundation of belief system that by its use opens new avenues of experience and growth in spirit; 2) spiritual willingness as the foundation upon which one must act.

SKI LIFT – 1) structure that elevates one so that they might ultimately descend; 2) climb to elevated height from which one's spiritual path is a steep descent.

SKIER – 1) one who's spiritual path is to suffer a swift descent after a meteoric elevation.

SKIING – 1) the journey to climb to elevated height from which one's spiritual path is a steep descent.

SKIN – 1) absorption and filtering mechanism; 2) point of contact with everything; 3) how one defends and protects one's self; 3) the symbol of one's vulnerability.

SKIRT – 1) belief system that obscures one's movement on one's path; 2) the veil of belief behind which no steps on the path can be seen; 3) belief system that makes life's purpose vaguer, unspecific.

SKIS – 1) means by which one climbs to an elevated height from which one's spiritual path is a steep descent.

SKULL – 1) wisdom that comes from contemplation of life, death and the temporal quality of life; 2) embracing man's vulnerability.

SKY - 1)man's connection to the heavens.

SKY DIVING – 1) one who amuses one's self by climbing to godlike heights in order to feel bliss during the fall back to earth saved from death by one's spiritual belief system; 2) the pattern when one leaves one's path via inspiration only to fall again; 3) the irony that even when one mocks spirit by trying to imitate it and is swiftly dashed back to earth, spirit will come to the rescue of those who embrace a belief system in spirit.

SKY WRITING – 1) the attempt to communicate spiritual concepts that are completely inspired.

SLAVE – 1) one who is forced by birth into living in service to others; 2) one who is permanently in a societal station below others.

SLEEP – 1) stage when one lets go of consciousness and the manifest realm to be united with spirit in the unconscious realm; 2) the name for direct, subconscious, communication with one's spirit self; 3) means of escape, running away; 4) state of total peace.

SLEEPING DOG - 1) companion available yet receiver of message is not open to companionship; 2) a companion is not available at that moment but is there.

SLEEVELESS – 1) a belief system that allows one to initiate and embrace naturally; 2) the ability to embrace the world without hesitation, filter, or protection of any sort.

SLEEVES ROLLED UP – 1) one who casts off belief system in order to live naturally; 2) uninhibited in life by one's belief system; 3) to act in one's own natural way.

SLIME – 1) one who's life has been subtly changed overall, so that those things one normally connects with cannot connect and slip to the side.

SLUM – 1) spiritual dwelling place the lower strata of society are relegated to.

SLUMLORD – 1) one who oversees the spiritual dwelling place the lower strata of society are relegated to.

SMALL INTESTINE – 1) way one assimilates the subtleties of one's life.

SMALL WOODEN BOAT – 1) creation made from life to become a vehicle for getting through change; 2) all of life is stripped down to survive change.

SMOKE – 1) confusion; 2) deception; 3) quest for spirit.

SNAIL – 1) represents being in the moment and being fully conscious of just the moment; 2) self-contained; 3) not looking far ahead; 4) must connect with one's place and anoint each moment with one's own essence.

SNAKE – 1) ability to seduce, beguile; 2) presenting temptation to others; 3) one who is double-tongue; 4) one who has an attitude that is poisonous and who consumes prey whole.

SNOW – 1) situation that is completely of spirit; 2) the pure spiritual state in the manifest world which is death; 3) condition in which nothing grows.

SNOW SHOE – 1) means of proceeding on one's path in situation that is completely of spirit; 2) traveling through a pure spiritual state in the manifest world; 3) being able to journey to and through death; 3) ability to continue on one's path even in conditions in which nothing grows.

SNOWBOARD – 1) that part of life itself that allows one to find one's path in a purely spiritual environment.

SOAP – 1) that which is added to change to purify through change; 2) those things one uses when subjecting self to change to assure one is cleansed.

SOAP OPERA – 1) dramatic and exaggerated fantasy of life; 2) a form of entertainment in which life's normal problems are exaggerated, and the time to solve them is collapsed, giving a false sense of hope and empowerment.

SOAP SCUM – 1) that which remains after a change in which one has added elements designed to purify; 2) those things that are discarded and shed when one has undergone a self-cleansing period of change; 3) after one has cleansed through change, then one must cleanse one's environment to be completely rid of those things no longer needed for spiritual growth.

SOCCER – 1) the interplay between one's direction on the path and commitment to spirit; 2) competitive comparison of movement on spiritual path between those who share a common spiritual commitment.

SOCCER FIELD – 1) the naturally abundant, societal place in which those with shared spiritual commitment compare movement on the path and the relationship between their direction on the path and that shared commitment.

SOCKS – 1) direction on path; 2) the manner in which one is going on one's path; 3) that which propels one forward and keeps one going on path.

SODA – 1) self-administered internal change that is pleasant, inspired but not healthy; 2) socially introduced internal change that is pleasant, inspired but not healthy.

SOFA – 1) shared moment in time; 2) a place for many to rest and repose; 3) several are still on their paths as their feet are on the ground; 4) a place to rest comfortably on belief systems and structures in life, designed to accommodate more than one; 5) a place to connect and share; 6) represents the need to come together and to connect with others; [VINYL SOFA] 7) a smooth place to rest (*not sleep*) on belief systems and structures in life that is desired by many people, a place to come together and to connect, rest and share; 8) this is not a place to change for with it there is a sense of stagnancy, of wasting time.

SOIL – 1) nourishment resulting from decay; 2) the practical foundation of manifest being.

SOLAR ECLIPSE –when self-deception blocks the light of spirit.

SONG – 1) one's own expression of one's eternal essence of spirit; 2) personal and inspired expression of spirit presence; 3) expression of spirit.

SONNET – 1) structured and exact pure spiritual message brought into manifest by power of music fused with conception of words; 2) organizing speech into a highly structured and traditionalized form that speaks from the heart and to the heart.

SORCERER'S STONE – 1) symbol for the obstacle anyone has who attempts to manipulate earthly powers; 2) the onas of disblief of the public when it comes to any practice of unseen powers.

SORCERY – 1) the practice of the art of manipulation of earthly powers; 2) practice of and belief in the combination of the power of nature, the occult and astrological powers can be directed to have predictable, tangible effect on the manifest world.

SOUL – 1) the spirit portion of our being; 2) the part of one's consciousness that is aware of spirit and seeks for spiritual growth; 3) part of one's every action, thought and intention that exposes an inner being filled with the elements of divinity, love and creativity.

SOUND - 1) the enduring spiritual essence of things.

SOUP – 1) self-administered internal change that nourishes and builds.

SOUTH – 1) that which directs one and urges one forward; 2) the base nature and the foundation of manifest self.

SOUTH AMERICA – 1) the portion of the universal commitment to manifest sexistence that represents the ancient resurrection of culture, civilization; 2) the portion of the universal commitment to manifest existence that represents the future resurrection of culture, civilization.

SOUTHERN HEMISPHERE – 1) bass or foundational half of commitment.

SPACE – 1) the void; 2) the eternal possibility; 3) nothing that contains everything; 4) all potential.

SPACE HEATER – 1) the aspect of one's spiritual dwelling place in the manifest that represents the usefulness of repression of feelings; 2) controlled and elective release of repressed feelings for useful purpose.

SPACE RACE – 1) universal urge to explore possibilities; 2) competitive angling to be the first to comprehend and explain the void.

SPACESHIP – 1) the full extention of ones gifts, including the timely release of rage built up from repressed emotions that thrusts one into the void looking for answers; 2) precious enterprise that employes all aspects of being enabling one to reach maximum potential.

SPEAR – 1) the need to enforce one's will on others; 2) the purpose of one's aggressive nature; 3) the inescapable urgency and emotion that accompanies ambition.

SPERM - 1) life essence; 2) spirit essence.

SPHERE – [*also see* **GLOBE, ORB**] 1) commitment; 2) recording one's experience of the relationships between things; 3) life's commitment to human growth; 4) that which speaks through color, atmosphere and smell; 5) commitment and dedication to something that one is loyal to; 6) elements that exist in the **LEVEL OF SPHERES** within the outer region of the astral plane.

SPHINX – 1) represents the embrace of ancient wisdom; 2) symbol of seeing through the veil; 3) mystery.

SPIDER – 1) something that bridges gaps that nothing else can bridge; 2) promise of poison; 3) the art of clever manipulation with the means of to capture and kill; 4) one's base nature as a creature of dark and of the land; 5) dark part of one's nature including the ability to entrap; 6) one's plotting and planning of things that aren't quite seen and designed to draw others in; 7) the conscious creation of a whole network with a purpose to create.

SPIDER WEB – 1) something that entangles when one gets close; 2) a complex cunning way of entrapping people and things.

spine itching – 1) one must act as if one's life is important; 2) one must actively change one'sentire life; 3) one must take direct action on one's mortality; 4) one must take direct action now, for one's life may soon end.

spine tingling – 1) feeling that one's life is important; 2) feeling that one's entire life must change; 3) feeling one's mortality; 4) feeling that one's life may soon end.

SPIRAL – 1) symbol for life as opposed to the body, and of the great mandala, the wheel of life; 2) constant chi that makes the manifest world happen.

SPIRAL SHELL – 1) mystery; 2) myth; 3) represents secrets to be unfolded.

SPIRAL STAIRCASE – 1) representation that life is the way to reach elevation through the evolution of humanity; 2) the double helix of DNA.

SPIRIT – 1) essential and immortal being of self; 2) that which is non-manifest; 3) not participating in space-time.

SPIRITUAL GARDEN –1) the place where one's consciousness goes just after death of the body; 2) it is where spiritual experiences happen at the end of the path.

SPIRITUAL LAW – 1) way in which the mechanics and flow of spirit works.

SPIT – 1) one's expression of the desire for things to change immediately.

SPONGE – 1) that which absorbs impact of change so that it will not have an effect on the world; 2) the ability to take in everything.

SPOON – 1) nurture; 2) nourishment; 3) the means to care for.

SPORTS ARENA – 1) location for competitive matching of skill in organized; 2) pre-arranged and mutually agreed upon tests.

SPORTS GLOVES - 1) activity to entertain self; 2) what one does in life to entertain self; 3) how one interacts while entertaining self.

SPRING – 1) extreme youth; 2) new beginning; 3) nature of manifest to regenerate; 4) the global balance extant in nature; 5) absolute efficiency of nature.

SPRINKLER – 1) one's effort to change the natural world in order to keep it abundant; 2) now evenly distributed and constant change brings forth the most out of life.

SQUARE – 1) structure in manifest created by man; 2) represents the number 4; 3) all creation achieved by utilization of elements of the manifest.

SQUATTING – 1) one's foundation is open, grounded and very stable; 2) one is strongly connected to one's path; 3) resting while remaining completely involved with one's path.

SQUIRREL – 1) basic element of human nature to gather and store things for future; 2) practical nature to plan for future contingencies; 3) one's effort to assure future nourishment, and ability to regenerate.

STAFF – 1) that which is mandatory in life and also supports; 2) those who support and aid one's efforts and are, at the same time, working under one's direction.

STAGE – 1) an element of life; 2) moment in space-time in which all things happen in a life; 3) platform of life itself on which one creates one's own significance through drama and practical efforts.

STAGE NAME – 1) self-identification when presenting product of one's life to public; 2) indication that one has divided one's self from one's occupation.

STAGNANT WATER - 1) represents a state of stagnancy coming from a lack of flow, growth or change; 2) one is in a state of stagnancy; 3S) lack of current flow or change.

STAIRWAY – 1) that path of progression one makes towards elevation; 2) if one should follow current pattern one will become elevated; 3) progress is possible, every step is a choice; 4) represents progression and regression; 4) yang way of achieving elevation.

STAMP (FOOT) – 1) conveyance of information by one's movements on one's path that inform anyone who is impacted by it; 2) delivery of information to others who observe one's direction on path; 3) instincts, essential nature of spirit as expressed through one's direction on path.

STAMP (POSTAGE) – 1) societal means of regulating flow of ideas and results from one's life; 2) one's means of working within society to share the results of one's experiences with another of one's specific choosing.

STANDING UP – 1) the act of connecting one's direction to one's path; 2) continuing on one's path after a rest or break.

STAR – 1) ideal; 2) distant source of light; 3) concept, idea, belief, goal, or ideal that can guide one through darkness; 4) that which provides light in darkest moments of life, causing one to be able to make it through the darkness; 5) that which sustains hope.

STARFISH – 1) universal mystery unfolding in one's life; 2) ancestral link to the universe (e.g., what is in the sea is in the stars).

STARS – 1) ideals.

STEAM ENGINE – 1) mechanism that uses a combination of repression, inspiration and enforced change that then causes and sustains forward motion and is powered by the joint efforts of the enterprise of mankind; 2) fusion of repression, inspiration and enforced change which supplies constant energy so that a structure in the manifest may continue to function; 3) represents circumstance in which a combination of repression, inspiration and enforced change keeps a person, place, idea, pursuit or attempt in motion.

steamer trunk – 1) system within a family of keeping traditions and lore alive from generation to generation; 2) tendency of individual or group to save or hoard memories; 3) collection of ideas, memories and indicators of personal significance one holds onto beyond their time of usefulness.

STEEPLE – 1) structure in **CHURCH** which represents direct link with divinity.

STEREO - 1)connection to spirit via manifest.

STICK – 1) minor detail of life that must be dealt with and cannot be ignored; 2) minor wand.

STICKY TAPE – 1) one-sided concept that binds things together temporarily and artificially; 2) any one-sided, near-invisible, artificial concept that binds things together due to the act of will of an uninvolved party.

STILTS – 1) using life status support haughtiness; 2) havingfalse sense of self; 3) feigned separateness from the human condition.

STINGER – 1) emotional reaction, applied in fear or panic, that poisons another.

STINGRAY – 1) that part of the base nature which hids behind simplistic wisdom and prepared to defend self even when there is no threat; 2) paranoia.

STINK – 1) evidence of the presence of a destrective, decrepid, fetid or degenerative element.

STIRRUPS – 1) precious means of making one's quest be the actual direction on one's path.

STOMACH – 1) represents how one assimilates the world; 2) one's greatest vulnerability.

STONE FLOOR - *1)*an obstacle or barrier that serves as one's foundation in life.

STONE ROOM – 1) ironic use of one's past barriers from which to create one's spiritual dwelling place; 2) the nature of man hold one's barriers in life close, and even revisit them even when one has already successfully overcome them.

STONE STAIRWAY – 1) represents that one way to achieve spirituality is to overcome barriers; 2) a way to reach elevation and access spirituality; 3) (walking down stairs, face front) having been elevated one then returns to manifest to deliver the message; 4) (walking down stairs, backwards) one retreats from elevation, and is loosing spiritual ground.

STONED – 1) state of repression and inspiration that distorts one's ability to think; 2) represents being in an inspired state of self-delusion mixed with fixation on self; 3) false sense of fascinating depth; 4) inspired state of inflated self-importance reflected in extreme paranoia.

STONES – 1) former barriers that have become obstacles.

STOOL – 1) craft; 2) focus on detail.

STOOL PIGEON – 1) opinion that harms another; 2) of the mindset to do the right thing but intentionally, and unnecessarily, harming another in the process.

STORM – 1) sudden state of inspiration; 2) making form from nuance; 3) creating order out of chaos that becomes enormously destructive; 4) power of nature that confuses state of inspiration into patterns of construction.

STORY – 1) use of words, images and symbols to convey a meaning; 2) sharing of one's point of view with many in a way that is entertaining, illuminating and inclusive.

STOVE – 1) place where one's feelings, normally held back, can serve to nourish; 2) that which sustains health, life, community.

STRAIGHT HAIR – 1) thoughts and ideas that have been made to be, or naturally are, clear and straight; 2) well maintained, organized and clear thoughts and ideas.

STRAWBERRY – 1) strong feelings; 2) emotions; 3) when feelings create new life .

STREAM – 1) change combined with repressed feelings can become force of inspiration to propel things forward; 2) minor natural change, often leads to larger more important change.

STREET – 1) common avenue that people go down; 2) society's path; 3) everybody's path; 4) not a personal or individual path.

STRING – 1) thought, idea; 2) idea that doesn't completely cover; 3) binds to bring things together that would normally fall separately; 4) essence of what brings something together; 5) idea, thought process; 6) idea that connects and holds something together.

STRING BAG - 1) one lets people know and see what one needs so people might understand.

STRIPES – 1) different aspects of something, intermittent; 2) *(vertical stripes)* core isn't matching actions or alternate approaches, not necessarily conflict; 3) *(horizontal stripes)* goes throughout being intermittently, 4) alternate states of being that change as one elevates.

STROLLER – 1) vehicle for moving new life forward; 2) vehicle for preparing for new project.

STUCCO – 1) rough man made barrier; 2) crude social regulation that restricts, contains or limits.

STUDIO APARTMENT - **1)**one's dwelling place of the soul that is in a single cube within urban life where each individual has their own singular space within an **APARTMENT BUILDING**.

STYROFOAM – 1) artificial, simplistic spiritual philosophy that is essentially hollow though gives the impression of being solid.

SUBCULTURE – 1) subset of societal order that represents sentiment common to many but not acknowledged by leadership.

SUBMARINE – 1) that which is contained within change but unaffected by it; 2) state in which traversing change is necessary but one has been guarded against being affected by it.

SUBMARINE SANDWICH – 1) symbol that life sustains life regardless of what is in that life, even if that is constant change.

SUBPLOT – 1) secondary thread that carries story forward; 2) peripheral or secondary plan or projection that is intended to be followed if primary is in default; 3) step by step secondary view of past, present or future event.

SUBTERRANEAN – 1) that which is beneath one's path; 2) the essence of practality; 3) that which allows direct access to spirit but lays within the most mundaine aspects of manifest existence.

SUBURB – 1) bordering the mainstream normal social structures and social behaviors, but different enough to have its own culture as well; 2) derivative sub-culture that is evolved sufficiently to be its own unique social order.

SUBWAY – 1) black market, and underbelly of society; 2) societal pathway aligned with the lower instincts of mankind.

SUMMER - 1) adolescence

SUN – 1) life-giver, illuminator; 2) that which makes one healthy and fulfilled and growing; 3) continuing of life (path of the sun from east to west), light, illumination of a path; 4) represents dynamic energy; 5) represents the principle of being able to generate, motivate, and stimulate.

SUNFLOWER – 1) abundant experience in life; 2) that which comes from the mind, and is of the mind.

SUNGLASSES – 1) elects to see the world as shaded or darkened *(specific color gives element that is shading view)*; 2) meant to alter or skew view of world.

SUNGLASSES IN HAIR - 1) has made decision to see world as it is, but block view of higher realms or spiritual point of view.

SUNLIGHT – 1) the truth of spirit; 2) divine illumination; 3) clarity of vision.

SUNRISE – 1) new beginning; 2) start of new journey; 3) beginning of a new cycle; 4) instigation of a belief; 5) origin of an idea.

SUNSET – 1) end of a journey; 3) end of a new cycle; 4) death of a belief; 5) end of an idea.

SUPERDOME – 1) societal half-commitment to entertainment; 2) reflects the fact that sporting competitions and mass entertainment events are only half of the picture, for they are also careful manipulations for profit; 3) mass entertainment of any kind ultimately undermines the culture of the society.

SURF – 1) use of a mobile platform in life that allows stability and forward movement through change.

SURFBOARD - **1)**mobile platform in life that allows stability and forward movement through change.

SURFING – 1) using of a mobile platform in life for stability and forward movement through change.

SURGEON – 1) one who seeks to change others from the inside, always in the name of healing though it can backfire; 2) one whose actions have a deep and changing effect on another.

SURROGATE – 1) a person, place or thing that acts as a substitute for something else, not necessarily similar; 2) use of a stustitution that is enscripted to service with a specific desired outcome.

SURROUND – 1) to take an action that will cause a desired effect no matter what course of action another has; 2) put into place a system or circumstance that will ensure certain precise responses.

SURROUNDED – 1) any direction on path will have same outcome; 2) there is no escape.

SURVIVOR – 1) one who has experience and developed skills from lessons learned; 2) state of being wise from experience.

SUSPECT – 1) one who is presumed to have done something particular; 2) likely person, place or thing responsible for particular event.

SUSPICION – 1) fear overruling heart; 2) when a preconceived or presumed interrelationship is believed in, yet has not yet been verified.

SWADDLING CLOTHES – 1) belief system based on openness, innocence and active contact with the heart; 2) indicates a state of innocence.

SWAN – 1) façade or illusion of calm in chaos; 2) represents Π – 1) the fibonacci spiral, an explosion of life; 3) a spiritual state, and the constant work required to maintain it; 4) one who must adjust to change, and does it in a calm state amidst the chaos; 5) one who is in the flow and mustconstantly adjust to remain in a calm spiritual state.

SWASTIKA – 1) original sign of luck and fortune; 2) in ancient Hinduism represented honesty, truth, purity and stability; 3) has become inverted and made the sign of dehumanizing corruption; 4) recent sign of man's inhumanity to man.

SWEAT – 1) how one changes the world; 2) how one is affecting change in the world that comes from the inside.

SWEATSHIRT – 1) protection that stays in place; 2) stable protection of both heart and assimilation.

SWELLING – 1) change that has not been fulfilled; 2) change that has occurred but not yet been fully processed; 3) ripe yet unfinished;) movement, growth or development that needs to be dealt with.

SWILL – 1) internalized change that has corrupted or perverted; 2) an offered change that is not pure and can cause damage.

SWIM FINS – 1) exaggerated artificial direction on the path that allows one to get through change with vigor; 2) means of accelerating changes in one's life by being resigned to that direction.

SWIMMING – 1) going through change without assistance, relying on self through change; 2) still reacting to the change, not solidly on shore yet.

SWIMMING POOL – 1) society's designated place for going through change without assistance, relying on self through change.

SWORD – 1) "the swords that pierce the heart"; 2) emotions; 3) clarity; 4) the ability to rid your life of unwanted and non-productive things; 5) cutting away everything except for the necessary.

SYDA YOGA – 1) global unity of spiritual purpose.

SYMPHONY – 1) the spiritual voice of society; 2) what happens when each one finds one's own voice and truth, then join together.

SYNAGOGUE – 1) place that is a creation of man made for the purpose of reflecting and embodying the presence of spirit; 2) spirituality and manifest meet in potential, and if manifest and spirit join together then the achievement is fulfillment of that potential.

T

TABLE – 1) communion place for meeting; 2) where people come together and share; 3) the place in life that elevates everybody to an equal place.

TABOO – 1) societal dictum that forbids; 2) community prejudice of behavioral exclusion; 3) activities, attitudes, events and places (usually considered quite normal elsewhere) that are forbidden.

TAIL – 1) structural elements from the past that balance one in their foreward movement; 2) counterbalance and anchor.

TAKING OFF – 1) giving in to inspiration; 2) being elevated by inspiration.

TAKING STEPS ON AIR – 1) very elevated, so much so that one is no longer on path; 2) one takes an inspired path without grounding; 3) so inspired that one is out of touch with reality.

TAN – 1) spirituality is practical when one has vast experience; 2) represents significance of earth experience to spiritual being.

TAP DANCING – 1) prevailing human spirit to celebrate even when repressed; 2) rebel of celebration.

TAP SHOE – 1) the precious element that connects those who will prevail when repressed to the forward movement on their path; 2) precious rebellion that that separates one from the dour path of society and allows the direction forward to be one of celebration.

TAPE – 1) artificial, one-sided concept that temporarily binds.

TAPE DISPENSER – 1) the source of artificial, one-sided concepts designed to bind, entrap or join unnaturally.

TAPE MEASURE – 1) society's system of thought to which all must compare; 2) the established system that measures the distance, height, depth, breadth or width of persons, places and things in the manifest.

TAPE RECORDER – 1) source of what one is willing to listen to; 2) spiritual vanity.

TAPESTRY – 1) the interweaving of a wide variety of ideas, thoughts, memories and concepts that reflect life; 2) an intricate belief system that exemplifies all of life in a single, simple scene.

TAR – 1) the essence of darkness that will change everything, bringing it to a state of absolute stagnancy; 2) those things which flow only by and of the manifest ultimately are dark and eventually stagnant.

TAROT ACE – 1) the essence of that suit's meaning; 2) that which is at the core of a widely applied principle.

TAROT KING – 1) the state of being fully accomplished and established; 2) one who has established and distinguished one's self in relation to a specific manifest path or realm; 3) one who has embraced full responsibility, impact, implication and potential of one's essential destiny.

TAROT KNIGHT – 1) having one's quest in sight and being active in its pursuit; 2) one who is actively pursuing that which is essential to one's own nature.

TAROT PAGE – 1) as yet unfamiliar and uninvolved with one's essential nature; 2) one who is vaguely aware of one's own nature but has not yet understood it signifies one's destiny.

TAROT QUEEN – 1) having become fully established in the aspect of one's destiny and then who looks to its continuance beyond one's lifetime; 2) that which is the larger benefit, extension or progenity of one's essential nature of being, and the sum total of all of one's accomplishments, honing of one's gifts and extrapolation of benefit for the world that potentially come from those gifts.

TATTOO – 1) accentuating one's natural boundary that creates the perfect combination of allowance and protection from change; 2) expressing one's self via one's natural boundary; 3) making public one's boundaries, in particular when it comes to growth, flow and/or change.

TAURUS – 1) one who holds and supports the established family structure; 2) one who takes on the purpose to provide a home for one's family; 3) one who likes luxury and open space; 4) one who is very sexual; 5) one who is sure of one's ideas and point of view, often to the point of blindness, prejudice and stubbornness; 6) one who is difficult to get going, yet once going is hard to dissuade; 7) represents full realization of self, one's journey of physically exploring the world; 8) one who can be "bull-headed", in both a positive and negative light; 9) one who gets things done, is reliable and persistent in completing projects, though may also be very stubborn and argumentative.

TAX – 1) societal fee for participation, protection and provision; 2) the cost of all that is provided to citizens of a society that they are free to use; 3) taking advantage of the enterprise by adding cost for the priveledge of having done something.

TAXI CAB – 1) assistance in achieving a goal without actually participating on the path to that goal; 2) one who takes advantage of the desire in another to have the illusion of reaching a goal without benefit of actually taking the proper path to that goal.

TEA – 1) formal setting for change, codification; 2) change in itself is nourishing and nurturing (learning to change that moves one forward, like school and graduation); 3) when change becomes agitated and is active, the presence of experiences and results from life become alive to nourish you and sustain you, nourishment, revitalization; 4) (cup of tea full) potential growth remains impossible until one assimilates that change; 5) (cup of tea empty) potential to change and grow exists, but as yet there is no direction, objective or plan; 6) (cup of tea partially filled) potential to change has begun to present itself, or has been half way assimilated.

TEARS – 1) cleansing of the soul; 2) the soul is moving and changing.

TECHNOLOGY – 1) essential manifest function that works of man are based upon; 2) that which an in-depth understanding of the manifest makes possible.

TEENAGER – 1) having one's quest in sight and being active in its pursuit; 2) one who is actively pursuing that which is essential to one's own nature.

TEETH – 1) anger; 2) how you express anger; 3) how one breaks something down; 4) how one gets what one desires with which to nourish one's self; [MISSING TEETH IN FRONT] 5) represents that one has no way to get what one needs; [MISSING TEETH AT SIDES] 6) one can get what one wants, but cannot do anything with it;

[MISSING MOLARS] 7) one can get what one wants, can do things with it, but cannot assimilate or internalize the benefit.

TEETH DRILLERS – 1) something one needs to deal with; 2) the original purpose is to attack anger, to break it down and destroy it.

TEETH FALLING OUT – 1) one believes that one has no power; 2) there is frustration and anger, and one believes that one can do nothing about the situation.

teeth itching – 1) one must actively show one's anger.

teeth tingling – 1) feeling the need to show one's anger.

TELEKINESIS – 1) indicates one has far more effect on the world around than one suspects; 2) a reminder that the most effective way of proceeding may not be traditional, visible or apparent.

TELEPATHY – 1) indicates that much of what is known is a gift from spirit through the knowing; 2) represents the direct connection between individuals can be much deeper than one might imagine.

TELEPHONE – 1) society offers a variety ways of communicating, many of which are indirect and not real; 2) communication from afar.

TELEVISION (TV) – 1) society offers a variety of ways of seeing each other, many of which are indirect and not real; 2) the illusion of seeing a person, place or thing as real when there is nothing real at all there.

TELEVISION SET – 1) societal mechanism that offers a way of seeing others that is indirect and not real; 2) the mechanism that produces illusion of seeing persons, places and things that are not real.

TEMPERATURE – 1) the effect of resistance a physical form has on the chi flowing through it.

TEMPLE – 1) place that is a creation of man made for the purpose of reflecting and embodying the presence of spirit; 2) spirituality and manifest meet in potential, and if manifest and spirit join together then the achievement is fulfillment of that potential.

TEN – 1) a complete set; 2) fruition of an earthly pursuit.

TENNIS – 1) the interplay between the combination of one's mandatory obligations and belief system with one's commitment to spirit; 2) competitive comparison of one's mandatory obligations and belief system with one's commitment to spirit.

TENNIS RACKET – 1) the combination of one's mandatory obligations and belief system that serves as one's interplay with spiritual commitment.

TENT – 1) belief system that serves as a temporary home of the soul; 2) belief system that gives a temporary place to dwell that could be a state of mind, a physical location, a transition.

TEPEE – 1) belief in an enhancement of an existing relationship that serves as a temporary home of the soul; 2) strength of connection such as a state of mind, a physical location, or a transition that gives a temporary place to dwell.

TEXT – 1) content of products and results from one's life that holds the potential to be known by others.

TEXTBOOK – 1) the collected statements, lessons, attitudes, analyses and anecdotes from life that provide guidance to others who study it.

THE GREAT Y – 1) mandate of all spiritual beings in the manifest to unite the divisions of the manifest world, and at the same time to bring into manifest the spiritual unity one represents; 2) duality becoming one, and one becoming duality; 3) represents the individual experience of living in life; 4) the voice of all wisdom gained from earthly experience.

THERMOMETER – 1) that which measures the amount of resistance to chi flow.

THIEF – 1) one who's actions take valuable things from others; 2) when one's actions make others feel that they have suffered a personal loss.

THIRD EYE CHAKRA – 1) being able to have vision; 2) having sight.

THORNS – 1) emotional protections that help one stay focused, be challenged and grow; 2) emotional outbursts that make one respect all of life.

THOUGHT – 1) one's construction in the manifest; 2) a projection of one's intellect that takes manifest form.

THREAD – 1) a continuous thought pattern; 2) that which connects things, things that make them come together.

THREE – 1) divine order; 2) natural order.

THROAT – 1) that which houses one's expression.

THROAT CHAKRA – 1) the ability to express the truth of your spirit essence; 2) one's spiritual expression.

THRONE - 1)position of authority.

THROW UP – 1) refers to one rejecting something one had taken in; 2) unwilling to accept a situation or person even when one had thought it possible.

THUNDER - 1)when light enters the manifest there is the result of music of inspiration.

TIC MARK – 1) a brief and lasting action that indicates the item nearest has been accounted for, recorded, inventoried or whatever else it might specifically be designated to mean in a case specific use.

TICKET – 1) guarantee that one will achieve, participate in or be given entry to a particular event, place or direction.

TICKING- 1) the regular little things that happen, 2) steady, constant communication of minor, neutral and unspecific ideas.

TICKLE – 1) to take action that energizes another; 2) to be fully dedicated to the experience of heightened energy in another; 3) to manipulate another, through one's actions, with a sudden influx of magnified energy.

TICKLING - 1) acting to energize another; 2) being actively dedicated to the experience of heightened energy in another; 3) manipulating another, through one's actions, with a sudden influx of magnified energy.

TIDAL WAVE – 1) sudden, absolute societal change that completely destroys the former way of living; 2) the absolute change that results from the global commitment to human existence has shifted and utterly changed; 3) the feeling at the moment of impact when global change arrives en force.

TIE – [verb] 1) to impose an idea or thought that forces a united state among people, places or things; 2) to complete and make momentarily effective the imposition of an idea that unites; [noun] 3) that idea or thought that can be used to force a united state among people, places or things; 4) that concept that is used to complete imposed unification.

TIGER – 1) wild and untamed psychic gift that is compelled by, or used to express, anger, 2) psychic state that unifies danger and aggression.

TIGHT PANTS AROUND ANKLE –movement separate from direction of path.

TIGHT ROPE – 1) concept about traversing the void that represents a singular path that very few will be able to follow; 2) ascedic, mystical path of concentration that takes one through the void; 3) the 5th ring of strategy in which focus allows balanced and relaxed traversing of the boid.

TIGHT WIRE – 1) concept about traversing the void that represents a singular path that very few will be able to follow; 2) ascedic, mystical path of concentration that takes one through the void; 3) the 5th ring of strategy in which focus allows balanced and relaxed traversing of the boid.

TILE – 1) platform structure of man's world that isn't conducive to change (it protects against change); 2) how proper use of barriers and obstacles can become one's actual path.

TIME – 1) one of two delimeters of manifest existence; 2) that which makes possible opportunities and challenges through growth, change, flow and progression; 2) illusion that separates events into seemingly linear progression.

TIN – 1) unobtrusive neutrality that is precious and malleable, but has no great value.

TIN CAN – 1) the fact that the extention or extrusion of one's gift creates the potential for experiences and possessions that are unobtrusive neutral but also precious and malleable; 2) extention or extrusion of one's gift creates the potential for experiences and possessions that have no great value

TINGLING – 1) anticipation; 2) sensing the need to take some sort of action; [arms tingling] 3) feeling the need to embrace; [hands tingling] 4) feeling the need to take action; [legs tingling] 5) feeling the need to move on one's path; [feet tingling] 6) feeling the need to change direction on one's path; [fingers tingling] 7) feeling the need to perform action with far reaching effect; [toes tingling] 8) feeling the need to reassess the ultimate goal of the direction of one's path; [head tingling] 9) feeling the need to think, or commit intellectually; [hair tingling] 10) feeling the need to think; [scalp tingling] 11) feeling the need to connect with divinity; [shounders tingling] 12) feeling the need to take on a task; [back tingling] 13) feeling the need to take responsibility; [chest tingling] 14) feeling an urge from the heart; [lips tingling] 15) feeling the need to change one's manner of expression; [tongue tingling] 16) feeling the need to further articulate one's manner of expression; [buttox or bottom tingling] 17) feeling the need to rest while remaining connected to one's path; [ears tingling] 18) feeling the need to seek counsil, wisdom or advice; [teeth tingling] 19) feeling the need to show one's anger; [palm tingling] 20) indication that money is coming one's way; [spine tingling] 21) feeling that one's life is important; 22) feeling that one's entire life must change; 23) feeling one's mortality; 24) feeling that one's life may soon end; [genitles tingling] 25) feeling the need to influence the foundation of another; 26) feeling the need to interact in intimacy; 27) sexual urge; [pelvis tingling] 28) feeling that one's foundation is particularly relevant; 29) feeling the need to rethink, question or address one's foundation; [nipples tingling] 30) feeling the need to nurture.

TIOLET – **1)** societal provision for changes that cleanse; 2) acknowledgment that one will always have need to grow through elimination of that which is unnecessary, no longer needed, and is practical to be rid of.

TIRE – 1) continuous, dark unfoldment of destiny that sustains one's vehicle of avoidance of one's path; 2) feature of destiny that sustains and makes easy one's attempt to avoid one's path while still embracing and racing toward one's goals.

TOAD – 1) one who is comfortable with sudden elevation and inspiration; 2) one who is able to be equally comfortable in manifest or spirit; 3) a true person of faith for it is one's nature to become inspired, or suddenly commune with spirit yet return to manifest with ease.

TOAD STOOL – 1) faith that nurtures and nourishes through sudden elevation and inspiration, feeling comfort in manifest or spirit, or communion with spirit; 2) resource of nature that nurtures and nourishes those comfortable with sudden elevation and inspiration; 3) that which nourishes and supports one who is able to be equally comfortable in manifest or spirit; 4) support fot the state of mind of one's nature to become inspired, or suddenly commune with spirit yet return to manifest with ease.

TOAST – 1) a restrained or inhibited portion of life that nourishes and sustains .

TOBACCO – 1) symbol of civilization; 2) represents communion with nature; 3) state of balance; 4) dance of yin and yang.

TOE IN WATER – 1) bridging the gap between the manifest and the spiritual; 2) represents being in a state where one is bridging the gap between the physical and the spiritual; 3) those without firm footing in either manifest or spiritual worlds, lost in concepts and ideals.

TOE RING – 1) precious goal or ultimate direction on path.

TOENAILS – 1) exact direction in which one is going.

TOES – 1) furthest reach of one's direction on path.

toes itching – 1) one must actively reassess the ultimate goal of the direction of one's path.

toes tingling – 1) feeling the need to reassess the ultimate goal of the direction of one's path.

TOGETHER IN BED – 1) person with whom one share's one's spiritual dwelling place; 2) person with whom one may interact in a way that shares and impacts one's foundation.

TOILET PAPER – 1) that which provides assistance and possibility of manifest act of spiritual cleansing.

TONGUE – 1) that which shapes speech in most elemental place of origin; 2) that which shapes the expression of ideas; 3) means of experiencing essential elements of that which will be assimilated.

tongue itching – 1) one must actively further articulate one's manner of expression.

tongue tingling – 1) feeling the need to further articulate one's manner of expression.

TOOLS – 1) those things, often precious, that assist our actions in life; 2) that which enhances and makes successful one's actions when one does not have enough strength to act alone; 3) represents precious willingness to be outside of ego and to reach out for help; 4) indication of need for willingness to be outside of ego and to reach out for help.

TOOTH ENAMEL – 1) strong spiritual element presented by anger; 2) represents responsibility to remain in spirit, even when showing anger.

TOOTH PICK – 1) elements of life that, when used in direct action, keep one's expression of anger healthy; 2) represents one's ability to break something down and to get what one desires but also nourishes; 3) actions by which to dissipate anger and make it healthy.

TOOTHBRUSH - 1) need for direct action to keep one's expression of anger healthy; 2) represents one's need for the ability to break something down and to get what one desires but also nourishes; 3) need for actions by which to dissipate anger and make it healthy.

TORAH – 1) resource for belief with which one aims one's life, as if an arrow, to have distinct, effective spiritual purpose; 2) source of inspiration that guides one to have distinct, effective spiritual purpose; 3) belief system concerning god by means of righteousness instruction; 4) source on a spiritual level teaches or instructs.

TORNADO – 1) represents a life that is calm in the center and carries inspiration that alters everything; 2) an inspiration that sweeps through society, restructuring and reorganizing through forceful inspiration.

TOUCHING – 1) making the action of reaching out to connect with something outside of and other than one's self; 2) represents the experience of joining with other.

TOWEL – 1) contains flow; 2) represents gathering experience; 3) means of controlling flow, growth or change; 4) mechanism to remove evidence of growth, flow or change.

TOWER – 1) nature of man's ego to wish to achieve oneness with god/ 2) tremendous ego that is futile; 3) represents a path of ambitious achievement that will ultimately end in catastrophic failure; 4) the way that ego produces humility.

TOWN – 1) concentrated organization of social behavior for a large community within a larger grouping of people; 2) small functions and events; 3) structured social life for a select group.

TOY – 1) items designed to allow one to practice skills without the full responsibility for outcome or impact; 2) that used to tease, joke with or amuse others.

TOY TRAINS – 1) non-serious societally predetermined path that strips individuals of their autonomy, denying one a unique individuality of path; 2) enforcement of singular path on the many that allows one to practice skills without the full responsibility for outcome or impact; 3) non-serious tract that allow one to practice skills without the full responsibility for outcome or impact while teasing, joking with or amusing others.

TOY WAGON – 1) non-serious replica of manifest structure for carrying a heavy load enabling one to practice skills without the full responsibility for outcome or impact; 2) way of practicing with life structures to ease burdens.

TRAFFIC – 1) indicates that the societal path one is on is typical and widely used; 2) one is on a path that is overused, hectic and draining; 3) one is following a typical path that may not be right for them.

TRAIL – 1) natural, but predetermined, path; 2) evidence that predecessors have taken this path before, leaving nothing more than evidence of passing; 3) path through life taken frequently enough to be a tantible alternative.

TRAIN – 1) societally predetermined path that strips individuals of their autonomy, denying one a unique individuality of path; 2) enforcement of singular path on the many.

TRAM – 1) societal method for overcoming major barrier; 2) acceptance of major barrier as a given, with prescribed societal path for overcoming it.

TRANCE – 1) indicative of one being in direct communication with spirit; 2) represents need to commune directly with spirit; 3) shows that one is capable of direct communication with spirit.

TRASH – 1) ideas, events, creations and structures that are no longer needed or useful; 2) outdated elements of the manifest; 3) that which is left behind after one has completed a portion of one's journey; 4) those things unnecessary and of no use.

TRASH CAN – 1) ideas, events, creations and structures that are no longer needed or useful; 2) outdated elements of the manifest; 3) that which is left behind after one has completed a portion of one's journey; 4) those things unnecessary and of no use.

TRAVEL – 1) represents need for, opportunity to be gained, or importance of a particular, elected path in life; 2) shows that what is needed can only be gained by departing one's normal place of journey; 3) that which can be learned from the experiences of others; 4) need for open mind to new experiences.

TRAVEL BAG – 1) represents those things one will need for a specific trip or a journey; 2) prepared for one's particular path; 3) prepared to depart one's normal place of journey; 4) shows that one is prepared to consider new experiences; 5) assurance that should one elect to seek a new or foreign path, all that is needed is in place.

TREAD MILL – 1) false and self-perpetuating path; 2) uselessness of following another's idea of one's path; 3) futility in societally prescribed paths that accomplish nothing for the one on that path; 4) tedium experienced when one is not on one's own proper path.

TREASURE – 1) that which is of great value in manifest life, and unexpected; 2) things so valuable that they are buried or hidden; 3) that which is of greatest value in life, but not readily found, recognized or obtained.

BURIED TREASURE – 1) that which is of such great value in manifest life that to preserve it for later generations it is hidden deeply in practicality and the mundane; 2) things so valuable to the future that they must be masked from current view; 3) that which is of greatest value in life but needed for future so that it is denied to the present.

HIDDEN TREASURE – 1) that which is of such great value in manifest life that to preserve it for later generations it is hidden deeply in practicality and the mundane; 2) things so valuable to the future that they must be masked from current view; 3) that which is of greatest value in life but needed for future so that it is denied to the present.

TREASURE CHEST – 1) that which contains things of such great value in manifest life that to preserve it for later generations it is hidden deeply in practicality and the mundane; 2) manifest creation that contains the things so valuable to the future that they must be masked from current view; 3) solid, manifest event to protect and preserve that which is of greatest value in life so that it will be available for future and denied to the present.

TREBLE CLEF – 1) societal organization of spiritual elevation; 2) means upon which expression of spiritual elevation is based; 3) agreed upon way of homogenizing spiritual elevation so all may participate.

TREE – 1) life; 2) one's life; 3) a particular life in its entirety.

tree TRUNK – 1) core structure of a life; 2) internal support for and sustainer of one's life; 3) practicality.

TRICK – 1) manifest action that dupes one into manipulation; 2) intentional manipulation that is masked in something entertaining, curious or tempting.

TRICKSTER – 1) one who performs manifest action that dupes another or others into manipulation; 2) one who intentionally manipulates others in a way that is masked in something entertaining, curious or tempting.

TRICYCLE – 1) spiritual vehicle that moves one forward in life, not quite connected to the path; 2) an opportunity for movement on the path that, because there is the element of spirit one can go forward; 3) triune empowers unity when used as both movement and direction, yet is not clearly one's truest path.

TRIP – 1) represents need for, opportunity to be gained, or importance of a temporary departure from one's current path in life; 2) shows that what is needed can only be gained by departing one's normal place of journey; 3) need for open mind to new experiences.

TRUCK – 1) powerful vehicle that accomplishes the large tasks of the will to alter one's path; 2) means of avoidance of path by rearranging or altering goal and/or terrain of path rather than actually interacting with one's journey on that path.

TRUCK DRIVER – 1) one whose actions empower and direct a powerful vehicle that accomplishes the large tasks of the will to alter one's path; 2) one who provides means of avoidance of path by rearranging or altering goal and/or terrain of path rather than actually interacting with one's journey on that path.

TRUCKING ROUTE – 1) societal avenue that accomplishes the large tasks of the will to alter one's path; 2) alternative societal path that rearranges or alters one's goal and/or terrain of path, allowing one to avoid interacting with one's proper path in life.

TRUE NORTH – 1) the direction that the truth of the heart leads one toward; 2) having to do with, or representing, that which guides one; 3) the specific direction, goal, or ideal of an individual.

TRUMPET – 1) idea, concept, ideal or proclamation that beacons all through inspiration of spiritual nature; 2) precious inspiration of spirit that alerts and calls all to action.

TRUNK – [steamer trunk] 1) system within a family of keeping traditions and lore alive from generation to generation; 2) tendency of individual or group to save or hoard memories; 3) collection of ideas, memories and indicators of personal significance one holds onto beyond their time of usefulness; [tree trunk] 4) practicality; [elephant trunk] 5) function of memory.

TRUNK OF TREE – 1) core structure of a life; 2) internal support for and sustainer of one's life; 3) practicality.

TRUTH – 1) one's individual certainty; 2) that which comes from the heart; 3) universal knowing available through the heart or voice of spirit; 4) that which communities, societies or groups proclaim is universal to all.

T-SHIRT – 1) belief system that informs the heart, one's assimilation of the world around and compels one to embrace the world naturally; 2) comfortable, convenient and mundane belief system common to many and unremarkable.

TSUNAMI – 1) sudden, absolute societal change that completely destroys the former way of living; 2) the absolute change that results from the global commitment to human existence has shifted and utterly changed; 3) the feeling at the moment of impact when global change arrives en force.

TUNNEL – 1) connection between this world and the spirit world; 2) deep internal connection to spirit world; 3) the spirit connection between things.

TURKEY – 1) opinion without inspiration; 2) mundane opinion that has soporific effect on those who assimilate it; 3) indicative of common beliefs based on opinion that cause individuals to be less aware of reality around them; 4) basis for contentment, perpetuation of status quo and provides justification for unwise, mundane and uninspired continuation of meaningless things.

TURNOVER – [VERB] 1) to explore a new option; 2) to observe or consider from new point of view; [NOUN] 3) inspired life, filled with nourishment, that is particularly enjoyable; 4) mainstay of life, with nourishment at its core, that is considered the most delightful and special part.

TURTLE – 1) signifies being one with the soul; 2) that which bridges and contains the material and the spiritual; 3) one who uses connection to spirit as means of hiding from the world; 4) state of isolation of those in religious order who are secluded and separate from life.

TWIN TOWERS – 1) manifest duality; 2) paradox; 3) balance between good and evil; [TWO TOWERS WITH A PATH BETWEEN] 4) balance of duality in the world; 5) represents that the choices one has in a life are always dualistic.

TWINS – 1) two individual experiences on parallel tracks in the manifest world lived in relation to each other; 2) mirror; 3) joining of opposites; 4) Law of Unity concept that that which one opposes, one strengthens.

TWISTED ANKLE – 1) when one has inadvertently gone in the wrong direction so that the connection between one's movement on one's path and direction on one's path is temporarily impared.

TWO – 1) the manifest realm; 2) state in which all things are in balance; 3) balance through duality as a given.

TWO TOWERS WITH PATH BETWEEN – 1) balance of duality in the world; 2) the choices one has in dualistic life; 3) any life that is a manifestation of duality (i.e., bisexuality; schytsophrenia; bigamy; of conflicting opinions; at war with one's self; dual standards; etc.).

TYPEWRITER – 1) that which allows one to take actions that will result in one's idea of wisdom to be available to others; 2) that which translates one's actions into a record of one's thoughts, beliefs and outlook.

TYPHOON – 1) state of inspiration and nuance that creates order out of chaos and becomes enormously destructive; 2) power of nature that confuses state of inspiration into patterns of construction.

U

UAE – 1) union of societal structures based on the aspect of the universal commitment to manifest existence of the human race; 2) those societal structures based upon the origins central religious concepts in the current era of human civilization since the last earth changes; 3) dominion of royal families in ancient lands.

UGLY STEP SISTER – 1) symbol for feeling of social disenfranchisement coming from superficial judgment against one; 2) the way one seeks to compensate for feelings of self-loathing by treating others badly; 3) insecurity based on superficial judtments.

ULTIMATE – 1) that which has developed to the maximum; 2) the pinacle achievement of a person, place or thing; 3) the limit of one's ability to dream, have vision or project.

ULTIMATUM – 1) expression of one's limits of endurance as projection of outcome should those limits be exceeded; 2) attempt to manipulate future outcome through threat of specific result; 3) utter lack of belief in spirit and the limitless bounty of grace.

UMBER – 1) deeply practical; 2) those practical things that are divisive, unique or punitive; 3) the essence of manifest practicality.

UMBILICAL – 1) symbol for the flow of generations through time; 2) temporal, and initiating, connection between origin and essence.

UMBRELLA – 1) anticipation of natural change with sudden, unpredictable onset; 2) one who is ready to deflect from changes that come from divine source; 3) signifies one who accepts the need to protect one's self on occasion; 4) shows anticipation for specific need for protection.

UNBUCKLED – 1) absence of means, sometimes precious, that secures that which connects or protects the intersection between foundation and assimilation; 2) state of being completely without any stricture that holds foundation and movement on path in synch.

UNCHECKED – 1) free from external authority; 2) in a state of earned trust; 3) when a person, place or thing has not yet been scrutinized by the applicable external authority.

UNCLE – 1) peripheral association that is extremely close and in union with one; 2) signifies peripheral familial lineage as relevant to one's specific moment in time.

UNCTUOUS – 1) represents that one is characterized by excessive piousness or moralistic fervor; 2) represents that one's external show of spirituality is overdone in an affected manner; 3) when one's manner is excessively smooth, suave, or smug; 4) one is sluggish to change, and avoids the impact of others' actions easily.

UNDER A BRIDGE – 1) one who has an opportunity to undergo change such that the past is integrated; 2) one who chooses to wipe out the past as one goes through change.

UNDERCURRENT – 1) hidden motive; 2) indicative of a state of change that contains a deeper change one may not be aware of; 3) represents that the things being expressed are masking a deeper message; 4) suggests that what is on the surface is insincere, misleading or false.

UNDERGROUND – 1) one who is actively seeking direct connection with spirit but unwilling to take actions that will assure it; 2) one who is hiding in half-hearted attempt at spiritual life; 3) avoidance of life through excuse of practicality.

UNDERMINE – 1) to intentionally disturb, discredit or contradict; 2) hidden motive to destroy that which is on the surface supported.

UNDERTOW – 1) to become victim to one's hidden motive; 2) to become ensnared in a deeper, hidden change one had not been aware was present; 3) becoming helplessly manipulated by the deeper motive another had; 4) being duped by a surface that was insincere, misleading or false.

UNDOCKED – 1) becoming disconnected from that which had been one's means of avoiding change; 2) to be overcome by the very change one was trying to avoid; 3) being adrift in a state of change.

UNDONE – 1) not connected; 2) represents loss of composure.

UNEMPLOYMENT – 1) the state of being outside of societal structures of productiveness and participation; 2) unable to care for one's self; 3) lack of opportunity to translate one's actions into manifest fluidity.

UNICORN – 1) spiritual mission that has vision itself as a goal; 2) representative of fanciful state; 3) one who sees spirituality clearly, is filled with vision, but is unable to make it manifest; 4) belief in non-manifest, and unobtainable, goals.

UNIFICATION – 1) essential principle of yin; 2) actively joined with another person, place or thing; 3) the state in which all are acknowledged, and can work in united effort; 4) loss of identity, individuality.

UNIFORM – 1) represents things appearing alike; 2) that which matches exactly something else; [CLOTHING] 3) shows one's choice of function in life; 4) represents the need for one to dedicate one's actions to something outside of self.

UNION – 1) those things joined by the essential principle of yin; 2) group that is actively joined other persons, places or things; 3) those who participate willingly in a state in which all are acknowledged, and can work in united effort; 4) a group who have, by their own choice, lost identity, individuality.

UNITED – 1) joined by the essential principle of yin; 2) those who are actively joined with another person, place or thing; 3) those currently in the state in which all are acknowledged, and can work in united effort; 4) those who have given over personal identity or individuality for a greater purpose.

UNITED NATIONS – 1) global structure through which extant societies join together to establish, maintain and enforce a standard of societal behavior on the large scale; 2) group of societies joined by the essential principle of yin; 3) group of governments actively joined with each other for their common good; 4) governments and societies currently in the state in which all are acknowledged, and can work in united effort.

UNIVERSE – 1) that which is everything manifest; 2) the entirety of being.

UNIVERSITY – 1) structure that insures that wisdom, expertise, ideas and skills are passed from generation to generation; 2) place of higher learning.

UNLOCKED – 1) joined but free; 2) that which is connected by mutual concent.

UNTIED – 1) things that had been, and may again be, joined together by a single idea; 2) state of being released from being held by an idea or concept for a period of time; 3) end of the term of a contract.

UNTOUCHED – 1) as yet unaffected by the actions of another; 2) pure and undisturbed; 3) independent of impact of the actions of others; 4) without prejudice from experience.

UNTUCKED SHIRT – 1) exposure of the limit of a belief system relative to one's heart, assimilation and embrace of the world; 2) evidence that one's operative belief system, relative to one's heart, assimilation and embrace of the world, can be altered or removed; 3) uncertainty about lasting commitment to a particular belief system relative to one's heart, assimilation and embrace of the world.

UP – 1) elevated; 2) divine; 3) inspiration.

UPSIDE DOWN – 1) represents that the world has fallen out of order; 2) one can't tell what has more weight, meaning or importance.

UPSTAIRS – 1) close to heavens; 2) ideas, thoughts that lead to elevation.

UPTURNED NOSE – 1) one seeks inspiration prior to commitment, acknowledgement or expression; 2) indicative that one finds one's self inspired but not others; 3) state of insecurity overcome by outwardly showing one's extreme association with inspiration.

UPWARD POINTING FINGER – 1) acknowledgment of divine, elevated, celestial or inspired.

URANUS – 1) commitment to sudden, unexpected changes; 2) one who thrives on dramatic twists and turns; 3) suggests that an unexpected change is coming.

USURP – 1) represents one seized and now holds (a position, office, power, etc.) by force; 2) one who lacks legal right to their position, authority or status; 3) one who uses without authority or right; 4) one has wrongfully used force.

V

VACUUM – 1) void; 2) that which drains life force from another.

VACUUM CLEANER – 1) mechanism that pulls things to the void; 2) mechanism that drains life force; 3) the force of spirit that pulls one to confront the void in order to cleanse.

VAGINA – 1) root chakra; 2) represents one's foundation is vulnerable, yet that should another intrude into that vulnerability the result will be an evolution of foundation that produces new life, new commitment; 3) connection to the earth.

VALHALLA –1) heaven fortress within the astral, so called by **NORSE** myth; 2) the journey's end for believers in sea-faring spirits of **NORDIC** extraction.

VAMPIRE – 1) one who uses anger to drain the emotional strength from others; 2) one who seeks to disable the heart of others through their anger; 3) represents that one's anger has the power to overcome one's heart.

VARNISH – 1) outer image; 2) façade.

VASE – 1) how one maintains experiences and displays them; 2) represents that one enjoys and celebrates one's experiences.

VAV – HEBREW LETTER] 1) represents divine light entering the void to make all things possible; 2) divine connection; 3) direct connection with infinite source.

VEGETABLE – 1) abundance of nourishment in nature; 2) alive but without self-purpose; 3) dedicated or commited to the nourishment of others only.

VELVET - 1) rich, lush belief system; 2) belief system that absorbs light; 3) substantial belief system that is strong, resilient, comfortable and elegant.

VENDING MACHINE – 1) manifestation that allows one's actions, in conjunction with societal norms, to produce nourishment for one's self; 2) neutral provision of access to needed items in society for those who so choose.

VENDOR – 1) one who sustains flow of societal chi via provision of needed items; 2) societal element that provides what one needs; 3) suggests that subject turn to others for what is needed, and be willing to do all that is required.

VENUS – 1) commitment to love, beauty, and creative power.

VERSE – 1) pure spiritual message brought into manifest by power of music fused with conception of words; 2) organizing speech into a form that speaks from the heart and to the heart.

LYRIC – 1) pure spiritual message brought into manifest by by union with music; 2) organizing speech into a form that speaks from the heart and to the heart only when combined with music.

LYRICAL – 1) that which has sense of spirit built in; 2) that which has as its essence flow, rhythm and emotion.

VERTICAL STRIPES – 1) core isn't matching actions or alternate approaches, not necessarily conflict; 2) **SHAKTI-PAD**.

VEST – 1) belief system that only impacts heart and assimilation; 2) one's method for dealing with feelings and interactions with others; 3) ground rules for engagement with others in meaningful ways.

VETERAN – 1) one who has had the active experience of conflict; 2) those who have survived standing for a principle in a conflict of principles.

VETERINARIAN – 1) one who cares for and heals the essential manifestation of a living creature; 2) one who studies the biological essence of an individual without consideration of human traits; 3) one dedicated to the health and well being of the basic manifestation of being.

VIDEO – 1) illusion meant to represent life itself; 2) illusion that imitates life based only on the presence of emminating spirit.

VIDEO GAME – 1) that which uses an illusion meant to represent life itself for entertainment only; 2) that which allows individuals to play with the illusion of life based only on the presence of emminating spirit.

VILLAGE – 1) concentrated organization of social behavior for a large community within a larger grouping of people; 2) small functions and events; 3) structured social life for a select group.

VINE – 1) element of life that endures; 2) that part of life, which when mature, holds one in place; 3) represents that in the past one began something that now traps one and makes one feel tied down.

VINYL – 1) smooth and synthetic belief system that creates illusion; 2) illusion of belief system with overall purpose to avoid, resist and deflect change, growth or flow.

VINYL COUCH – 1) a smooth place to rest *(not sleep)* on belief systems and structures in life that is desired by many people, a place to come together and to connect, rest and share; 2) this is not a place to change for with it there is a sense of stagnancy, of wasting time.

VINYL SOFA – 1) a smooth place to rest *(not sleep)* on belief systems and structures in life that is desired by many people, a place to come together and to connect, rest and share; 2) this is not a place to change for with it there is a sense of stagnancy, of wasting time.

VIOLIN – 1) the soul; 2) the manifest vessel that houses and expresses the soul; 3) represents a life of spiritual service to others.

VIRGIN – 1) state of unused potential; 2) purity in that one has not yet learned lessons that come from exploring and making vulnerable one's foundation; 3) unused potential to bring things to life.

VIRGIN MARY – 1) possessing message of peace, kindness, gentleness, forgiveness; 2) the **EMPRESS**, thus provides opportunities to grow; 3) originator, and benefactress, of all that happens in our lives that gives us opportunity to grow comes from her.

QUAN YIN – 1) possessing message of peace, kindness, gentleness, forgiveness; 2) the **EMPRESS**, thus provides opportunities to grow; 3) originator, and benefactress, of all that happens in our lives that gives us opportunity to grow comes from her.

EARTH MOTHER – 1) possessing message of peace, kindness, gentleness, forgiveness; 2) the **EMPRESS**, thus provides opportunities to grow; 3) originator, and benefactress, of all that happens in our lives that gives us opportunity to grow comes from her.

DIVINE GODESS – 1) possessing message of peace, kindness, gentleness, forgiveness; 2) the **EMPRESS**, thus provides opportunities to grow; 3) originator, and benefactress, of all that happens in our lives that gives us opportunity to grow comes from her.

MOTHER EARTH– 1) possessing message of peace, kindness, gentleness, forgiveness; 2) the **EMPRESS**, thus provides opportunities to grow; 3) originator, and benefactress, of all that happens in our lives that gives us opportunity to grow comes from her.

VISION – 1) one's ability to be shown by spirit; 2) opening to spiritual view of life; 3) gift from spirit and the Empress that gives direction, guidance and clarity.

VISION CHAKRA – 1) represents one's vision; 2) potential to have vision through one's third eye.

VITAMINS – 1) building blocks of the physical body; 2) those essential elements that sustain and support life.

VOID – 1) ultimate reality; 2) the nothing in which everything exists; 3) absence of nourishment, absence of companion; 4) represents that everything one does is a choice; 5) challenge to embrace nothingness and the void and thereby understand that what one has is a miracle; 6) origin and destination; 7) ultimate consistency is the void, rather than the identity; 8) the omnipresence of reality is simply chaos.

VOLCANO – 1) represents the fact that every commitment houses a potential for growth, change, feeling and an earthly surge to an elevated state of inspiraton; 2) the coming to fruition of a commitment that creates new paths and potentials.

VORTEX – 1) the flow of all of life; 2) the manifestation of exponential growth, flow and potential; 3) represents that beneath all of manifest reality is simply the flow of chi.

VOTE – 1) to take an action that represents one's intention; 2) represents that one's actions that are honest expressions of self may alter the course of society; 3) the individual, through actions of one's deep truth, can impact and change the manifestation of society.

VOW – 1) represents a declaration of one's commitment ; 2) voicing sacred intention ; 3) public commitment to live by one's beliefs.

VOYAGE – 1) represents need for, opportunity to be gained, or importance of a temporary departure from one's current path in life; 2) shows that what is needed can only be gained by departing one's normal place of journey; 3) need for open mind to new experiences.

VULTURE – 1) opinion that is nurtured and perpetuated by the destruction of others ; 2) represents one who is inspired and nourished by the misfortune and destruction of others ; 3) one who seeks to destroy through expression of inspired gossip.

WAFFLES – 1) the offering of many creations that will nourish one's soul if they are assimilated; 2) manifest actions that are the tangible results of putting one's repressed feelings to practical use.

WAGON – 1) vehicle that doesn't move on its own; 2) something that moves because it is pulled; 3) represents one's ideas, attitudes and other life constructs that cannot be functional unless led by an external force.

WAIST – 1) complete realm and extent of one's assimilation; 2) represents need to acknowledge and act upon what one has assimilated.

WAITING – 1) represents specific opportunity in one's life; 2) having access, through patience and meditation, to receive that which spirit intends; [WAITING 1 HR] 3) patience, meditation and openness are essential; 4) indicates that this is one's hour of spiritual instruction, it is very important to the individual; [WAITING 2 HRS] 5) represents the presence of spiritual instruction through a bureaucratic, man made process; [WAITING 3 HRS] 6) focus, meditation and mindful patience will deliver spirit unto your heart; [WAITING 7 HRS] 7) patience and meditation are required for a very long time; 8) ultimately patience will deliver great spiritual awakening; [WAITING 8 HRS] 9) the attempt to perfect patience will lead one to the highest achievement of man in the manifest; [WAITING 10 HRS] 10) the essence of patience, meditation and focused mindfulness is spiritual completion.

WALKER – 1) represents the absolute preciousness of being of assistance to the elderly; 2) wisdom is found in one's willingness to support one's self on one's path; 3) represents humility in making use of the precious structures of the manifest in order to continue on one's path in times of strife and weakness.

WALKING – 1) progressing on one's path; 2) the means by which one makes progress on one's path.

WALKING DOWN STAIRS, BACKWARDS – 1) one is retreating from elevation; 2) one is loosing spiritual ground.

WALKING DOWN STAIRS, FACE FRONT – 1) having once been elevated one then returns to manifest to deliver the message.

WALKING ON AIR – 1) very elevated, so much so that one is no longer on path; 2) one takes an inspired path without grounding; 3) so inspired that one is out of touch with reality.

WALKING ON WATER – 1) represents tenacity and elevation as means of continuing on one's path when it is changing constantly; 2) one must accept change, growth and flow as one's designated path.

WALKING STICK – 1) tenacity in life is found through using all one can to keep going; 2) one must always take actions to continue on one's path; 3) forward movement on one's path is mandatory.

WALL – 1) manmade barrier; 2) when one crosses a manmade barrier, one understands something more about one's life.

WALLET – 1) the way in which one identifies one's self in, and to, man's world; 2) means of societal power; 3) ability to move and function in society; 4) represents what one's class is; 5) suggests one consider how one presents one's self.

WAND – 1) necessary tool to redirect or channel forces; 2) represents ability of one to channel force (either natural or spiritual) for one's purposes; 3) required ritual, tool, device or process that allows one to facilitate the delivery of spirit, or manipulation of natural energies, in the manifest.

WANING CRESCENT MOON – 1) state of delusion involving eroding self-confidence; 2) approaching self-view of oblivion.

WANING GIBBOUS MOON – 1) state of delusion in which, having recently fallen from a **TOWER** state one 's confidence is eroding and if uninterrupted will achieve a self-view of oblivion in time.

WANING MOON – 1) deceiving one's self by viewing self as less than what is accurate.

war – 1) ultimate form of ego and pride manifested through ideal-driven conflict; 2) conflict resulting from creativity mixed with fear and pride; 3) the active experience of ego-based conflict; 4) a conflict of principles.

WARRIOR – 1) one who has based life on the ultimate form of ego and pride manifested through ideal-driven conflict; 2) one who enters into conflicts resulting from creativity mixed with fear and pride; 3) those who live in the active experience of ego-based conflict; 4) one who wagers one's own life within a conflict of principles.

WASH – 1) to change a person, place or thing as one wishes; 2) to enforce an environment in which growth is inevitable and will flourish; 3) to intentionally create flow where there was none before.

WASHING MACHINE – 1) mechanism with which one can change a person, place or thing as one wishes; 2) an environment in which growth is inevitable and will flourish; 3) a place or mechanism in which one can intentionally create flow where there was none before.

WASP – 1) clandestine and aggressive activity of accomplishing what one needs by taking the most out of each experience in life; 2) persistence, aggression and intrusion; 3) tenacity of inspiration that has the specified goal of getting what one needs for one's self, and ready at any moment of opposition in the quest having emotional barb ready with which to disable and harm the opposing force.

WASP STING –emotional action that disables and harms any who might oppose one's clandestine and aggressive activity of accomplishing what one needs by taking the most out of each experience in life.

WATCH – 1) societal indicator of time; 2) represents one's relationship to time; [BLACK WATCH] 3) one's devotion to time keeps intercedes between one's embrace of the world and one's actions by imposition of stagnation, uniqueness, judgment or divisiveness; [METALLIC WATCH] 4) inditation that time is considered precious and is used to intercede between one's embrace of the world and one's actions.

WATER – 1) change, flow or growth; 2) represents that manifest life is about growth, change and constant flow; [STAGNANT WATER] 3) represents a state of stagnancy coming from a lack of flow, growth or change; [TOE IN WATER] 4) represents being in a state where one is bridging the gap between the physical and the spiritual; 5) those without firm footing in either manifest or spiritual worlds, lost in concepts and ideals; [BOILING WATER] 6) represents being in a state of agitated flow, growth or change; 7) actively changing, growing or flowing; 8) state of evolving growth, change or flow in which many inspired commitments are made, though none last; 9) chaotic growth, change or flow that will continue until nothing more can occur; 10) indicates that one is forcing growth, flow or change to become inspiration due to repressed feelings that must become expressed.

WATER SLIDE –1) when one uses change, flow or growth to practice skills without the full responsibility for outcome or impact while teasing, joking with or amusing others; 2) represents that one is using their path of growth, change and constant flow in manifest life to practice skills without the full responsibility for outcome or impact while teasing, joking with or amusing others

WATER SPOUT – 1) naturally occurring intrusion into one's life in which growth, flow or change comes in contact with inspiration; 2) becoming suddenly subject to inspired growth, change or flow due to the intrusion of natural forces.

WATER WORKS – 1) indicates one is taking change, growth or flow and manipulating or altering it so that it will appear to be under one's own control; 2) unnatural manipulation of change, growth or flow accepted and wanted by society; 3) making change, growth or flow occur within a fixed boundary; 4) containing growth, flow or change to make it seem easy to take in.

WATERBOARDING – 1) torturing another by creating the illusion they are perishing due to absolute change, alteration of state or absolute flux; 2) creating a state of absolute fear in another by sumulating their transition from manifest to spirit, the ultimate change.

watercolor – 1) represents that one is artistically showing to the world their own growth, change or flow by means of leaving a residual impression of the nature of that event; 2) suggestion that one express one's growth, change or flow in life to others.

WATERCOLOR PAINT – 1) represents the residual impression of the nature of events in one's life that gives evidence to the world of one's growth, change or flow; 2) suggestion that one use the residual impression of the nature of one's life process in order to express one's growth, change or flow in life to others.

WATERCOLOR PAPER – 1) represents an expression of one's wisdom on which the residual impression of the nature of events in one's life gives evidence to the world of one's growth, change or flow; 2) suggestion to present, in tangible terms, the wisdom gained in one's life.

WATERCOLOR BRUSHES – 1) represents the mandatory need to show the world the residual impression of one's own growth, change or flow; 2) suggestion that one make the mandatory express one's growth, change or flow in life to others.

WATERFALL – 1) represents encouragement that change, growth and flow can overtake any obstacle no matter how profound; 2) shows that while growth, change or flow may not really change the barrier, it isn't stopped by it either; 3) suggestion that through growth, flow or change one can have a major fundamental change; 4) indicates one will successfully overcome a barrier and even change one's the foundation.

WAVE – 1) one takes actions that are an inspiration in themselves; 2) a work of inspiration; 3) represents that when growth, flow or change meets stable grounds, with persistence it can break down barriers and give one wisdom; 4) an event of growth, flow or change serve to generates itself.

WAVING HAND – 1) one takes actions that are an inspiration in themselves; 2) a work of inspiration.

WAX – 1) represents that which, with emotion, produces growth and change, but without feelings becomes brittle; 2) shows there are two ways—of the heart and of the mind—and the path of the heart is smoother and produces a easier and greater result.

WAXING CRESCENT MOON – 1) changing state of delusion from seeing one's self as completely nothing, but not yet able to see the light of self accurately.

WAXING GIBBOUS MOON – 1) deluded state in which one views one's self as spiritual, good, great and expecting to achieve full greatness.

WAXING MOON – 1) growing delusions of grandeur as form of self-deception.

WEALTH – 1) hoarding that which is meant to flow freely may produce power, but with it comes fear, delusion and suspicion; 2) represents society's Tower challenge.

WEASEL – 1) represents that one is superficial and more drawn to the illusion of light than light itself; 2) desire to be free of responsibility through evasive actions.

weather – 1) the constant growing, changing and flowing of all things; 2) the nature of inspiration surrounding the universal commitment to manifest existence.

wedding – 1) ritual of joining paths and bodies in manifest life; 2) state of sharing all one is, has and will become with another; 3) celebration of love through outward presentation of ritual.

wedding ring – 1) precious, ongoing and continuous joining of paths and bodies in manifest life; 2) represents the precious, ongoing and continuous celebration of love through the joining of two lives.

wedge of cheese – 1) spiritual element of that which is made from inheritance and essence of life; 2) having access to the the prepared and spiritual evolution from the essence of life; 3) spiritual food made from life essence.

weed – 1) represents the overabundance of that which imitates; 2) indicates that what one is doing or encountering is inauthentic and persistent; 3) calls one to discern between that which is authentic and that which is not, and then remove the inauthentic.

WEEK – 1) an abundance of days; 2) societal cycle of days.

WEEKEND – 1) time of rest from obligations; 2) society's presumption that members must rest.

WEEPING WILLOW – 1) a life that is flexible; 2) the fullness of experience available when one is openminded and flexible.

WEIGHT – 1) represents something solid or substantial in the manifest; 2) things that are unresolved, challenges and 3) represents the importance of a thing.

WELL – 1) cooperation of man and nature to ensure growth, change and flow; 2) represents that change, growth and flow are all essential parts of the practical foundation of life, but can only be accessible when man cooperates with nature.

WELLSPRING – 1) the abundant and flowing continuoum of ideas available to man; 2) represents that should one just seek, abundance will be instantly found.

WEST – 1) ultimate tendency of things to go into darkness; 2) represents the direction of the path; 3) where things inevitably end; 4) destiny of the new as it progresses into the future.

wet suit – 1) artificial belief system that seeks to ensure there will be no growth, change or flow in one's life; 2) self-induced protection against growth, change or flow; 3) indicates one is in an unnatural state of aversion to growth, change and flow.

WHALE – 1) the major message that comes from absolute change, growth or flow in life; 2) one goes through absolute change in order to truly understand something; 3) indicates that one's path through change, growth and flow ultimately gives one an understanding of All That Is; 4) represents the wisdom that is the result of absolute growth, change or flow.

WHEAT – 1) sustenance of life; 2) shaft of life.

WHEEL – 1) r o t a = t a r o t; 2) destiny and fate; 3) stands for the Great Mandala, the Wheel of Life; 4) indicates to prepare for that which comes in life, the unexpected; 5) represents the inevitability of one's fate.

wheelchair – 1) represents that even when one loses one's way in life, destiny will be fulfilled; 2) the koan that one is always on one's path of fate, even when one is not on it.

WHIM – 1) spontaneous following of one's intuition or one's heart; 2) proceeding without thought.

WHIRLPOOL – 1) when absolute change, growth or flow becomes the flow of all of life; 2) the inexcapable manifestation of exponential growth, flow and potential; 3) represents that behind all growth, change and flow in manifest reality is simply the flow of chi.

WHISK – 1) precious action that infuses anything with inspiration; 2) represents that it is both mandatory in life and precious to take actions that bring inspiration to all things.

WHITE – 1) pure spirit; 2) the state of death; 3) indicates spirit is coming to one's life; 4) speaks of situation filled with things that change one and cause feelings are in fact divine.

WHITE CANDLE – 1) the spiritual life of an individual.

WHITE GOLD – 1) represents how precious is spirit that allows self-reflection.

WHITE HANDKERCHIEF - 1) spirituality in the hand that is of service; 2) meaning outgoing action that conveys, "I will help you, I will deliver to you."

WHITE HOUSE – 1) dwelling place of the soul is of pure spirit; 2) indicates that only in absolute spirit will one feel completely home.

WHITE LINGERIE – 1) indicates that choosing spirituality on the deepest level is the way.

WHITE LIPS – 1) one's manner of expression is pure spirit.

widow – 1) represents that one's place of commitment is eternal; 2) one's love lives on even after the one loved has joined spirit.

wig – 1) suggests that one's thoughts are false; 2) indicative of one who imitates the thoughts of others; 3) represents that one is covering one's own thoughts with those of another or that are completely artificial just to keep appearances.

WILDFLOWER – 1) chaotic experience that nobody plans for; 2) abundance found in chaotic, impromptu but natural experiences.

WILL – 1) represents the power of the mind; 2) the destructive force of the intellect.

WILLFUL – 1) one who only uses the power of the mind; 2) state in which all is destroyed due to the preponderance of the mind and intellectual belligerence.

WIND – 1) inspiration.

WIND SOCK – 1) belief system of circular thinking that is easily inspired; 2) self-repeating beliefs that ill pick up the inspiration of the moment and conform to it.

WINDMILL – 1) structures in life that capture inspiration and put it to good use; 2) represents the need to make use of inspiration; 3) suggests that the inspiration in one's life is ripe for conversion into actual progress or creative use.

WINDOW – 1) represents ability to understand something new, something different; 2) suggests one open to new concept; 3) potential for new understanding goes two ways; 4) points to presence of potentiality and the idea that in following a potential something else becomes possible.

WINDOW PANE – 1) view of potential new ways of thinking is only possible through the filter of structures in the world, or earlier accomplishments; 2) framing new perspective in ancient wisdom gives unique perspective.

WINE – 1) self-imposed emotional change or flow can lead to confusion; 2) when celebration results from having let one's emotions flow by artificial means, often regrets follow.

WINGS – 1) individual ideas, bits of gossip or opinions collectively have the potential to fly free on inspiration; 2) the pursuit of inspiration as a means of creating a connection with the heavens, but that actually take one off of one's path.

WINTER – 1) old age; 2) nearness of pure spirit; 3) seeking of comfort in death.

wire – 1) indicates precious ideas and lasting values; 2) represents a sense of ideas continuing; 3) a single idea that makes everything inter-relate.

wiskey – 1) intensely practical, self-imposed change, growth or flow that leads to deluded state; 2) when one's teacher is one's own view of practicality, growth will be skewed and one will become insane.

WITCH – 1) one person skilled in manipulating the manifest, meditative, clairvoyant and astral planes, as well as in herbal matters; 2) one wh o is manipulative of this reality; 3) one who uses forces of the manifest to enact one's will.

WARLOCK – 1) one person skilled in manipulating the manifest, meditative, clairvoyant and astral planes, as well as in herbal matters; 2) one wh o is manipulative of this reality; 3) one who uses forces of the manifest to enact one's will.

WIZARD FINGER POINTING UP – 1) suggests taking note of how the planetary dance affects the manifest on earth.

WOLF – 1) one who is an aggressor; 2) represents that one is finding what one needs, and is actively getting what one wants; 3) the searcher, hunter.

WOMB – 1) internal commitment to life; 2) the origin of all things.

WOOD – 1) the practical substance of life.

WOODEN – 1) made from life itself; 2) practical.

WOODEN BENCH – 1) taking life and with it creating something that elevates one and upon which one can rest; 2) practical societal provision that is for the good of many.

WOODEN BOX – 1) practical events and structures one makes that contain those things one holds as separate, specific or of particular usefulness.

WOODEN CHAIR – 1) single moment in time that is pratcical; 2) a place to rest and repose; 3) one is still on one's path as one's feet are on the ground; 4) place to rest that is made from life.

WOODEN FLOOR – 1) cycle of life is what supports you.

WOODEN HAIRBRUSH – 1) method of organizing thoughts that comes from life lived and, when used, is necessary.

WOODEN SHOES – 1) practicality that connects or disconnects one from one's path; 2) practical vehicle one chooses to carry one forward.

WOODS - 1) many lives united by geographical location or common purpose; 2) society that gathers naturally because of the involuntary nature of the geographical location.

WOOL – 1) collection of ideas held by the faith-filled; 2) ideas that unite those members of a faith who work together.

WORD – 1) shared and inspired manifestation that represents a person, place, sentiment, idea or event.

WORK – 1) the performance of actions required to accomplish a stated task; 2) those actions required by one in charge of a group.

WORK FORCE – 1) those assigned the performance of actions required to accomplish a stated task; 2) those whose collective actions are required by one in charge of a group.

WORKER – 1) one assigned to performan actions required to accomplish a stated task; 2) one member of a group whose collective actions are required by one in charge of a group; 3) suggests one must become better aligned with one's specific purpose or intended task.

WORLD – 1) universal commitment to human existence; [UPSIDE DOWN WORLD] 2) indicates that one's world has fallen out of order; 3) indicates that one can't distinguish what element has more weight, meaning or importance.

UPSIDE DOWN WORLD – 1) indicates that one's world has fallen out of order; 2) indicates that one can't distinguish what element has more weight, meaning or importance.

worm – 1) represents parts of life that can only exist in entirely practical environment; 2) symbol of organic flow of death into new life; 3) indicates transitory states; 4) reminds one that after death one is reintegrated into the biosphere.

WOUND – 1) tear in the natural protection that guards against too much change; 2) breaking down of the boundary between flow of feelings contained within and one's outer protective barrier.

WOVEN FABRIC – 1) belief system made up of intricate intersection and interrelationships between a great many different ideas and points of view coming together in time to form a solid network of thought.

WREATH – 1) societal recognition; 2) means of celebrating outwardly; 3) way of marking achievement.

WRESTLING – 1) ironic conflict in which one and another embrace each other yet each still tries to dominate; 2) suggests looking at all aspects of a thing before making a choice or decision; 3) suggests it may be time to stop weighing aspects and come to a finishing point.

WRINKLES – 1) when one's natural boundary shows the scope and depth of one's experience; 2) evidence of successful movement beyond conflicts; 3) the map of one's life; 4) indicates wisdom through experience.

WRIST – 1) the union of one's embrace of the world and one's actions; 2) the transition from embrace to action; 3) that which divides or separates one's embrace of the world from one's actions.

WRIST WATCH – 1) indicates that elements or considerations of time form the relationship between one's embrace of the world and one's actions; 2) suggests one must re-evaluation the presence of time in one's life as it is becoming too predominant an issue in the translation of embrace into action.

WRITER – 1) one whose actions result in the expression of one's gained wisdom or specific point of view; 2) one who mainly expresses one's self to others through examples and reflections of one's wisdom and experiences.

WU WEI – 1) suggests Buddhism as a path one might follow; 2) represents that one interacts with each next thing encountered in place of having a premeditated plan for life; 3) flowing on one's path.

XENOPHOBIA – 1) represents that one's insecurity of identity is grounded by specific societal, governmental or social identity which fears and resents others not so affiliated; 2) suggests one might be of closed mind and heart to others due to arbitrary or possibly irrelevant affiliation.

XEROX – 1) means of copying the wisdom, ideas and concepts of another ; 2) to mimic the beliefs and expressions of others ; 3) insincerety ; 4) show of respect for others.

X-RAY – 1) indicates the ability to see the interior structure of an individual; 2) suggests one look to the underlying structure of the thing one is encountering.

XYLOPHONE – 1) when one does the mandatory actions in life and in so doing strikes against those precious and mandatory elements of the world, spirituality will result; 2) indicates that the road to spiritual expression is to simply do all that is mandatory in one's life.

Y

Y – 1) symbol of The Great Y; 2) mandate of all spiritual beings in the manifest to unite the divisions of the manifest world, and at the same time to bring into manifest the spiritual unity one represents; 3) duality becoming one, and one becoming duality; 4) represents the individual experience of living in life; 5) the voice of all wisdom gained from earthly experience.

YACHT – 1) in the process of change, represents luxurious means of survival; 2) indulgent way of dealing with change; 3) exclusive vehicle of getting through change; 4) a half commitment to a particular vehicle to survive change; 5) vehicle used to navigate, survive and manage change is solid and strong, can contain many.

YAH – 1) inspired expression of alignment with The Great Y; 2) supplication to The Great Y; 3) celebration and extolling praise on The Great Y.

YANG – 1) that which has definition and a goal; 2) hierarchy and division by exclusive category; 3) that which is active in setting and maintaing boundaries.

EXCEYARD – 1) represents the space of one's earthly existence and therefore the space of one's earthly responsibilities; 2) indicates need to divide or define one's domain; 3) represents one's need to focus on one's own path.

yarn – 1) ongoing belief that is derived from the unified beliefs of many; 2) singular focus and idea; 3) how one sees one's experiences, ideas, accomplishments, life and purpose.

yea sayer – 1) represents one who always agrees; 2) indicates one must review one's own opinions, thoughts and beliefs and represent them accurately; 3) suggests that one may be, or one may have fallen victim to, one who always agrees and thus misrepresents self.

year – 1) astronomical cycle in manifest; 2) measure of one's advancement and growth by returning to the same place in time but one cycle later; 3) represents need to take personal inventory.

YEARN – 1) represents wanting badly; 2) expression of insecurity in which one will only feel complete in possession of specific person, place or thing; 3) suggests one must become more faith filled.

yellow – 1) intellect; 2) ego; 3) mental process; 4) intellectual concept.

YELLOW HOUSE – 1) represents one for whom the dwelling place of the soul is an intellectual process.

YELLOW JACKET – 1) one's protection is in the intellectual or egotistical; 2) one's anticipated need for protection is based on expectation derived from memory and its projection.

YELLOW LIPS – 1) one's manner of expression is intellectual; 2) one expresses one's self in terms of ego, mind, concept or idea.

yes – 1) sense of permission and support; 2) freedom from inhibition.

YIN – 1) inherent interconnection between all persons, places and things; 2) unification of individual uniqueness; 3) harmony among diversity; 4) inclusive and embrasive.

YOD – 1) tenth letter of Hebrew alphabet meaning 'hand'; 2) refers to the action that brings something into being; 3) that which inituates.

yogi – 1) represents one who practices alignment of one's self with the manifest; 2) suggests the need for centering; 3) in elevated form is one who has mastered the manifest.

yogurt – 1) the living essence of life; 2) the nourishment and nurture that comes as one assimilates the spiritual essence of life.

YOSEMITE – 1) to identify foreign group by experience of interaction with them; 2) prejudiced view based on experience; 3) limited view to isolated interactions.

YOUTH – 1) the promise of immaturity; 2) potential; 3) future hope.

YUD – 1) represents the infinite point; 2) symbol for the power of the infinite to contain finite phenomena within, and then express them to apparent external reality; 3) initial point, the essential power of the yud, is the "little that holds much; 4) the first letter of the name of god; 5) the infinite point from which everything flows.

yule – 1) pagan festival of many important celebrations; 2) represents present day Christmastime.

yule log – 1) passage in time of important celebrations that call back the sun to rule the skies once more; 2) symbol for ability to create heat in the cold.

Z

ZEALOT – 1) represents a fanatic; 2) suggests one is acting like a member of a radical, warlike, ardently patriotic group.

ZEBRA – 1) suggests one is of polarized nature; 2) reoresebts one who switches between extreme and opposite states with such regularity that one keeps one's self in balance.

ZENITH – 1) highest vertical point on the celestial sphere above a given position or observer; 2) represents a highest point or state; 3) suggests culmination.

ZEPPELIN – 1) inspired commitment that is vapid and hollow yet able to transport and travel great distances without being found out, mainly due to the outward appearance of neutrality.

ZERO – 1) represents the void; 2) suggests all possibility.

ZIG-ZAG – 1) movement that is pulled from side to side as it progresses forward; 2) represents a meandering path forward; 3) indirect movement in general forward direction that has a "stop and go" feel to it; 4) indicates one is pulled by outside forces and though contining on one's path, it is inefficient progress.

ZION – 1) symbol for a religious or spiritual center, specifically of the Jewish people; 2) represents the final gathering place of true believers.

zip line – 1) precious idea that tightly connects two opposite points of view and, by taking practical and mandatory action, allows one to traverse inspiration and thereby connect to both points; 2) successful idea used in negotiation to bring peaceful coexistence between opposing forces; 3) the preciousness that connects all things no matter how diverse or how opposed; 4) law of unity that states opposites hold each other in place.

zipcode – 1) societal place marker; 2) manifest way of identifying one's location.

zipper – 1) represents ability to unite all that is precious and close the divide; 2) action that closes the gap between opposites by recognizing that which is cherished by each side.

zodiac – 1) represents the earth-centric view of significant heavenly bodies; 2) represents organization of significant heavenly bodies near enough earth that their gravitational pull exerts defining pulls on all earthly beings; 3) suggests that one's precise location has huge impact on one's nature; 4) where one is defines what one is.

ZOO – 1) organized place of abundance for the benefit of members of the society that supports and displays the essential manifestation of living creatures; 2) area specifically set aside for activities and events surrounding the biological essence of an individual without consideration of human traits; 3) place, activity, or group marked by the chaos or unrestrained behavior that represents the basic manifestation of being.

zoo keeper – 1) one who maintains the organized place of abundance for the benefit of members of the society that supports and displays the essential manifestation of living creatures; 2) one who keeps the area specifically set aside for activities and events surrounding the biological essence of an individual without consideration of human traits; 3) supervisor of the place, activity, or group marked by the chaos or unrestrained behavior that represents the basic manifestation of being.

zoroastrianism – 1) represents a system of belief based on the eternal struggle between a being that is good and a being that is evil; 2) suggests that one's internal struggle is not only perpetual, but represents one's balance.

ZYGOTE – 1) essential element of commonality that holds the potential to develop into a commitment; 2) represents the idea that any two things joined together have the potential to form a commitment.

This edition of the Mystics Dictionary of Spirit Language was published in 2012. Subsequent updated editions will be published periodically, and each most recent edition will govern all pervious editions. Be sure to check that you have the most recently published edition.